THE
LAST OUTLAWS

ALSO BY TOM CLAVIN

Follow Me to Hell

The Last Hill (with Bob Drury)

To the Uttermost Ends of the Earth (with Phil Keith)

Lightning Down

Blood and Treasure (with Bob Drury)

Tombstone

All Blood Runs Red (with Phil Keith)

Wild Bill

Valley Forge (with Bob Drury)

Being Ted Williams (with Dick Enberg)

Dodge City

Lucky 666 (with Bob Drury)

Reckless

The Heart of Everything That Is (with Bob Drury)

The DiMaggios

Last Men Out (with Bob Drury)

That Old Black Magic

The Last Stand of Fox Company (with Bob Drury)

Halsey's Typhoon (with Bob Drury)

THE
LAST OUTLAWS

THE DESPERATE FINAL DAYS OF
THE DALTON GANG

TOM CLAVIN

ST. MARTIN'S PRESS
NEW YORK

First published in the United States by St. Martin's Press, an imprint of St. Martin's Publishing Group

THE LAST OUTLAWS. Copyright © 2023 by Tom Clavin. All rights reserved. Printed in the United States of America. For information, address St. Martin's Publishing Group, 120 Broadway, New York, NY 10271.

www.stmartins.com

Filigree art on title page: © Nora Hachio/Shutterstock.com

Map credits: Midwest During the Dalton days (front matter) © Jeffery L. Ward; Oklahoma Territory 1890 (Act III), courtesy of Oklahoma Historical Society; Coffeyville, October 1892 (Act IV) © Jeffery L. Ward

Library of Congress Cataloging-in-Publication Data

Names: Clavin, Tom, 1954– author.
Title: The last outlaws / Tom Clavin.
Description: First edition. | New York : St. Martin's Press, 2023. | Includes bibliographical
    references and index.
Identifiers: LCCN 2023024746 | ISBN 9781250282385 (hardcover) |
    ISBN 9781250282392 (ebook)
Subjects: LCSH: Dalton Gang. | Dalton family. | Outlaws—West (U.S.)—
    Biography. | Outlaws—Kansas—Coffeyville—History—19th century. | West (U.S.)—
    History—1890–1945. | West (U.S.)—Biography.
Classification: LCC F595.D15 C53 2023 | DDC 978/.020922—dc23/eng/20230324
LC record available at https://lccn.loc.gov/2023024746

Our books may be purchased in bulk for promotional, educational, or business use. Please contact your local bookseller or the Macmillan Corporate and Premium Sales Department at 1-800-221-7945, extension 5442, or by email at MacmillanSpecialMarkets@macmillan.com.

First Edition: 2023

10 9 8 7 6 5 4 3 2 1

To James, Kathryn, and Vivienne Vunkannon

CONTENTS

MIDWEST DURING THE DALTON DAYS

CANADA

Lake Sakakawea

Bismarck ★

NORTH DAKOTA

SOUTH DAKOTA

— *Lake Oahe*

Pierre ★

NEBRASKA

Missouri River

Omaha ●

Lincoln ★

Platte River

KANSAS

Dodge City ●

Cimarron ● ● Kinsley

Topeka ★

Coffeyville ●

Ingalls ● ● Tulsa

Guthrie ● ● Stroud

Oklahoma City ★ ● Morris

OKLAHOMA Boley ● Henryetta

Ardmore ● ● Mill Creek

MINNESOTA

Minneapolis ●

St. Paul ★

Northfield ●

Menomonie ●

Mississippi River

WISCONSIN

Madison ★

IOWA

Des Moines ★

Chicago ●

ILLINOIS

Springfield ★

St. Louis ●

MISSOURI

Southwest City ●

ARKANSAS

Arkansas River

Little Rock ★

Mississippi River

Lake Superior

Lake Michigan

Lake Huron

MICHIGAN

Lansing ★

L. Erie

Columbus ★

Indianapolis ★

INDIANA

OHIO

Ohio River

Frankfort ★

KENTUCKY

Nashville ★

TENNESSEE

Atlanta ★

ALABAMA

GEORGIA

Denton ●

Fort Worth ●

Cisco ● ● Dallas

TEXAS

Sonora ●

Sanderson ●

Round Rock ●

Austin ★ ● Houston

LOUISIANA

Jackson ★

Montgomery ★

MISSISSIPPI

Baton Rouge ★

★ Tallahassee

FLORIDA

Rio Grande

MEXICO

Gulf of Mexico

0   200   400

Miles

© 2023 Jeffrey L. Ward

AUTHOR'S NOTE

The men in the Dalton Gang and its immediate spin-off, the Doolin-Dalton Gang, were not literally the "last outlaws." The occupation of outlaw exists to the present day, though few can still be found atop horses. As this book details, some members of these two gangs did not meet a violent end until into the twentieth century—one man, in fact, was gunned down in 1924, during an era when outlaw was being replaced by gangster. And one can point to the rotating members of the various Hole-in-the-Wall gangs in Wyoming and Utah in the 1890s, whose days of depredations continued into the next century.

But the Dalton brothers and their accomplices represented a Wild West that was waning in 1892 when the Coffeyville raid put an exclamation point on the demise of the hard-riding outlaws who had come of age during and after the Civil War. The Daltons operated—or attempted to operate—as if decades had not passed and Winchester-wielding bank and train robberies still provided a way to make a living instead of what they truly were: last hurrahs. Outlaws did not die with the Daltons . . . but the romantic glow of an iconic figure of the American West certainly did.

PROLOGUE

The event, like the Wild West itself, was a distant memory. But Emmett Dalton was about to turn sixty, and the ailments were piling up. If he did not set foot in Coffeyville now, most likely he never would. And some of the people, especially the survivors of that deadly day of almost forty years earlier, still wanted a display of atonement. Emmett could do that. A part of him even wanted to, though deep down he believed all the years in prison was plenty of punishment.

To be honest—which could be difficult for him at times—Emmett enjoyed the attention. His return to Coffeyville generated headlines. As *The Kansas City Star* would report in its April 29, 1931, edition: "Emmett Dalton, leader of the notorious Dalton gang that thirty-nine years ago was the terror of the Southwest, returned Sunday to revisit the scenes of his career as an outlaw." He was certainly not the leader—Bob was—but close enough.

Emmett had a practical and somber reason too. Otherwise, it would appear unseemly after all this time to just pass through the town in southeast Kansas where in October 1892 eight men had been shot to death. There could still be grieving widows and children, even mothers here. Two of those murdered men had been his older brothers Bob and Grat. Ever since, they had lain with Bill Power in a common grave in the city's Elmwood Cemetery. Even more of an insult, the only marker the grave had was a length of lead gas pipe. Today, when Emmett got there, he expected to find the fine marker he had paid good money to create.

As he stood on the sidewalk in the center of Coffeyville, two men approached him. "How do you do, Emmett," said one of them. He identified himself as E. W. Morgan, and he had been eleven years old on that blood-soaked day in October 1892. The other was Charles Gump. He was seventy-two now, and as he extended his hand, he told Emmett that it had been struck by a bullet during the gun battle. "But no hard feelings," Gump cheerfully assured him.

It occurred to Emmett that just by still being alive and the last of the Dalton Gang, he was a celebrity to these people. And still a source of wonder, given that the last time he had been in Coffeyville, he had been shot twenty-three times yet did not die. The dying was done by eight other men. Sure, it did not hurt that Emmett and his wife, Julia, had driven east from their home in Hollywood, and he was indeed in the motion picture business, where he was encountering many more bandits than back in his outlaw days.

Ironically, gangster movies were all the rage now. As Emmett and Julia were preparing for their trip, people were lining up in Los Angeles to see the young actor Jimmy Cagney in *The Public Enemy*. Emmett looked the part of a Hollywood producer, which he still aimed to become. He noted the two men admiring his fresh-bought blue suit and the sharp crease of his trousers.

As he released Gump's hand, the pain in his own arm returned, and the citizens could see it on Emmett's face. "The old wounds bother me a lot," he explained. "You know, during the event"—he did not like the word *raid* or *robbery*—"one of the bullets was planted right there in my arm. It shattered the bone some. The doctors wanted to cut the arm off, but I was only a kid and hotheaded, and I told them that if I was going to die, as they said I was, I would be buried all together."

He could not stop talking. "It has never healed. It is an open sore yet and I have to bandage it every morning." He grinned at the gathering crowd. "Outside of that, I'm all right."

Someone shouted out, "Are you rich?"

"It depends on what you call *rich,*" Emmett replied, further warming up to being the center of attention. "If you mean a million, we haven't got it. But we are comfortable. One thing you can say, I've made more money in two or three years of real estate deals than the Dalton gang ever made in all years of our deviltry."

He reached out his good arm. "Just say that whatever I've got I owe to my wife, the most wonderful woman in the world. Come here, Julia." She stepped closer. The newspapers would describe her as "a refined and charming woman with graying hair."

A young man with a notebook and pencil leaned in and queried, "Is this Julia, the sweetheart of your boyhood you tell so much about in your book?"

"This is she," he answered. "This trip we are making now is our second honeymoon. After we leave here, we are going to drive to her old house in Oklahoma."

The Julia portrayed in his books was an invention, but few if any in Coffeyville knew that. Emmett had ceased caring much about the past a long time ago. The thousands of days and nights in the penitentiary had helped with that.

The young reporter followed them to the Elmwood Cemetery. Emmett realized there really was not much to be done. Even if he was willing to get on his hands and knees, he had not brought any grave-tending implements. But more important, the new marker was where it was supposed to be. It listed in descending order Bob

Dalton, Grat Dalton, Bill Power, and October 5, 1892. During the installation, workers had not removed the length of pipe.*

Emmett doubted any kin remained who cared about Power. At least for Dick Broadwell, family had carted his lead-filled body away a couple of days after the event.

"Poor Bob," he murmured, gazing at the granite headstone. "He was the finest figure on horseback I have ever seen. He was the bravest, coolest man I have ever known, both as a United States deputy marshal and as an outlaw. Between Bob and me was a bond of wonderful affection; I would have died for him. There he lies." After taking a step to one side, Emmett added, "Poor Grat. Here he sleeps, an aimless, discontented boy who grew into a fierce fighting man."

No one mentioned Frank Dalton. He was the good brother, the deputy marshal who had died heroically. His grave was at the Elmwood Cemetery too. But Emmett avoided it. He had barely known Frank, but he had ridden with Grat and Bob. And probably best not to let the others here compare Frank's handsome headstone to the rather plain one of the outlaw brothers.

Emmett also thought of his brother Bill. He should be lying here as well because surely what had happened in Coffeyville killed him too. Instead, Bill Dalton occupied a lonely piece of ground a couple of thousand miles away, with not even his wife nearby. He had been the last of the Dalton outlaws.

Emmett was giving the reporter what he wanted—and, conveniently, it was the truth. As cloudy images drifted through his mind of shooting and shouting and desperately trying to haul his dead brother Bob up onto his horse, Emmett told the young man, "I am the last survivor of the old-time frontier outlaw, and I, too, am

---

* A few years after Emmett's return to Coffeyville, the headstone was stolen. For another thirty years, as it had done before, the pipe was the only marker on the grave. In the late 1960s, the city had a replica marker placed at the grave. It was stolen in 2010 but found four months later and returned to the site.

doomed to die as all those others did, from a bullet, for this bullet wound in my arm will carry me off one of these days."

As he stepped slowly away from the grave, he added, "I challenge the world to produce the history of an outlaw who ever got anything out of it except that"—pointing to the new marker—"or else to be huddled in a prison cell. And that goes for the modern bandit of the skyscraper frontier of our big cities, too. The machine gun may help them get away with it a little better and the motor car may help them in making an escape better than to ride on horseback, but it all ends the same way. The biggest fool on earth is the one who thinks he can beat the law, that crime can be made to pay. It never paid and it never will, and that's the one big lesson of the Coffeyville"—he finally added—"raid."

Emmett glanced at his wife, and Julia's expression indicated he may have already gone too far and he ought to stop. Just as well, because suddenly Emmett felt all of his years and a chill despite the late-April sun as he recalled two forever-intertwined days. One was in November 1887, when he was sixteen years old, and his mother and her younger children received the news about Frank and the Daltons' hopes for a law-abiding life were suddenly and cruelly dashed. The other day was directly connected: October 5, 1892, when the Dalton Gang attempted the most daring robbery of the American West . . . and died trying.

He took Julia's arm and they began walking toward the cemetery gates. For the last of the Daltons, there now was an urgency to leave the past behind.

THE DALTONS

CHAPTER 1

MAYHEM IN MINNESOTA

As daring as the raid on Coffeyville in 1892 was, there was a precedent involving men who were kin to the Dalton boys. It had taken place sixteen years earlier, far from Kansas.

Jesse and Frank James were the most well-known members of the James-Younger Gang who flourished after the Civil War, but the bandits were as much led by Cole Younger as the James brothers. At various times, the gang included Cole's brothers Jim, Bob, and John as well as their brother-in-law John Jarrett. There were also Clell Miller, Arthur McCoy, another set of brothers, George and Oliver Shepherd, and yet another one, William and Tom McDaniel, along with Charlie Pitt and Bill Chadwell. Most hailed from Missouri.

This roundup of roughnecks had begun as a group of Confederate bushwhackers who had participated in the bitter partisan fighting in Missouri during the war. Afterward, the men continued to plunder and murder, though the motive shifted to personal profit rather than for the fight for Southern independence. But the loose association of outlaws did not truly become the James-Younger Gang until 1868 at the earliest, when the authorities first named Cole Younger, Jarrett,

McCoy, and the Shepherd brothers as suspects in the robbery of the Nimrod Long Bank in Russellville, Kentucky.

After that, they were off to the races. For the next eight years, the James-Younger Gang was among the most feared, most publicized, and most wanted company of criminals on the American frontier. Though their crimes were reckless and brutal, many members of the gang were afforded a romantic aura in the public eye that earned them significant popular support and sympathy. And they got around—the gang was suspected of having robbed banks, stagecoaches, and trains in Kentucky, Tennessee, Iowa, Kansas, Minnesota, Texas, Arkansas, Louisiana, Alabama, and West Virginia as well as Missouri.

Who were they and why did they seem to relish a violent life of crime? Some of them did not start out poor. The Younger brothers grew up as the sons of a prosperous slave-owner father in Jackson County, Missouri. Thomas Coleman (the one known as Cole), James Hardin, John Harrison, and Robert Ewing were four of the fourteen children of Henry and Bursheba Younger. Henry was from Kentucky and had met his wife in Kansas City. In Jackson County, he became successful as a land speculator and businessman as well as a farmer. He could afford to have his children educated, especially his sons.

But Missouri was not to have a peaceful future for many years. Its turmoil began with the border war with Kansas. Many residents and lawmakers in the latter wanted it to enter the U.S. as a state free of slavery, while many families in Missouri were slave owners and wanted the same for their western neighbor. Though Henry Younger owned a couple of slaves, he supported the free-state movement in Kansas. This position, however, was no protection against Kansas Jayhawkers who crossed the border to attack Missouri farms.

The irony, then, was that as the pro-Union Henry's livestock was being stolen and property damaged, his sons were becoming Southern sympathizers. Finally, Cole set off to join the guerillas led by William Quantrill. This could have resulted in being only a temporary allegiance, especially once Cole saw the consequences of Quantrill's depravity, but in July 1862, his brother Henry was killed by Union militiamen. After that, there was no turning back.

After a year of hard riding with the Confederate bushwhackers, Cole was a willing participant in the August 1863 raid on Lawrence, Kansas. The town was ransacked and left in flames and some two hundred men and boys were gunned down or burned to death. The following year, James Younger replaced his brother in Quantrill's band so that Cole could join the Confederate army. As a captain, he led troops in campaigns in Louisiana and then as far west as California. He was there when the war ended and had to make his way back to Missouri.*

Alexander Franklin James, known to all as Frank, and his younger brother Jesse were not related to the Youngers but grew up in the same "Little Dixie" area of western Missouri. Their mother, Zerelda, was an outspoken supporter of Southern independence.† Frank and later Jesse, at age sixteen in 1864, joined up with Quantrill's raiders. Both also rode with the spin-off guerilla leaders Archie Clement and "Bloody Bill" Anderson. After these freewheeling and morally compromised days as bushwhackers, it is highly unlikely the James boys would have found work other than as outlaws.

In the final days of the Civil War, Frank surrendered to Union troops in Kentucky. Jesse was in the process of doing the same in Missouri when he was shot through the lung. In an unforeseen twist,

---

* In May 1865, a month after the surrender at Appomattox, Quantrill was badly wounded during an ambush by Union soldiers. Several of his men were captured, including James Younger. Quantrill died the following month. Younger was sent to prison but was soon released.
† According to Hollywood, the death of Mrs. James at the hands of Union sympathizers was the catalyst for the renegade career of Frank and Jesse. However, while an incendiary attack on her home (see page 8) cost the thrice-married Zerelda James part of an arm and the life of her eight-year-old son, Archie, this did not occur until a decade after the war ended. She eventually relocated to Oklahoma and died at eighty-six in 1911.

this led to romance because Jesse was nursed back to health by a cousin also named Zerelda and the two married. Domestic bliss did not tame Jesse: He and Frank soon needed another gang to ride with, and the Younger brothers provided that.

Cole and James Younger had returned to a family farm in ruins and no trace of their former prosperity despite the efforts of their brothers John and Bob and their mother and sisters. This loss coupled with the anger toward Reconstruction with its ongoing presence of Yankee troops persuaded the Younger boys to pursue a different line of work. They joined the ranks of Confederate soldiers turned outlaws. In the case of the Youngers, they were especially good at it, even more so after they teamed up with the James boys.

Particularly in Missouri, banks had become the symbols of subjugation and financial ruin, so these institutions became the targets of the outlaws' wrath. The first robbery by the James-Younger Gang was of the Clay County Savings Association in Liberty. Their new career had an auspicious beginning, as the thieves rode off with over $60,000, which was a very handsome haul in February 1866.*

No surprise, then, that the emboldened gang wanted to keep at it. During the next decade, with a changing cast of characters, some of whom were also former bushwhackers, the James-Younger Gang terrorized businesses and law-abiding citizens, and it frustrated lawmen throughout the South and Midwest. Best estimates are that the robbers raided a dozen banks, seven trains, and four stagecoaches. Fear and frustration were not the only result—at least eleven men were killed, beginning with a bystander, George Wymore, in Liberty.

An especially tragic event during this reign of terror occurred in January 1871. Two lawmen tried to arrest John Younger in Dallas County, Texas, and he killed them both. Another highlight, or lowlight, came five months later when the gang robbed a bank

---

* Some accounts contend that this was the first daylight, peacetime bank robbery in the U.S.

in Corydon, Iowa. One consequence was the bank contacted the Pinkerton National Detective Agency in Chicago, the first involvement of the famous company in the pursuit of the James-Younger Gang.

Allan Pinkerton dispatched his son Robert, who joined a county sheriff in tracking several gang members to a farm in Civil Bend, Missouri. A short gunfight ended indecisively as the bandits escaped. Displaying journalism ambitions, soon afterward, Jesse wrote a letter to *The Kansas City Star* claiming Republicans were persecuting him for his Confederate loyalties by accusing him and Frank of carrying out the robberies. "But I don't care what the degraded Radical party thinks about me," he wrote. "I would just as soon they would think I was a robber as not."

What would have been a major confrontation in the history of the American West was narrowly avoided on September 23, 1872, when Jesse James and Cole and John Younger robbed a ticket booth of the Kansas City Industrial Exposition, amid thousands of people. They took some nine hundred dollars and accidentally shot a little girl in the ensuing struggle with the ticket-seller. In attendance and arriving on the scene just as the trio hurried off was Wild Bill Hickok, who often lived in Kansas City when he was not out on the trail.

Instead of a gunfight, a significant outcome of the robbery was that the editor of *The Star,* John Newman Edwards, wrote what became a famous editorial titled "The Chivalry of Crime." It said about the gang, "They rob the rich and give to the poor"—giving the unreformed bushwhackers a Robin Hood sheen.

The cast of Younger brothers was reduced in March 1874. On the eleventh, a Pinkerton agent, Joseph Whicher, was found shot to death alongside a rural road in Jackson County, where the brothers grew up. Two other agents, John Boyle and Louis Lull, accompanied by Deputy Sheriff Edwin Daniels, posed as cattle buyers to try to track the Youngers down. On the seventeenth, the trio was stopped and attacked by John and Jim Younger on a rural stretch of road.

Daniels was killed instantly, Lull and John Younger wounded each other, and Boyle and Jim Younger escaped. John Younger died soon after the shoot-out, but Lull lived long enough to testify before a coroner's inquest before succumbing to his wounds.

More attempts to capture the gang were unsuccessful. Finally, on the night of January 25, 1875, Pinkerton agents surrounded the James farm in Kearney, Missouri. Frank and Jesse had been there earlier but had left. The Pinkertons threw an iron incendiary device into the house, which exploded when it rolled into a blazing fireplace. It was after this vindictive attack that injured Zerelda and killed her son Archie that Allan Pinkerton abandoned the chase for the James-Younger Gang.

The final act of the James-Younger Gang—one directly connected to what would happen in Coffeyville—took place in Minnesota on September 7, 1876. The gang set out to rob the First National Bank of Northfield.

Why would Jesse, Frank, Cole, and the rest travel so far away from familiar surroundings? The idea for the raid came from Jesse and Bob Younger. Cole tried to talk his brother out of the plan, but Bob refused to back down. Reluctantly, Cole agreed to go, writing to his brother Jim in California to come home. Jim Younger had never wanted anything to do with Cole's outlaw activities, but he agreed to go out of family loyalty.

The Northfield bank was not really worth the trip of 375 miles straight north. It was a perfectly ordinary rural bank, though rumors persisted that General Adelbert Ames, son of the owner of the Ames Mill in Northfield, had deposited $50,000 there. A possibility is it had been selected because of its connection to two Union generals and Radical Republican politicians: Ames, and his father-in-law, Benjamin Butler. Ames had just stepped down as governor of Mississippi, where he had been strongly identified with civil rights for freed slaves and had recently moved to Northfield to be near his father. The New Hampshire–born Butler had been a major general in the Union army.

Instead of wearing out their horses, Cole, Jim, and Bob Younger, Frank and Jesse James, Charlie Pitts, Clell Miller, and Bill Chadwell took a train to St. Paul in early September. After a layover there, they divided into two groups, one going to Mankato, the other to Red Wing, on either side of Northfield. They purchased horses and scouted the terrain around the towns, agreeing to meet south of Northfield along the Cannon River on the morning of the seventh.

At two that afternoon, the gang attempted to rob the bank. Northfield residents had seen the unfamiliar men leave a local restaurant near the mill shortly after noon. The outlaws ate fried eggs that, according to later testimony, were washed down with whiskey. Bob Younger, Frank James, and Charlie Pitts crossed the bridge by the Ames Mill and entered the bank. Jesse James, Cole and Jim Younger, Chadwell, and Miller stood guard outside. Two were standing by the bank's front door, and the other three were waiting in Mills Square to guard the gang's escape route.

Suddenly, a man named J. S. Allen shouted, "Get your guns, boys, they're robbing the bank!"

Once local citizens realized a robbery was in progress, several took up arms from local hardware stores. Shooting from behind cover, they poured deadly fire on the outlaws. During the gun battle, a medical student, Henry Wheeler, killed Clell Miller, shooting from a third-floor window of the Dampier House Hotel, across the street from the bank. Another man, A. R. Manning, who took cover at the corner of the Scriver building down the street, killed Bill Chadwell.* Cole was shot in his left hip, Bob suffered a shattered elbow, and Jim was shot in the jaw. The only civilian fatality on the street was thirty-year-old Nicholas Gustafson, an unarmed recent Swedish immigrant, who was killed by Cole at the corner of Fifth Street and Division.

---

* With no other takers, Chadwell's body was collected by Henry Wheeler. When the latter opened a medical practice, the skeleton on display was that of the outlaw.

While all this was going on outside, inside the bank, Joseph Heywood, the assistant cashier, refused to open the safe and was murdered for resisting. The two other employees in the bank were teller Alonzo Bunker and assistant bookkeeper Frank Wilcox. Bunker escaped from the bank by running out the back door despite being wounded in the right shoulder by Pitts. The three robbers then ran out of the bank after hearing the shooting outside and mounted their horses to make a run for it, having stolen only several bags of nickels.

A posse was formed quickly to catch and perhaps hang what was left of the James-Younger Gang. A cross-country chase was on.

CHAPTER 2

MIDWEST MANHUNT

Near Mankato, the surviving gang members split up. The Younger brothers and Charlie Pitts went one way, and Frank and Jesse James went another. The latter turned out to be luckier, as the posse continued after Cole and company.

Eighty miles and two weeks later, the not-to-be-denied Northfield posse caught up to and pounced on their prey near Madelia, still in Minnesota. In the ensuing gun battle, Pitts was killed, and the Youngers, after being filled with even more lead, surrendered. Though some citizens were sorely tempted to do so, the brothers were not hanged and were instead soon tried for murder. After the guilty verdicts, the outlaws were sentenced to twenty-five years in the state prison at Stillwater. Bob did not see the end of his prison term, dying in 1889. Jim was paroled in 1901 and immediately fell in love with Alice Miller, a newspaper reporter. Barred from marrying her by the strict terms of his parole, Jim died by suicide. Cole was also paroled in 1901 and managed to get by, dying fifteen years later.*

---

* During his incarceration, Cole Younger founded *The Prison Mirror*, what is believed to be the longest-running prison newspaper in the U.S. After receiving a

Compared to the shot-up Youngers and the dead Miller, Chadwell, and Pitts, the James brothers had gotten off easy—Jesse took a bullet in one thigh, and Frank was hit in one leg. The injuries did not prevent them from galloping out of Minnesota, and they kept going. Somehow, despite hundreds of pursuers and a nationwide alarm, Frank and Jesse managed to keep riding all the way back to Missouri.

The Northfield disaster seemed to have knocked the stuffing out of the James boys, though, and they quit their outlaw ways. They relocated and lived quietly in Nashville. Frank, in particular, thrived in his new life, farming in the Whites Creek area. But Jesse did not adapt well to peace, so this mundane existence lasted only until 1879. A restless Jesse, with a hesitant Frank in tow, pulled a new gang together and returned to robbing banks, trains, and stagecoaches, beginning on October 8, when they took on a train near Glendale, Missouri.

It was the holdup of a Chicago and Alton Railroad train in September 1881 that put the new governor of Minnesota, Thomas Crittenden, in such a lather that he convinced the state's railroad and express executives to put up the money for a large reward for the capture of the James brothers. In a related event, that December, when a gang member, Wood Hite, was killed during an argument, one of the men arrested for the crime was Bob Ford. He made a deal that in return for being let off the hook and being promised the reward, he would become a member of the James Gang.

As it turned out, he did more than betray the James brothers. Ford shot Jesse in April 1882 at the latter's home in St. Joseph, Missouri. Ford and his brother Charley surrendered to the authorities, pleaded guilty, and were promptly pardoned by Governor Crittenden. Escaping a fate similar to his brother's, on October 4, Frank

---

pardon, Cole teamed up with Frank James to perform in a touring Wild West show and he wrote *The Story of Cole Younger,* in which he portrayed himself not as an outlaw but as an avenger of wrongs done to the Confederacy.

James surrendered to Crittenden. Supposedly, Frank turned himself in with the understanding that he would not be extradited to Northfield to face charges there. The only two times that Frank was brought to trial for the gang's activities, he was acquitted.

Frank James was done with the outlaw life for good. In addition to teaming up with Cole Younger as a pre-vaudeville act, he kept up a lifelong correspondence with Bat Masterson, whom he had befriended in the 1870s, and he hosted curious visitors to Jesse's grave at the James family farm. Like Cole Younger, Frank died at the age of seventy-two, in 1916.

CHAPTER 3

DALTON DESCENDANTS

Some members of the Dalton clan believed that they were descended from a Viking family. As the Dalton researcher Nancy B. Samuelson reports, there is also some evidence to support the belief that a branch of the family later settled in France and a Dalton descendant was a member of the army under William the Conqueror, who sailed west in 1066 to earn his name. However it happened, Samuelson writes that "by the thirteenth century the name was well established in the British Isles."

Flash-forward several hundred years to the 1630s when Daltons can be found in New England. The American Revolution and its aftermath represented a change of fortunes and relocation of at least some of the family thanks to Tristram Dalton. Born in what is now Newburyport, Massachusetts, Dalton graduated from Harvard College in 1755, in a class that also included John Adams. Afterward, he studied law and was admitted to the bar, but did not practice, instead pursuing a career as a merchant.

Dalton's father was a ship captain turned merchant, involved in trade with Europe and the West Indies, and upon his death in 1770, Tristram inherited an estate and local businesses that made him a wealthy man. He was not significantly involved in politics until 1774, when the tensions between the colonists and Great Britain increased. Dalton was elected to the Massachusetts Provincial Congress and was an active proponent of independence. During the American Revolution, his contributions included provisioning ships from his merchant fleet for the Penobscot Expedition.

This adventure was a flotilla of nineteen warships and twenty-five support vessels that sailed from Boston on July 19, 1779, for the upper Penobscot Bay in the District of Maine carrying an expeditionary force of more than one thousand American colonial marines and militiamen. Also included was a one-hundred-man artillery detachment under the command of Lieutenant Colonel Paul Revere. The expedition's goal was to reclaim control of mid-coast Maine from the British, who had captured it a month earlier, naming the territory New Ireland. It was the largest American naval expedition of the war. The fighting took place on land and at sea over a period of three weeks. The result, alas, for Dalton and the mission's other supporters was the worst naval defeat the U.S. would suffer until Pearl Harbor 162 years later.

Tristram Dalton was elected to the Continental Congress in 1783 and 1784. He was also elected as a delegate to the state convention on the adoption of the United States Constitution. In 1788, he was chosen as one of Massachusetts's first U.S. senators, along with Caleb Strong. Strong won the draw for the longer of the two terms, leaving Dalton with a short two-year term. In the 1791 election (senators were then chosen by vote of the state legislature), Dalton ran a distant fourth.

He and his wife, Ruth Hooper, the daughter of a wealthy Marblehead merchant, lived in New York City, then moved to Philadelphia. When the site of the nation's capital was selected, Dalton speculatively purchased land in Washington, D.C. His crystal ball failed him, because Washington real estate did not appreciate, plus he had invested through an unscrupulous agent. The unhappy combination wiped out most of his fortune.

Thanks to a patronage job, Dalton eked out a living until he died at age seventy-nine in 1817. Somewhere along the way, probably during his ill-fated Washington foray, he encountered a branch of Daltons living in Virginia. Tristram and Ruth had ten children, so one might think the Massachusetts Daltons spawned the Virginia Daltons, but according to one account, of those ten children, only three lived to adulthood, all daughters. In any event, according to Samuelson, Tristram had been "a known associate of George Washington and other prominent Virginia families." And, probably not coincidentally, "so were some of the early Virginia Daltons."

Another Dalton descendant of interest was Benjamin Dalton. He was the son of James and Agatha Dalton of Pitts County, Virginia. In April 1815, he married Nancy Rabourn in Montgomery County, Kentucky. Presumably, Benjamin had served with U.S. forces in the War of 1812, because in 1879, at the age of eighty-six, Nancy filed for a widow's pension. One cannot explain what took her so long, because by then, her husband had been dead for forty-four years.

During the couple's twenty years of marriage, they produced five (possibly six) children. One of them was James Lewis Dalton, born in Montgomery County in 1826. He claimed to have attended college, but what is certain is at age twenty, he enlisted in a Kentucky infantry regiment. He served for a year in Mexico during the Mexican-American War, his contribution to the fighting being as a fifer. Exactly a year after enlisting, while his regiment was in New Orleans, Dalton was mustered out. Four years later, in March 1851, he married Adeline Lee Younger, who probably had no idea of how harsh her long life would be.

It could be said that James Dalton—or Lewis, as he was most often called—married up. Adeline was the daughter of Charles Lee Younger, whose brother Henry Washington Younger had fathered the four boys who would comprise the Younger Gang. Many years later, in his autobiography, Cole Younger claimed that his family "had always been prominent. It was born in the blood. My great-grandmother on my father's side was a daughter of 'Lighthorse Harry' Lee whose proud memory we all cherish." His mother, Bursheba, was the daughter of a man who had fought in General Andrew Jackson's smashing victory over the British at New Orleans in January 1815. His maternal grandfather "was a grand nephew of Chief Justice John Marshall of Virginia."*

Right from the beginning of their marriage, Lewis and Adeline Dalton were busy making babies. He did not stay nearly as busy providing for them. Lewis was keenly interested in horses, and he roamed the racetracks of Kansas, Missouri, and Oklahoma. Sometimes, he brought his wife and then older sons. When Lewis was home, he and Adeline continued to produce child after child—they would have fifteen in all. Ironically, when Lewis and Adeline married, he was a saloonkeeper, but at his sober wife's insistence, he gave up what would have provided a steadier income and lifestyle. The saloon life suited him better too, being an easygoing and attractive man who enjoyed meeting people.

"Father was six-feet-one-inch barefoot, and, in his prime, weighed two hundred and twenty pounds," recalled his son Littleton. "He was a fine looking man: black eyes, clear, rosy complexion and curling, coal-black hair." Adeline, he said, was "stocky, with blue eyes, florid complexion and dark, almost red hair."

Lewis also, alas, enjoyed gambling even more than people, especially on the horses. He had other skills and good qualities, such as being a carpenter and a musician, and as a farmer, he would read the Bible and pray when morning chores had been completed. But betting on the horses kept him moving around a lot, either on to the next racing venue or eluding the people from the last one to whom he owed money. Over the years, the family settled for various periods

---

* Adeline Younger had a half brother named Thomas Coleman Younger, whose third wife, Augusta Inskeep, was related to Benjamin Simms, who was Zerelda James's second husband. Augusta was also an aunt of the outlaw Johnny Ringo of Tombstone infamy.

of time in the Denver area; Lawrence, Kansas; Cass, Bates, and Clay counties in Missouri; in the Indian Territory of Oklahoma; and in Coffeyville, Kansas.

Adeline Younger Dalton was, clearly, a woman of unbreakable will and determination. She kept the family and the family homes together, birthing and caring for those fifteen children. By temperament as well as necessity, Adeline was the disciplinarian, but her children also remembered her as a kind and caring mother. She had to be quite resilient, given that nine of her children would die during her lifetime, four of them from gunshots.

Lewis Dalton would live to experience only one of those violent deaths. He was living in Kansas, near Dearing, when he died, at the age of sixty-four. In his wife's obituary in *The Kingfisher Free Press*, it was reported that "in 1890 the family started to Oklahoma in a covered wagon to make their home. Mr. Dalton died July 16, 1890, from a sudden attack of Cholera morbis, about a week out on their trip."

That obituary would not be published for many years, because when Adeline arrived in Kingfisher with her younger children, she had many years left. They would not be easy ones, though, thanks to four sons whose reputations would rest on being outlaws.

CHAPTER 4

"THIS CATASTROPHIC CONTEST"

The Dalton children were born and grew up during an especially tumultuous time in the shared history of Kansas, Missouri, and Oklahoma—one that had begun centuries earlier, well before they became neighboring states.

Indigenous peoples were present in the region by the last ice age. The first recorded history dates back to the expedition of the Spaniard Francisco Vázquez de Coronado. The governor of Mexico had commissioned him to trek north in search of the Seven Cities of Cibola, keeping an eye out especially for Quivira, rumored to be the richest of the cities. After wintering in New Mexico, Coronado and his would-be conquerors headed east. They got lost in the dangerously dry Staked Plains of Texas. Rather than risk his entire command, Coronado sent some of his men back to New Mexico. With the remaining thirty soldiers, he and an Indian guide turned north. They eventually crossed the Arkansas River near what is now Spearville, Kansas. On a foray farther east, Coronado and company also wandered around some of what is now Oklahoma.

In the seventeenth century and early eighteenth century, French explorers roamed the area. Around this time, Comanche and Kiowa entered the region from the west and Quapaw and Osage peoples moved into what is now eastern Oklahoma. Both Spanish and French colonists were left on their own in 1803, when all the French territory west of the Mississippi River was acquired by the U.S. in the Louisiana Purchase, which included most of Kansas. The subsequent Meriwether Lewis and William Clark Corps of Discovery was the first official U.S. expedition to reach Kansas. Their July 4, 1804, celebration was held near the present site of Atchison. It is in one of that expedition's journals that the word *Kansas* is found, probably connected to Lewis and Clark encountering the Kaw tribe.

Explorations led by Lieutenant Zebulon Pike and Major Stephen Long and others meandered through portions of eastern Kansas and Oklahoma. In their wake came other explorers and hunters and, inevitably, settlers. Also inevitably, as more of the U.S. was being populated by people of European descent, to make room, the federal government forcibly removed tens of thousands of Indians from their homelands in Kansas and other territories and transported them to the area that included present-day Oklahoma.

The Choctaw was the first of the Five Civilized Tribes to be exiled from their longtime hunting grounds. The tragic event known as the Trail of Tears was the removal of the nation in 1831, although the term is also used for the Cherokee removal, when seventeen thousand members of the tribe and two thousand of their black slaves were deported.

Meanwhile, the increasing number of white people were trying to figure out their landholdings and political shifts. Missouri was a slave state, and the proslavery population in Kansas wanted that territory to enter the union the same way. Competing for the hearts and minds of those who would decide were "free-staters," composed mostly of antislavery residents. The conflict represented the turmoil expanding in much of the rest of the United States.

"Kansas was the center of this catastrophic contest," writes Charles C. Howes in his *This Place Called Kansas*. "Both sides were fully organized, and both sides were determined. The result was five years of internecine strife in Kansas, followed by four years of bloody warfare between the North and the South." The term *Bleeding Kansas* described the years of violence in the territory that continued during the Civil War.

Many families, like the Daltons, lived in fear, caught between competing interests, not all of them having to do with partisan battles. "There were booze and bootleggers and whiskey runners and prostitutes by the hundreds," Littleton Dalton told Frank Latta for his book *Dalton Gang Days*. "The old Whiskey Trail, also called the old Border Ruffian Trail, which ran by our home, was strung with graves. I believe there was an average of a murder a night between Kansas City and the Red River."

During the savage four-year war among the white people, many Indian tribes were forced to choose sides or did so because there was some financial or political benefit to doing so. For example, the Five Civilized Tribes supported and signed treaties with the Confederate military during the Civil War because they were promised their own state if the South won. Among other benefits to the tribes, such sovereignty would allow them to continue slavery in their territories.

Soon after the war ended, cattle ranches in Texas strove to meet the demands for food in eastern cities. The lengthening railroad lines in Kansas promised to deliver the ranchers' beeves in a timely manner. Cattle trails and more ranches developed as cowboys drove herds north, sometimes illegally through Indian Territory. By 1881, four of five major cattle trails on the western frontier were slicing through the territory.

The increasing presence of white settlers in Indian Territory prompted the U.S. government to establish the Dawes Act in 1887, which divided the lands of the tribes into allotments for individual families, encouraging farming and private land ownership among the Indians but expropriating land to the federal government. In the process, railroad companies purchased or at times simply took nearly half of Indian-held land within the territory for outside settlers.

Then came the "land runs," or "land rushes." They were held for settlers where certain territories were opened to occupation, starting at a precise time. Usually, land was open to settlers on a first-come, first-served basis. Those who broke the rules by crossing the border into the territory before the official opening time were said to have been crossing the border *sooner,* leading to the term sooners, which eventually became a nickname for all Oklahomans.

Why was this particular territory so desirable? By the late 1880s, much of the best land in the established states was already occupied. In the large swaths of Oklahoma reserved for Indian tribes, the land was not covered by sod houses and farm fields and ranches nearly as much as in neighboring Kansas and Texas. Pressure mounted on politicians as would-be settlers coveted the millions of acres of buffalo grass and fertile soil that Oklahoma offered.

However, the territory was already occupied, wasn't it, by those tribes? As colonial and U.S. governments had amply demonstrated for over two centuries, treaties were made to be broken. A powerful argument was that such enviable acreage was being wasted on people who did not properly know how to exploit their property. *The Oklahoma War Chief,* published in Caldwell across the Kansas border, thundered its unhappiness that in 1883 the Cherokee Nation had leased land to a group of cattle ranchers for five years at $100,000 annually, which would earn each member of the tribe just three dollars a year. What a waste, when that area could be covered with high-yielding farms.

And what about those ranchers who had arranged such a one-sided deal? The Cherokee land had been "filched from the people by the cattle kings," sputtered the Caldwell newspaper, who added that all those acres were "fattening countless herds of stock at two cents an acre!"

The answer was not to break the lease and return the land to the

Cherokee but to better exploit it and do so more democratically by opening it up to everyone. After all, as General Nelson Miles advised the War Department, "The Indian Territory is now a block in the pathway of civilization. It is preserved to perpetuate a mongrel race far removed from the influence of civilized people—a refuge of the outlaw and indolent of whites, blacks and Mexicans."

The result of all this fulminating was that enough lawmakers agreed to draft the Dawes Act of 1887. It would allow for the western half of "Indian Country" (all land except the home of the Five Civilized Tribes) to be settled.* On March 3, outgoing President Grover Cleveland signed the act into law, and three weeks later, President Benjamin Harrison declared that April 22 at noon would see the opening of Oklahoma to settlers.

All the pent-up pressure would be let loose that day. In the weeks leading up to it, roads through Texas and Kansas to the border were packed with people on wagons, horses, mules, and every other kind of conveyance. Each traveler knew that he had to get in the best position possible to jump off fast when the signal was given and to grab a parcel before the next guy did.

As noon on the twenty-second approached, "They were lined up by the thousands, mile upon mile, north to south, east to west," according to Glenn Shirley in *West of Hell's Fringe*. "The rich and the poor, the refined and the ignorant—all touched elbows in this horde who waited now for the sound of starting bugles and carbines. Most of the people were making the run on horseback. There was everything from mules to race horses, some saddled, many bareback. Open buggies, fringed carriages, prairie schooners, light farm wagons, carts, racing sulkies, and even a few five-foot bicycles stood wheel to wheel in that curious assemblage. Hundreds of people had

---

* Also approved that year was a line of the Santa Fe Railroad to be built right through the territory, from Arkansas City to Fort Worth, further intruding on previously protected land.

come on foot, trusting to sturdy legs and good lungs to win a piece of land."

At noon, the dams burst. By nightfall, every available parcel had been claimed in the Oklahoma District, totaling 1,920,000 acres.* Yet many of the one hundred thousand would-be settlers had missed out, either because they were not fast or strong enough or they had been injured or even killed by rampaging animals and vehicles. Still, in one afternoon, the population in the territory had increased by sixty thousand. Guthrie, which had been nothing more than a railroad stop, suddenly had fifteen thousand citizens; Oklahoma City had five thousand and Kingfisher had three thousand. Brand-new tent-filled towns ranging in population from a hundred to a thousand had sprouted across the territory. Around campfires that night, plans were already being made to form local governments, which would include a law-enforcement system.

The latter would mean having the federal government appoint U.S. marshals for the newly populated portion of Oklahoma, who in turn would appoint deputy marshals. It was expected that elected sheriffs and their deputies would be few and far between and would probably at best be a mixed bag of competent and reluctant lawmen. And once men were arrested, what of a judicial system?

For years, that system had been under the purview of Isaac Parker in Fort Smith, Arkansas, who was often referred to as "Hanging Judge" Parker—for good reason.

---

* Some so-called sooners had managed to slip in and claim prime parcels, and most of them got away with it.

CHAPTER 5

THE JUDGE AND HIS HANGMAN

Until his death in 1896, the white-bearded visage of Judge Parker was the face of frontier justice. He did as much—and probably more—than anyone to promote law and order in what remained of the frontier in Middle America.

Parker was born in 1838 and raised on the family farm in Barnesville, Ohio. He had a good education, including a private school, then he taught in a county primary school. He switched paths at seventeen and began "reading the law" with an established firm. Four years later, he passed the Ohio bar exam.

Parker moved to St. Joseph, Missouri, where he joined his maternal uncle's law firm of Shannon and Branch. In December 1861, he married Mary O'Toole, with whom he had sons Charles and James. During the following year, he opened his own law firm and represented clients in the municipal and county courts. Parker also ran successfully as a Democrat for the part-time position of city attorney for St. Joseph. He served three one-year terms beginning in April 1861, keeping the position even after he had enlisted in the Sixty-First Missouri Emergency Regiment, which fought on the Union side.

In 1864, Parker left the Democratic Party because of his staunch opposition to slavery. As a Republican, he ran for county prosecutor of the Ninth Missouri Judicial District, and as a member of the Electoral College, he voted for the reelection of Abraham Lincoln. Four years later, Parker won a term as judge of the Twelfth Missouri Circuit. He did not stay in that position long, though, because in 1870, he was elected to Congress. One of his more progressive efforts was sponsoring a bill designed to allow women to hold public office in U.S. territories. The measure failed, but still, a local paper wrote of him, "Missouri had no more trusted or influential representative in Congress during the past two years."

Such endorsements persuaded Parker to run for a Senate seat. But the political tide had shifted in Missouri; it seemed unlikely that the legislature would elect a Republican to the Senate. Instead, in March 1875, President Ulysses S. Grant nominated Parker to a seat on the U.S. District Court for the Western District of Arkansas. It had been vacated by Judge William Story, who resigned under threat of impeachment for allegations of corruption. Parker would be a breath of fresh air—except to criminals.

His first session as the district judge in Fort Smith was on May 10, 1875, and on that same day, he commissioned as a deputy U.S. marshal Bass Reeves, who began a busy career as one of the first African American lawmen west of the Mississippi River. During his first session, Judge Parker presided over the trial of eighteen men, all of whom were charged with murder. After fifteen were convicted, Parker sentenced eight of them to a mandatory death penalty. He ordered the condemned to be executed at the same time on September 3. One of those sentenced to death was killed trying to escape. The governor commuted the sentence of another to life in prison because of his youth. The rest were hanged—two days after Parker told a reporter for *The St. Louis Dispatch* that he favored the abolition of capital punishment. Even so, his tenure as the "Hanging Judge" had gotten off to a fast start.

Parker's court had final jurisdiction over federal crimes in the Indian Territory, as there was no court available for appeals. The Five Civilized Tribes and other Native American tribes in the Indian Territory had jurisdiction over their own citizens through their tribal legal systems and governments. Federal law in Indian Territory applied to non-Indian U.S. citizens.

Parker was kept busy. The Western District of Arkansas court was to meet in four separate terms each year, but it had such a large caseload that the four terms ran together. Parker's court sat six days a week and often up to ten hours each day. Finally, in 1883, Congress reduced the jurisdiction of the court, reassigning parts of the Indian Territory to federal courts in Texas and Kansas. Still, the increasing number of settlers moving into the Indian Territories continued to burden the court's workload. In his "spare time," Parker also served on the Fort Smith school board and he was the first president of St. John's Hospital.

Judge Parker's reign in Fort Smith lasted as long as he did. In 1895, Congress voted to remove the remaining Indian Territory jurisdiction of the Western District, effective September 1 of the next year. Despite or because of a reduced caseload, Parker died two months later, at age fifty-eight.

One cannot leave off discussing the Hanging Judge without mention of the man who did most of the hanging, and he would be dubbed, appropriately, the "Prince of Hangmen." It is safe to assume George Maledon will not be surpassed as the man who executed—at least legally—the most people in U.S. history.

Born in Germany in June 1830, Maledon, along with his family, immigrated to Detroit, where he grew up, then he became a police officer in Arkansas. He served in a state artillery battalion during the Civil War. Afterward, he served as a deputy sheriff and worked as a "turnkey" in the federal jail in Fort Smith. Glenn Shirley described Maledon as a "wispy, black-bearded Bavarian with a tight lip and a brooding eye. He had little education, but was as quick as a cat, an excellent shot with the two pistols he carried, and liked prison work." In 1872, he was appointed a special deputy responsible for the execution of condemned prisoners. Befitting his new profession, he always wore black.

During the next twenty-two years as the Hanging Judge's hangman, Maledon was the consummate professional. He executed more than sixty prisoners, and that number would have been higher if not for having to shoot five prisoners who attempted last-minute escapes. During the early years, the hangings were events open to the public, and thousands of onlookers gathered to witness them in a convivial atmosphere. Maledon's solemn professionalism and the wide-ranging behaviors of the condemned made for riveting theater.

Maledon prided himself in killing quickly. The ropes he used were made of the best hemp fiber handwoven in St. Louis to keep them from slipping. The ropes were treated with an oil substance, then stretched on the gibbet with two-hundred-pound bags of sand, then oiled again, which helped shrink them from 1.25 inches to 1 inch in diameter, which was best for knotting. He would affix the knotted rope in a way that the prisoner's neck would immediately break. This, Maledon believed, was more humane than the prisoner kicking and twisting as he strangled to death.

The largest group Maledon executed at once consisted of those six men who were hanged in Fort Smith on September 3, 1875. As early as the week before, people had begun to arrive for the spectacle, including reporters from St. Louis, Kansas City, and Little Rock newspapers, whose accounts would receive national distribution. By the time the six prisoners were marched to the gallows, the audience consisted of at least five thousand people. There was much cheering as the six swung.

After a productive career, it did not end well for Maledon. He did retire in 1894 and open a grocery store, but he was back in the Fort Smith court the following year when his eighteen-year-old daughter, Annie, was murdered. The accused man, named Carver, was her boyfriend—well, she thought he was her boyfriend, but when she went with him to Muskogee, Oklahoma, she found he was already married. Angry about her protests, Carver shot her. Annie was taken to Fort Smith, where she died.

Carver was arrested, found guilty of murder, and sentenced by Judge Parker to die. No doubt Maledon would have gladly come out of retirement to do the deed himself. But with a new lawyer, Carver appealed his conviction to a higher court. It was not overturned, but the sentence was changed from death to life in prison. To distract himself from being so distraught all over again, the former hangman loaded up a wagon with various execution artifacts and left Fort Smith. He toured towns in Arkansas and Oklahoma, telling tales about the outlaws whose necks he broke and displaying ropes and photographs. Maledon became a rather popular showman.

In his seventies, his health began to fail. There was no retirement home for old executioners, so he wound up in one for elderly soldiers in Humboldt, Tennessee. He died there in 1911, in his eighty-first year.

The Oklahoma and southeastern Kansas region the Daltons were born and came of age in had known more than its share of bushwhacking, war, feuding, and banditry. That by itself, though, does not explain why four of the Dalton boys became outlaws, with their siblings becoming for the most part law-abiding citizens. One of them even became a sort of poster boy for upright lawmen.

In a Hollywood movie, Frank Dalton would have been one of the men with a posse tracking down his bandit brothers . . . if he had lived long enough. That he died young and the way he died can be connected directly to what became the Dalton Gang.

CHAPTER 6

A HEROIC DALTON DEATH

I claim no literary excellence for this book—none is needed," wrote Emmett Dalton in his first and more reliable memoir, *Beyond the Law*, published in 1918. "But I do claim that every statement herein contained, regarding myself and my brothers, is absolutely true in every detail and is the first true and only authentic history ever written about us."

Well, the surviving bandit brother can claim all he wants, but the fact is not everything Emmett wrote was true. There were also falsehoods by omission, in that first book and its 1931 follow-up, *When the Daltons Rode*. As much as he admitted what the Dalton Gang did was wrong, Emmett continued to paint his brothers as victims of their times: "The James Boys, the Youngers, the Daltons, with the exception of myself, have gone on to their reward or punishment. For the moral point of view there is no justification for the things that were done, I shall attempt none except to say that the environment of those days was different from the present time, and it is hard for a person born and raised in this day to understand the conditions as they existed then."

And Emmett had to be careful because he had become a legitimate businessman and did not want to publish anything that could once more put him behind bars.

His father, Lewis, did more than breed and race horses, he gambled on them—meaning there was less left for Adeline and their children. That included his very presence in their lives, which was infrequent.

Many years later, Lit Dalton's feelings toward his father had not softened: "It's a tragedy to have to blame your father for the failure of four of your brothers, but I just can't get around it. He trailed the boys around with him after a string of racehorses, associating them with the worst riff-raff in the country. The example in gambling that he set them offset all the good habits he held up to them."

The durable Adeline apparently did not hold her husband's absences against him, at least not for very long, as the couple produced ten boys and five girls. The firstborn was Charles, in 1852, the last born were the twins Simon and Hannah, born in 1879, a span of twenty-seven years, and the last of that brood to pass away was Leona in 1964. The generation of that branch of the Daltons began when Franklin Pierce was president and ended when Lyndon Johnson was in the White House.

Of the brothers in this narrative, from oldest to youngest: Littleton Lee "Lit" Dalton was born October 1857, and was named for Uncle Littleton Younger. He lived and worked in California for many years, as a sheepherder and cattleman and a saloonkeeper. Lit had sporadic contact with his family back east, yet in his later years when interviewed, what he could not remember or did not know, he simply invented.

Franklin Dalton was born in 1859. See more about him later in this chapter.

Gratton Hanley "Grat" Dalton was born in 1861. According to Emmett, he was the most "pugnacious" of the Daltons, easy to anger and sensitive to insults, even imaginary ones.

Mason Frakes "Bill" Dalton was born in 1863. He too went out to California. There in June 1885, he married Jane Bliven and they had two children. A talented guitar player with the gift of gab, Bill had political ambitions until his brothers' deaths turned him to crime.

Robert Rennick "Bob" Dalton was born in 1869 and named after an ancestor who had been killed by Indians in Virginia in 1765. Six feet tall, blue eyes, sandy hair, Bob was considered the most handsome of the Dalton boys and became the gang's leader.

Emmett Dalton, born in 1871, was named for the Irish orator Robert Emmet. He would follow Bob wherever he went, except to an early grave.

Until Adeline's permanent move to Oklahoma, as all the children came along and grew up, the Dalton family lived in southeast Kansas or in Missouri. About being near the two states' border, Lit could remember nothing but "fight, fight, fight" during his early years. There was "fighting, shooting, and killing all of the time."

During the Civil War, Emmett wrote that "the very soil was fertilized with atrocity." Redlegs, Jayhawkers, Quantrill's Raiders, and Missouri border ruffians as well as more formally organized Union and Confederate forces fought all over this territory and left little but chimneys standing in many areas. Where the Daltons lived during the war became known as the "Burnt District" as a result of General Thomas Ewing's infamous Order No. 11 issued in August 1863: "All persons living in Jackson, Cass, and Bates counties are hereby ordered to remove herewith." The area was almost entirely leveled, and even the crops were burned. The Dalton home remained standing but was shot full of holes. During raids in the area, some of the Dalton children fled the house to hide in the bush.

The Indian Territory was the American frontier at its worst after the war. The area was referred to as "Robbers' Roost" and the "Land of the Six-Shooter" at least as often as it was called Oklahoma. Crime was rampant, and a familiar phrase was, "There is no Sunday west of St. Louis—and no God west of Fort Smith."

Despite all these frightening and distressing experiences, the older Dalton sons led mostly steady lives—well, compared to their Younger relations and, later, their younger brothers. Then Frank Dalton became the success story of the family. In 1884, he was commissioned as a deputy U.S. marshal, serving under Judge Parker. Frank quickly developed a reputation as being a brave lawman and was involved in shoot-outs and high-risk arrests over a three-year period.

The incident on November 27, 1887, changed everything. This is not an exaggeration. It is reasonable to believe that if Frank Dalton had been able to continue as a lawman and perhaps had a distinguished career, there would have been a positive impact on his brothers. Instead, his violent demise had the opposite effect.

Many people learned of it from an account in *The St. Louis Globe-Democrat,* which began, "A bloody tragedy took place this morning in the Cherokee Nation, in which United States Marshal Frank Dalton, Dave Smith and Mrs. Lee Dixon were killed."

Frank and his two possemen had completed their latest mission for Judge Parker's court two days earlier when they had turned a group of recently arrested prisoners over to the jailers in Fort Smith. Frank had then recrossed the Arkansas River to set up camp in the bottoms with his two companions—his brother Bob and Bud Heady, who at twenty was two years older than Bob.

Not having any particular place to go, the three men were still there the next day, a Saturday, when another deputy marshal, Jim Cole, arrived in the late afternoon. He carried with him two writs against Dave Smith, one for larceny and the other for selling whiskey in the Indian Territory. Rather than return to Fort Smith for the night and then come back again, Cole stayed at Frank's makeshift camp.

The following morning, Sunday, was a cold one, barely brightened by weak sunlight. Frank and Cole warmed themselves as best they could with the remnants of the discreet campfire. Cole said he knew where Smith was holed up, so he would take the lead. This could mean trouble because he and Smith had had a previous dustup, and the latter had threatened to kill the deputy marshal. Cole and

Frank Dalton left Bob and Heady behind asleep in their tent, as they expected that it should not take four men to arrest such a low-rent outlaw as Dave Smith.

Frank took pride in his appearance and thought it made for a more effective lawman. As David Allin writes in *The Dalton Boys,* "It didn't hurt any that Frank looked the part, just like the heroes on the covers of dime novels. Tall, lean, and handsome with the steely eyed gaze of a man who had seen it all, Frank wasn't afraid of anything. His suit was always clean and neat, and his tall boots were always polished. On his head he wore a neat grey hat with a short rounded crown and a flat narrow brim."

The two lawmen tried to stay warm as they rode through the late-autumn landscape of leafless bushes and trees and abandoned logging camps. They finally arrived at a clearing containing a structure that was half logs and half tent. A woman was tending the campfire in front of it. When Frank Dalton and Jim Cole paused to study the scene, the woman walked into the tent cabin. The two men eased closer to the campfire, then dismounted. They drew Winchesters out of the saddle holsters and strode toward the tent cabin, Cole circling so there was one lawman at the front and the other at the back.

He used the tip of his rifle to push aside the tent flap. The barrel was grabbed from inside. Cole tried to back away, and as he did so, the woman emerged, the end of the barrel clutched in one fist. She began shouting at him. Hearing the commotion, Dalton stepped around to that side of the cabin. Dave Smith came out behind the woman. He too held a Winchester. Seeing Dalton, Smith shot him in the chest.

As the wounded lawman staggered off, Cole backed away, jerking his rifle free and accidentally firing. But he also tripped over a tent rope and fell to the ground in a sitting position. Smith turned and fired at him too, hitting the deputy marshal. Cole wasn't dead, but Smith thought he was, so he went after Dalton. By this time, three other men had run out of the cabin. One kept going, while the other two ducked back inside. Cole saw Smith lower his rifle as though Dalton were on the ground. Smith pulled the trigger a moment before Cole raised his Winchester and shot him. Smith fell facedown.

From inside the cabin came the sound of a gunshot. Not waiting for an explanation, Cole got up, fired again, this time at the tent cabin, and began to run away. Behind him, he heard a woman wail, "Lord a mercy, I'm killed!" Cole kept running.

He took cover behind a thick tree at the edge of the clearing. From there, he and a gunman inside the cabin exchanged shots until Cole ran out of ammunition. Apparently uninjured was the woman who had first been seen at the campfire, who was now back outside and shouting incoherently. To Cole, there was nothing else to be done, and he could not tell how badly he was wounded. Scurrying from tree to tree until he thought he was out of danger, Cole went to find his horse. He would hurry to Fort Smith to get help.

Miraculously, Frank Dalton was not dead. Dave Smith was—Cole had shot true. Now emerging from the cabin was a teenage friend of Smith's named Will Towerly. He held a pistol but stuck it in his pants and picked up Frank's Winchester. Towerly wandered over to a tree stump behind which Frank had taken cover. Seeing the tall boy looming above him, Frank managed to rise up on one elbow and pleaded, "For God's sake, don't shoot. I'm already a dead man."

Towerly considered this for a few moments, then casually pulled the trigger. Hit, Frank collapsed. Towerly stepped closer and shot the deputy marshal in the head. Satisfied, finally, he went and got his gear out of the tent, marched to a small pen, saddled up one of the horses inside of it, and rode away.

When they felt it was safe to do so, several nearby residents approached the tent-cabin to assess the carnage. The woman who declared herself dead had told the truth. She would be identified as the wife of Leander Dixon, who was also inside the cabin and wounded in the shoulder. He was the brother of the woman who at some point had stopped shouting and was now identified as the recently widowed Mrs. Smith.

As Emmett later lamented, "Frank is dead. A martyr to his duty and the custom and environment of a wild time. Reckless day that took its toll hundreds of good and bad and by the same method—a quick shot, a quivering form, one final twitch—and then silence forever."

When a posse of lawmen from Fort Smith arrived, they chose to leave it to the relatives of Smith and his sister-in-law to bury their own dead. They carefully wrapped Frank Dalton's mangled body in blankets and began the grim journey to Coffeyville.

CHAPTER 7

THEY GOT THEIR MAN

Coffeyville sits north of the border, and its counterpart in Oklahoma, South Coffeyville, is only a mile away.* Its earliest distinction in American history was being a sort of rest stop on a trail created by Osage Indians led by Black Dog in 1803. It was hard to confuse this particular headman with other members of the Hunkah band, as Black Dog was seven feet tall, weighed three hundred pounds, and was blind in his left eye. He was apparently a restless—or curious—man, because he led hunts to as far away as Santa Fe.

During the Civil War, members of the Osage tribe camped in a valley west of the Verdigris River. They crossed the river to trade with white men. In 1869, Coffeyville was founded. It was named after Colonel James A. Coffey, who had journeyed down from Humboldt, Kansas, to establish a trading post on the west side of the river.† Not having to cross the river had made the post popular among the Osage.

---

* In Coffeyville's early days, South Coffeyville was known as Stevens Switch.
† Another army officer, named Blanton, had also helped found the town. To name it, a coin was tossed. How that turned out is why it is named Coffeyville instead of Blantonville.

More white people found the site congenial too, including farmers, who began tilling the surrounding fields. Streets were laid out, and homes began to be built. Coffeyville was incorporated as a city that following year . . . well, almost. Its charter was voided as illegal, so it was reincorporated in 1873.

Seemingly as restless as Black Dog, Colonel Coffey did not stick around long. He had more business to conduct and trading posts to develop elsewhere in Kansas. The final stop of his fifty-one years was in Dodge City, where Wyatt Earp and Bat Masterson enforced the law in the mid-1870s, and Coffey, upon his death in 1879, was buried in the city's Maple Grove Cemetery.

There was another Coffey connection: The town's first school was in the colonel's house and taught by his daughter Mary. An actual school opened in 1870, and by then, the Methodist church had been constructed. There was much excitement the next year because of a three-way race by railroads to secure a right-of-way into Indian Territory. The competition was won by the Missouri, Kansas & Texas Railway (also known as the "Katy" line). Coffeyville continued to grow as a commercial center thanks to the railroad, the cattle trade, grain and flour milling, and successful surrounding farms.

According to Robert Barr Smith in *Daltons!,* for a time, Coffeyville "looked a lot like the other bawdy, raucous Kansas cow towns, with the obligatory contingent of saloon owners, gamblers, and con men. With them came the calico queens—whores, that is—to service the Texas cowboys who pushed the herds north. 'Red Hot Street' [was] a clutter of shanties, shacks, and tents, and it qualified as the sin strip of Coffeyville. [It] echoed nightly to the roistering and quarreling of the young cowpunchers, mixed in with a goodly number of teamsters, soldiers, and Indians, all of them out to paint the town red."

As the city's cow trade waned, along came another way to make money. In 1881, on West Ninth Street, a man was digging a water well and he struck oil. At about the same time, farmers reported oil oozing up from beneath their plows. A sure sign of prosperity and confidence was the ceremony in the spring of 1885 celebrating the opening of the First National Bank of Coffeyville. And by then, the weekly *Coffeyville Journal* had been publishing for a decade.

It was to Coffeyville that Frank Dalton's body was brought for burial. At the time, Adeline and her younger children were living in Robbins Corners, six miles to the west. According to Lit Dalton, "Mother spent the last of her savings to erect a fine marble headstone at Frank's grave" in the Elmwood Cemetery.

Two days after Frank Dalton's death, U.S. marshal John Carroll sent a telegram to Heck Thomas with the news of the deadly shootout and the assignment to find William Towerly. The telegram was waiting for the deputy marshal when he arrived in McAlester, Oklahoma. He was on his way to Fort Smith with three wagons full of prisoners and was assisted by six guards. Not wanting to risk the delivery to Judge Parker, Thomas chose to remain with the prisoners. He selected two of the guards, Bill Moody and Ed Stokely, to go after Towerly.

The lawmen knew that Towerly lived near Atoka in the Choctaw Nation, so that seemed the best place to begin looking for him. Moody and Stokely took a train to Atoka, and upon arrival, they rented horses. Before sunup the next morning, they were in position to discreetly observe the Towerly home, which contained the killer's parents and sister. There was no sign of Will Towerly during the day, but the lawmen saw him slip into the house late that night. His father stayed out on the porch, maintaining a cold vigil while his son slept inside.

Early the next morning, the younger Towerly hurried out of the house, heading for his horse and carrying a sack of food. His escape was short-lived. Moody and Stokely emerged from the brush and ordered Towerly to drop the sack and raise his hands. Instead, he pulled out a pistol. Both lawmen fired, and bullets struck Towerly in the leg and shoulder. When he fell to the ground, he lost his grip on the six-shooter.

Given that Towerly had just murdered a fellow lawman, one would think Moody and Stokely would shoot to kill. However, they were mindful that the federal government paid per prisoner brought to the Fort Smith jail—live ones, not dead ones. The hope here was to incapacitate and disarm Towerly. That turned out to be a fatal miscalculation.

Stokely leaped forward to grab the gun . . . but he was not fast enough. Towerly got hold of it again and began firing. Stokely was struck at least twice, with one bullet going through his heart, and he was dead when he hit the ground.

Meanwhile, the rest of the Towerly family had become involved. The younger Towerly tossed his father the pistol and shouted for him to reload it "and throw it back so I can kill the other damned marshal!" Moody was trying to fend off the curved fingers of Mrs. Towerly and her daughter, who were competing to be the first one to scratch his eyes out. They did succeed in dragging him away from the younger Towerly, who they then hauled into the house and slammed the door.

Moody still had his Winchester, however, and he used it to break through the front window. With an open shot, he aimed and fired at Towerly. It cost him money, but Moody finally ended the young murderer's life. That afternoon, Stokely's body was put on a train and shipped to his family in Marietta, Georgia.*

---

* In March 1889, Moody, now a deputy marshal, was a member of a posse sent to serve a warrant for murder on a man living near Tulsa. As they approached the dwelling, the suspect opened fire from inside, striking Moody and another member of the posse. Moody died. The apprehended suspect was found guilty and sentenced to ten years in prison.

CHAPTER 8

DEPUTY DALTONS

Frank was not the only Dalton brother to wear a badge, or what was called then "to ride for Parker." However, he was the only one to die a lawman. The story of the lawing done by Grat, Bob, and Emmett Dalton begins with the previously mentioned William Story, Judge Parker's predecessor.

In 1871, Story had been nominated to the federal bench in Fort Smith by President Grant. He did not stay in that position long. A combination of suspected corruption and allowing murder suspects out on bail persuaded the powers that be in Washington to replace Story with Isaac Parker. For him, the more deputy marshals the better because he had an especially tough and large territory to tame. There were as many as two hundred deputy marshals rounding up suspects for the judge, but they were doing so across the length and width of seventy-four thousand square miles.

Being a deputy marshal was far from an enviable occupation. It was "tough anywhere, but in the Indian Territory it was brutal," explains Dalton family researcher Nancy B. Samuelson. "The area had become a refuge for fugitives from justice, bushwhackers, guerillas, and every other undesirable one could imagine. There were few laws in this territory to regulate things and what laws did exist were often confusing. The federal court had jurisdiction over whites and the various tribes had jurisdiction over the Indians. When disputes involved both whites and Indians the situation became completely muddled."

However, early in his lawing career, Frank Dalton took the role seriously and was good at it, and that, coupled with few other job opportunities, enticed his brothers to try their hand at lawing. No doubt another reason was Adeline and her younger children needed food on the table, with Lewis Dalton continuing his wandering ways while pursuing the ponies. Being able to make some kind of living was probably why Grat and Bob continued as officers after Frank's lead-filled demise.*

Inspiring much of the crime in Indian Territory was whiskey. First, it provoked all manner of violent incidents; second, it was a crime itself to possess whiskey in the territory. And worse, what was sold was often of such poor quality that it could kill people. If the sellers were low on genuine whiskey, they would make their own from several unsavory ingredients, including Perana, a high-alcohol patent medicine. Members of the tribes were especially affected by these concoctions, and it did not enhance the law-abiding behavior of others either.

Given the combination of the rotgut being peddled and its vast expanse harboring many hiding spots, it's no wonder that the Indian Territory had more than its share of notorious criminals. Two in particular attracted the attention of not just lawmen but much of the United States: Blue Duck and Ned Christie.

Bluford Duck was born Sha-con-gah in 1858 in the Cherokee Nation. As a teenager, he was already riding with gangs across the Oklahoma Territory, specializing in armed robberies and cattle

---

* All told, during the years of Judge Parker's jurisdiction, sixty-five deputy marshals were killed in the line of duty.

rustling. Blue Duck became romantically involved with Myra May-belle Reed, and when she married outlaw Sam Starr, becoming Belle Starr, she and her husband formed their own gang, which Blue Duck joined. He is believed to have ridden with the gang through most of the latter part of the 1870s, although his involvement with them was off and on.*

On June 23, 1884, while riding drunk in the Flint District of the Cherokee Nation, and in the company of outlaw William Christie, Blue Duck came upon a farmer named Samuel Wyrick. For no apparent reason, the two riders opened fire on the farmer, killing him. They then reloaded and fired on a young Cherokee boy who had witnessed the murder, missing him but shooting his horse. Soon after, Blue Duck and Christie were captured and taken before Judge Parker in Fort Smith. Both were convicted, although Christie was later cleared of the charge and released.

Blue Duck was sentenced to hang, but later that sentence was reduced to life in prison. He was sent to Menard Penitentiary in Illinois. He was assisted in an unsuccessful appeal by Belle Starr. In 1895, when he was diagnosed with tuberculosis and given only a short time to live, he was granted a pardon and released. Blue Duck died shortly thereafter at just thirty-seven in Catoosa, Oklahoma, where he was buried.

William Christie had a brother named Ned who had a more eventful criminal career. He was born in 1852 in the Cherokee Nation, the son of Watt and Lydia Christie, who had survived the Trail of Tears. They were of the Keetowah band, one of the most traditional of Cherokee peoples. As a child and young man, Christie was

---

* A possible connection to the Daltons was that supposedly Belle Starr, while living in Texas, offered her home as a hideout to the James-Younger Gang, whom she had known from her early days in Missouri. It has also been reported, though not persuasively, that before Blue Duck, Belle had been involved with Cole Younger or was even briefly married to his uncle Charles Younger.

a marble champion, stickball player, and a popular fiddle player. He could speak both Cherokee and English.

A big man at six feet, four inches, Ned Christie became a blacksmith and gunsmith. In 1885, he was elected to the tribal senate and was an advisor to the principal chief. Concerned about trying to protect Cherokee national sovereignty, Christie strongly opposed giving the federal government land to construct railroads through their territory. In addition, federal legislators were proposing to force the Cherokee and other tribes to end their practice of holding communal land and to accept allotment of the tribal lands to individual households.

Christie's opposition to such positions, which were supported by powerful whites in the region, began to earn him some enemies. Not helping his tenuous situation was that he had a hot temper, especially after drinking whiskey. It was no surprise when he was charged with manslaughter in the death of William Palone, another Cherokee. However, in the tribal court at Tahlequah, Christie was found not guilty and released.

In May 1887, U.S. deputy marshal Daniel Maples led a posse into Indian Territory seeking sellers of whiskey. A prime suspect was Bud Trainer, who had a record of selling the stuff and was known for violence. After spending the day unsuccessfully seeking Trainer, Maples and posse member George Jefferson started back to their camp near Spring Branch Creek, outside Tahlequah. Maples was shot from ambush and died the next day of his wounds. Other marshals suspected that Trainer had shot Maples, and began arresting his associates. Christie was implicated when an acquaintance, John Parris, told lawmen that the Cherokee leader had been involved in the murder.

Friends convinced Christie to hide. Fearing a trial before white people in a U.S. court, he fortified his house to resist arrest. Christie's home was in the Rabbit Trap community of the Goingsnake District in the Cherokee Nation, where he lived with his wife, Nancy Greece, and their thirteen-year-old son, James. Judge Parker sent more marshals to arrest him. Christie wrote a letter saying that he was willing to surrender if Parker would promise to release him on bail so that he could seek evidence to prove his innocence. Parker did not respond to the letter, and Christie did not surrender. And apparently, the marshals chose to leave Christie alone rather than storm the house.

Two years passed. When Jacob Yoes was appointed as the U.S. marshal in Fort Smith, he viewed the defiant Christie as unfinished business. He assigned Heck Thomas to lead the effort to bring in Christie. Three other deputy marshals assisted him, and, curiously, Bud Trainer, who may have made a deal with the court. Thomas decided to burn Christie out. The marshals set fire to Christie's blacksmith shop, and flames spread to the cabin. Nancy Christie and their eighteen-year-old nephew, Little Arch Wolf, escaped the cabin. Ned Christie was wounded by gunfire.

Thomas and the posse left the scene, believing that Christie was dead; they could return later to look for remains when the fire was out. However, Nancy Christie got to the burned-out cabin first and found her husband alive. She took him to a local white doctor who, with the assistance of a Cherokee medicine man, saved his life.

Upping the ante, a recuperated and bitter Christie and his friends built a fort for protection. The fort was double-walled with logs and had sand packed between the two walls. It also had gunports for rifles and was amply stocked with food, water, and ammunition to withstand a siege. The U.S. government increased the reward for Christie's capture from $500 to $1,000.

This time, Marshal Yoes sent a posse of six deputies to Christie's new home. This group withdrew after two men were wounded in a firefight. Yoes proposed a military-style raid on the fort. An expedition of fifteen men set out, led by Deputy Marshal Gideon "Cap" White, a former captain in the Union cavalry during the Civil War. An army post in Kansas agreed to loan White a cannon for the expedition.

One morning, Ned Christie woke up to find White's force

surrounding his fort. After the first exchange of rifle fire, the marshals allowed the women inside to leave. Then the lawmen loaded a double charge of powder into the cannon, which turned out not to be a good idea because the next shot blew up the barrel. They pushed a wagonload of dynamite against one wall of the fort and detonated it. The explosion destroyed part of the structure and set the rest afire. Christie was fatally shot as he escaped the burning ruins.

His body was tied to a door for transport by train to Fayetteville, Arkansas. There the lawmen were photographed with Christie's body as a trophy. They then brought the body by train to Fort Smith to claim their reward from the court. (This had been a dead-or-alive warrant.) More people had their pictures taken next to Christie's body, and the Cook photography studio took a photo to reproduce and sell as postcards. Christie's body was finally released by authorities to his family, who buried him.

It was into this cauldron of criminality and despite Frank's violent death at just age twenty-eight that the three younger Dalton boys first sported badges. Grat had worked for Frank as a guard but hadn't really taken to it. At the time of his brother's murder, Grat was in California, having accompanied his father on one of Lewis's horse-racing excursions. After Grat's return, he was given Frank's position as a deputy U.S. marshal.

This appointment was more sentimental than sensible. Grat already had a well-earned reputation as a drinker and brawler. He lost his temper easily and frequently—all in all, not a good combination for a frontier peace officer. Bob Dalton was also made a deputy for the Western Arkansas District. Emmett rode along as a posseman.

The first Dalton "gang" consisted of three brothers who rode on the right side of the law. That did not last long. As Emmett was to rationalize, "The Dalton Gang was born of injustice, or what seemed like injustice."

CHAPTER 9

BEYOND THE LAW

It was not long before things went wrong for the Dalton brothers as lawmen.

In August 1888, Bob, still only nineteen years old, set out to track down Charley Montgomery. As Emmett put it, "Montgomery was a ne'er-do-well, who came from no one knows where and lived no one knew how."

The word was that Charley was masquerading as a deputy marshal, and this was after having fed false information to Grat about a few recent crimes and then stealing two pistols in Coffeyville. Bob, considered the smartest of the brothers, had discovered Montgomery's location in Timber Hills. Believing that Grat was busy gambling in Coffeyville, Bob decided to skip alerting his older brother, and instead, he put together his own posse. He did not want to risk that Montgomery would escape the territory.

While approaching the cabin where Montgomery was hiding, the posse began taking fire from the far side of it. In an attempt to flank Montgomery, Bob ran to the southwest corner of the house with a shotgun. When he rounded the corner into the front yard, he ran straight into the fugitive, who was running toward Bob with his pistol raised. Montgomery fired at Bob but missed, even though he had been close enough to leave powder burns on the lawman's face. A moment later, Bob fired his shotgun and killed Montgomery.

One would think this was a justified killing, but the legal ground was muddy. Unlike Grat, Bob was not a sworn deputy, and he had not waited to obtain a warrant for Montgomery's arrest. Thus, the fact that Grat was not present meant that Bob could be charged with murder like any other citizen. This sure seemed unfair—and, tauntingly, Bob would show the sign of the powder burns for the rest of his life.*

Making the lives of U.S. deputy marshals—and those who worked for them—even more miserable, as an incentive to take prisoners alive, a marshal would have to bury a suspect himself or pay to have it done when one was killed if no kin could be found. Thus, Bob was forced to pay eighty dollars for Montgomery's burial and then show up for a preliminary hearing two weeks later, charged with killing him. The hearing lasted until late November, but finally, the testimonies from Bob and posse members about self-defense trumped the technicalities, and they were officially cleared.

However, the event had earned Bob a reputation as a reckless killer, and that stuck to him like a damp shirt wherever he went. It was this stigma dogging him plus guilt over the killing itself that was blamed for Bob becoming a drinker, though he would never match Grat shot glass for shot glass. The alcohol Bob began to regularly sample in Indian Territory was not only bad for his liver but further eroded his reputation and put him on thin ice with the marshal's office in Fort Smith.

So it was a pleasant surprise in January 1889 when Bob was sworn in as a deputy marshal. This promotion could signal a fresh start for

---

* Many histories of the Dalton brothers include the unfounded—though alluring—story that Bob and Charley Montgomery were involved in a love triangle with a woman, and Bob deliberately killed his rival. In some circles, that might make Bob look better, but the fact is he screwed up.

the Dalton brothers. Still, given the paltry pay, it was understandable that Bob took on a second job as a member of the Osage Nation police force. Unlike the U.S. Marshals' office, the Osage Police paid a monthly salary. Bob hired Emmett under him to guard prisoners. Emmett was two years younger than Bob and looked up to him. Since they were closer in age in comparison to their other siblings, Bob and Emmett had been almost inseparable in childhood and remained close as teenagers.

What appeared to be a promising situation did not stay that way long. It was true of every deputy marshal on the frontier that not only was the pay inadequate, it could also be months before it was issued by the federal bureaucracy in Washington, D.C. The impact on the Daltons was that for awkward stretches of time, the only income the brothers had was what Bob could share on his Osage Police paydays. Inevitably, debts piled up, as did the feelings of frustration.

There was another unfortunate incident that further blemished Bob's nascent lawing career. In April 1890, a deputy marshal had been shot and wounded near Claremore, Oklahoma, and the suspect was a part-Cherokee man named Alex Cochran. A telegram that found Bob in Tulsa ordered him to track the man down. Bob and Emmett got on a train, and when they arrived in Claremore, Grat, who had received a similar message, was waiting for them.

The brothers did not have to go far. As they walked through town, a local merchant named Davis Hill met them to say that Cochran had just been at his shop to buy a box of cartridges. Even more promising, Hill pointed to a rider down the street and assured the Daltons that he was the suspect. Bob was the first one on a horse and took off in pursuit.

Once Bob was close enough, he halted and dismounted and shouted for Cochran to stop. "Instead of stopping," Emmett observed, "the man put spurs to his horse and started to run." Aiming his Winchester and justly confident in his marksmanship, "Bob shot twice, and the horse wheeled to the right and ran all the faster. Then

Bob shot twice more. And the horse fell. By this time Grat and I had arrived, and we walked up to where the horse and rider lay."

An understandable yet still terrible mistake had been made. The rider was the teenage son of Alex Cochran, who had been on an errand for his father. If Bob had not been as good a shot, the boy would still be alive. The deputy marshal had done nothing criminal and he had been given erroneous information, yet his shaky reputation as a lawman took another hit.

No matter: Bob would not be a deputy marshal much longer. His financial frustration did not change under a new marshal, R. L. Walker. He "always had some excuse," Emmett recalled about Walker. "The government had not made the appropriation. The money would be coming along soon. But 'soon' never materialized."*

In September, Bob went to Marshal Walker's office to complain about the shortage of pay. The response was being fired. For as long as he could, Bob kept this information to himself and continued with the Osage Police and, with Emmett, kept out of sight by patrolling the outer reaches of the Osage Nation. This also provided a fresh and more reliable source of revenue.

For the next several months, the two brothers would stop any suspicious wagon they could find and would frequently discover stashes of illegal liquor. Rather than making any arrests, Bob chose to fine the culprits himself as well as confiscate their liquor. This was, of course, illegal, but the victims could certainly not turn to the law with their grievances. As for Bob, Emmett rationalized, "Is it any wonder that the thoughts of a young fellow who had gained a fairly good start in life should turn to retaliation and revenge?"

When once more a new marshal took office, Grat was retained as a deputy marshal, but the best Jacob Yoes could do for Bob and

---

* Years later, it was discovered that Bob Dalton was owed $181.80 for his work as a deputy marshal during the tenure of the previous U.S. marshal, W. C. Jones. The federal government had sent Jones $136.35 of this, but not a penny of it was passed on to Bob.

Emmett was to offer them positions as possemen for Deputy Floyd Wilson. They accepted, but while waiting to be called upon, Bob and Emmett returned to the outer Osage Nation. Their downfall came on Christmas Day.

Witnesses observed Bob being accompanied by two bootleggers to a holiday celebration held by a group of Osage. During the gathering, jugs of whiskey were openly sold. Worse for Bob, he partook liberally and became quite drunk. An Osage chief named Chi-sho-wah-hah, who owned the home, reported Bob to the marshal. Warrants were issued to Deputy Lafe Shadley for the arrest of both Bob and Emmett on January 7, 1890. Shadley was a friend of the Daltons, and instead of enforcing the warrant, he warned the boys to go into hiding deep in the Indian Territory.

This they did, relying on friends and family for food and shelter. But this was lonely living, and after enough of it, Grat and Deputy Wilson easily convinced Bob and Emmett to turn themselves in. On March 26, they both appeared for their hearing. Emmett was discharged, but Bob was told to appear in the district court at Wichita in a few months. He was released after Deputy Shadley raised the $1,000 bail.

By this time, Grat had his own legal troubles. Earlier that same month, a report was filed about an assault committed by Grat against a man named Delonsdale in Tulsa. The two had gotten into an altercation in the street shortly after Grat had woken up feeling the effects of a long night of drinking and gambling. According to newspaper accounts, he got into an argument and pistol-whipped Delonsdale. Eventually, this would result in him too being fired as a deputy marshal.

For a time, despite the legal clouds hovering over them, Bob and Emmett tried to continue to work as possemen under Grat and Deputy Wilson. Then it was in April that Yoes fired Grat. Bob and Emmett continued working under Deputy Wilson, but they soon gained the impression that they were no longer welcome. On June

20, 1890, Bob told Deputy Wilson that he and Emmett were quitting, and the two left Tulsa.

Worried that he would be found guilty at his upcoming trial, Bob discussed a plan with Emmett to travel to their brother Bill's ranch in California and that he would write to Bill and Lit Dalton to see if they could find them some work. Bob, still bitter at the Osage chief Chi-sho-wah-hah for snitching on him for drinking at the Christmas party, suggested getting revenge by stealing the chief's mules and then using the proceeds to fund their trip. Emmett was reluctant, but then, as usual, he was persuaded to go along with Bob's plan.

In July, Bob and Emmett stole two of Chi-sho-wah-hah's mules and twenty other unguarded horses they came upon in the Osage Nation. They then drove the impromptu remuda into Indian Territory and tried to sell them to a man from Fort Smith. When the man started asking too many questions, Bob and Emmett took the mules and horses and headed on toward Kansas, where they found a buyer. The brothers found the venture so profitable that they decided to steal another forty horses while still in Kansas.

There had to have been a better idea: When they arrived in Columbus, the Dalton brothers had to dodge several questions about the many brands on their stock. When their buyer, W. W. Scott, showed up, he offered them way below market price. Not having another buyer and wanting to get rid of the illegal stock fast, Bob and Emmett were forced to accept the price. Expecting cash, they were further disappointed when they were handed a check and told to take it or leave it. It got worse: When an irritated Bob took the check to the bank and endorsed it, he used his real name.

And worse still: Apparently not dismayed enough by the previous transaction, Bob and Emmett rounded up another twenty horses in the Osage Nation with the intention of once more selling them to Scott. On their way to the stockyards, however, Bob and Emmett passed the train depot, where they noticed Scott and the owners of the previously stolen remuda, men named Rogers and Musgrove, in conversation. The two men had just finished proving ownership to Scott of their stolen stock and were preparing to drive their reclaimed animals away. Spotting the Dalton brothers, the three men began to point and shout. Bob and Emmett barely escaped, leaving the newly stolen stock behind.

Word got around fast, and several stockmen pulled together a posse to go after the horse thieves. Bob and Emmett thought it prudent to disappear. The two hid out for several months on the bluffs of the Canadian River some seventy miles northwest of Kingfisher, in a dugout they had made on a ranch owned by a man named Jim Riley. They somehow got a message to Grat, who tried to send them food, horses, and ammunition.

This too did not turn out well. Grat was nabbed for aiding and abetting the suspects and tossed into the same jail in Fort Smith where he used to deposit prisoners. He was released after just two weeks—not because of the kindness of the court but because it was hoped he would lead lawmen to his brothers. However, Bob and Emmett had grown tired of hiding and were able to take a train to California. They aimed to pursue the plan to work at their older brother Bill's ranch near San Miguel in California and lie low until they were mostly forgotten in Kansas and Oklahoma.

Bob and Emmett did find their way to Bill's ranch. The lying-low part proved more difficult to achieve.

CHAPTER 10

REUNION IN CALIFORNIA

Before more of the tale of the Daltons' descent is told, now is a good time to discuss two of Bob Dalton's talents—being a marksman and a ladies' man.

Of the six Dalton brothers, by far the most accurate with a gun was Bob. Some of that was indeed talent, and the other was he worked at it. The venerable lawman Heck Thomas (much more about him in Act II) once declared that Bob Dalton was "one of the most accurate shots I ever saw." An exclamation point to this was that Bob fired his rifle mostly from his hip instead of his shoulder.

He did not overlook trying to improve his prowess with a pistol. From time to time, he'd find a youngster who for a quarter would toss cans in the air while Bob drew and fired. One newspaper account claimed that Bob could hit a can three times, also shooting from the hip, before it hit the ground.

Part of the legend of the Dalton Gang was Bob's love life—or love lives. While it has not been disputed that Bob fancied the ladies and they fancied him back, his well-known flames were mostly fabricated. One was a cousin named Minnie. Another was Flora Quick, who might also have been Tom King.

If the few accounts can be believed, Flora Quick was one of the more fascinating characters of the American West. She was the daughter of a prosperous farmer who died when she was fifteen, leaving her with $13,000 and his 2,300 acres. Eager to share the wealth, a man named Ora Mundis married her. Once the cash was gone, so was the husband.

Now having to fend for herself, Flora Mundis began stealing horses, possibly in addition to being a prostitute because she and a friend, Jessie Whitewings, opened a brothel in Guthrie. Jessie used the alias of Ed Bullock, and Flora chose to go with a male nom de plume too, christening herself Tom King. By that name, she acquired a deserved reputation as an expert horse thief. One newspaper article reported King sitting in an Oklahoma City jail, dressed in men's clothing, on a charge of horse-stealing.

But not for long. She formed a gang with fellow inmates Ernie Lewis and Billy Roach. What she could do a lot better than they could was seduce the guard, grabbing his gun during the encounter. She locked him in her cell and released the two prisoners, and they took off. But the eighteen-year-old Tom King was recaptured a few days later. No worries, she was soon free. It was reported at the time that either she eloped with a deputy sheriff or she was pregnant and was released.

Either way, Flora/Tom headed west to Arizona and ended up in the rowdy mining town of Clifton. She took up with a Chinese man and began calling herself China Dot. She soon traded him in for a man named Bill Garland. In late January 1903, the two were high on opium and quarreling, which turned out to not be a healthy combination: He shot her four times then used the fifth bullet on himself.

Nowhere in the Flora Quick/Tom King story can Bob Dalton be found. Plus, her heyday, such as it was, occurred well after Bob's demise.

However, there was a woman who may have actually existed and had an intimate relationship with Bob: Eugenia Moore. According to Emmett, when he and Bob realized a wise move was to ride west, away from the Fort Smith jurisdiction, they decided to try New Mexico before going on to California. Maybe they could get that elusive fresh start there.

The brothers stopped to eat at a hotel in Silver City and decided to stay on a few days: "There by accident or fate enters one of the most important members of what was later to be known as the 'Dalton Gang'—one who played her part to perfection but, like the rest, was destined to lose in the end," Emmett contended. "Bob was introduced to Miss Eugenia Moore. She was also of north Missouri." Supposedly, she had come to New Mexico to be a schoolteacher and "was from a fine old Missouri family" and "was a beautiful young lady, about twenty-two years old, pure of mind, a fair telegrapher, unusually intelligent and courageous," reports Emmett.

Grat's love life was focused on prostitutes—sometimes still referred to as "soiled doves"—when he was not too broke or too drunk to patronize them. Bill, as mentioned, had married Jane and was, until reunited with his brothers, a devoted family man. Let's not leave Emmett out—or more accurately, Emmett made sure not to leave himself out of the gang's legend. His young and eventually lifelong love was Julia Johnson.

Emmett claimed that while riding one evening, he was passing by a small church and heard organ music wafting from it. Intrigued, he detoured to the building, and upon entering, he spied a young woman providing the lovely music. He thought she too was lovely, and a romance blossomed. Alas, none of this is true. Emmett was indeed married to a woman named Julia for the rest of his life, but when he met her, he was in his thirties and was a former prison inmate.

Quite smitten with Bob, Eugenia Moore was persuaded to take a train east to Guthrie and wait for him there. He and Emmett chose to stay in New Mexico longer and rode on to Santa Rosa. There the brothers became involved in a "Mexican monte" game that would result in what Emmett asserted boldly—and inaccurately—in his first memoir was "Our First Crime," conveniently forgetting the horse-stealing back in Oklahoma.

By 10:00 that night, there were more than forty men "gambling, drinking and dancing, and all armed." The brothers had determined that the game was rigged. They drew their pistols, but one participant managed to run out of the saloon, possibly with some of the proceeds. Bob declared to the crowd, "You people don't know how to treat strangers, so we'll teach you how strangers should be treated."

With that, Bob grabbed "all of the crooked proprietor's bank roll." After exiting and climbing onto their horses, Emmett claimed, "we let out a fusillade of shots into the air which sent every one scurrying for cover."

It was probably best to return to plan A and hightail it to California.

Though born Mason Frakes Dalton, he was also William Marion Dalton and known as Bill. Well into adulthood, it appeared that he was following in the lawful footsteps of the older Dalton boys—Ben, Cole, and Lit, who had ventured out to California to find work away from the dangerous border country they had grown up in.

Bill had visited California a few times with his father on his horse-gambling journeys. But in 1884, at twenty years old, he came to stay (or so he intended). Because his older brothers were there, Bill looked for work in the San Joaquin Valley and found a job with them as a mule skinner.* His next job would ultimately prove more satisfying: Bill worked for a man named Bliven in Livingston and fell in love with the boss's daughter, Jane. She and Bill married and had two children, Charles and Gracie Dalton.

With his wife's brother, Clark Bliven, Bill went into business.

---

* The occupation was not as unsavory as it seems. A mule skinner was a mule driver, whose job it was to keep the mules hauling materials to and from work sites. The term *skinner* was common slang during the time for someone who could "skin," or outsmart, the mules into behaving in the way that was needed.

It did well enough that he bought land and built a home thirteen miles southeast of San Miguel. Bill was such an upstanding citizen that he became involved in politics, which included being a Democratic Party committeeman in Merced County. The future looked bright . . . until his two younger brothers appeared on his doorstep.

When they had first arrived in California, Bob and Emmett had visited Lit near Fresno and had bragged to him about robbing the stockmen in Oklahoma and their close-shave getaway. "They thought their escape as funny as could be," Lit told Frank Latta, author of *Dalton Gang Days.* "Some of it was funny, all right, to hear them tell it, but I sure burned them up about it."

Lit had lectured the two fugitives about the trouble they were getting into. When he relayed his concerns to their brother Bill, the latter made the case that as long as he didn't break from the boys, he could steer them away from trouble. Send 'em along, he advised.

Jane Dalton could not have been overjoyed to see Bob and Emmett at the front door, but her husband refused to turn his brothers away. He apparently bought the story that they had been unfairly accused of crimes in addition to being mistreated by the U.S. Marshals system. Perhaps a stay in California was more than a time-out; it could be an opportunity to start over in a legitimate occupation. The steady ways of an older, family-man brother could be a good influence. And that would go for Grat too, when he showed up.

After his release from the jail at Fort Smith, Grat had stayed at his mother's home in Kingfisher for several weeks. The original Dalton house there was built partway into the bank of Kingfisher Creek. It had been constructed with heavy timber with walls and the roof made of sod. Much of the home's heat emanated from Adeline's cookstove in the kitchen. Separately, there was a bunkhouse, which is where visiting Dalton children slept. A third structure on the property was a dugout barn. Lit recalled, "The country between the place and the town of Kingfisher was as barren and level as a floor. You could see a man afoot for a mile or more."

Adeline was worried her sons were headed down the same path as her infamous relatives, so she urged Grat to follow the boys and to look after them. Dutifully, Grat took the train to California, arriving in January 1891. He too first went to visit Lit, and the two talked about the trouble their younger brothers were in. And while he was at it, Lit probably gave Grat the same lecture he had given to Bob and Emmett. It would turn out to do just as much good.

When Grat got to Bill's ranch on the Estrella River, another Dalton brother was also there: Cole. He and Bill tried to keep their brothers busy with ranch work. It seems they had even more energy than the workday soaked up because when not driving mule teams and tackling other sweaty tasks on the ranch, Bob, Emmett, and Grat spent their time gambling and getting in over a dozen bar fights at saloons in San Miguel, Paso Robles, and San Luis Obispo. This put them in a money squeeze because it did not take long to go through most of the several hundred dollars they had swindled from Scott for the stolen horses. Plus, instead of being able to pay his younger brothers, Bill gave them two of his horses. Before long, the boys were staring at being flat broke.

That was when Bob decided to rob a train.

During a pensive moment, he must have realized that he was not cut out to be working for wages for the rest of his life. True, it is a leap to go from some frustration about the near future to becoming desperadoes, but that appears to be what happened. Bob figured that if they made enough money train-robbing, they could then escape to South America. A U.S. dollar was then worth three or four pesos, and Bob felt that with a sufficient haul, the boys could live large on South American ranches. Emmett was initially against the idea of robbing a train, but as usual, without much arm-twisting, he agreed to follow Bob's lead.

And thus the outlaw adventures of the Dalton Gang truly got underway.

---- ACT II ----

THE GANG

CHAPTER 11

RAILROAD ROBBERS

In February 1891, hoping to help his brothers find steady work, Bill Dalton wrote a letter to the superintendent of the nearby Muller and Lux Ranch, having heard it was hiring. After that was confirmed, Bill borrowed a horse and saddle from one of his hired men for Grat and two saddles from his neighbors for Bob and Emmett. The three left, telling Bill they were headed to their new jobs at the ranch. No doubt Bill stopped congratulating himself the next day when he discovered that his brothers had made a trapdoor out of the ceiling in the closet of his house to get into the attic. Most likely, he did not tell his wife, Jane, that this implied his brothers would be back.

Still, it was possible that Grat, Bob, and Emmett intended to give the Muller and Lux jobs a try. They made their first stop in Cholame, where they watered their horses, got drinks, and, just in case there was a dry stretch of road, bought a flask of whiskey. They then pushed on, but somewhere along the way, their thoughts, perhaps influenced by the whiskey, turned away from finding work and toward what could be easier money. They came up with a rather convoluted way to get it.

The first step was to find a better horse than the nag Bill had borrowed for Grat. When the three brothers reached Malaga, about four miles south of Fresno, Emmett remained there while Grat and Bob kept riding fifteen miles northeast to the ranch of Clovis Cole, where Lit had been working. Before arriving, though, Bob rode back to Malaga with Grat's horse in tow, to make it appear as if Grat had walked all the way to the Cole spread.

"I was asleep in the bunk house when I heard a single knock outside my bunk," Lit recalled. "The knock was repeated twice, about a half minute apart. This was a signal we brothers had used among us for many years. So I knew that one of the boys was outside and that he needed help." It was Grat, and he "had a fishy story."

Grat claimed that his horse had gone lame and that he had walked the rest of the way from Malaga, where the boys were waiting, to see if Lit could furnish him with a fresh horse. Ironically, a stranger might have obliged, but Lit knew his brothers and, suspecting that Grat was up to no good, he refused to lend one of his boss's horses. Instead, he borrowed a rig and drove Grat back to Malaga, apparently hoping he could find out what the other Daltons were up to and, if necessary, talk them out of it.

Bob and Emmett were killing time in a ranch barn a mile west of Malaga, and after Grat and Lit joined them, they talked until morning. Lit offered to help Grat sell his horse so he would have some money. He did so but could get only sixty dollars for it.* Lit returned to the Cole Ranch, and Bob and Emmett rode off, leaving an irritable Grat behind.

He was not alone long. After contemplating his few options, Grat hoisted his saddle and took a train to Traver, where he caught up to Bob and Emmett. The reunited brothers played poker all night there and then traveled to Tulare to do the same. (We have to assume that Grat rode with Bob or Emmett, whichever had the more durable

---

* The well-meaning Lit may never have learned that he had sold a horse Grat did not own, thereby perpetrating a crime.

horse.) Along the way, the Daltons asked about the Southern Pacific Railroad pay car that routinely made its way down the valley from Oakland to Bakersfield. This train's arrival was always accompanied by a crowd of gamblers and prostitutes looking to make money off the recently paid employees. An idea was hatched.

The next stop for the three brothers was Delano, where they spent their time at the saloons. They all used assumed names, even though several men had recognized Bob and Grat from the days when they would travel with their father's racehorses and from when they used to gamble and get in bar fights in Tulare. Grat also kept his distance from Bob and Emmett, pretending to not know them, and slept and ate in different places from them because he felt he was too easily recognizable. The reason for such subterfuge was they had decided to rob the next Southern Pacific train with a pay car attached—though they kept getting into bar fights, which was not the best way to go unnoticed.

The trio of would-be bandits became a duo when Grat lost his remaining cash playing cards. Broke, and with his brothers unable to stake him to anything, he gave up on trying to buy a new horse. He thus missed out on the crime . . . though he would still wind up paying a price for it.

In Delano the morning before the robbery, Bob and Emmett had several drinks, bought fifteen sandwiches wrapped in newspaper, and two quarts of whiskey. Thus fortified by 10:00 a.m., the two brothers rode toward Alila, one of the train's stops. Taking advantage of the shade in a secluded spot a half mile outside of the town, they ate half their lunch and emptied one of the whiskey bottles. That night, probably a bit woozy in their saddles, Bob and Emmett rode to the Southern Pacific line.

They tied their horses to a telegraph pole and walked up the tracks to Alila. When the train pulled into the station, the brothers snuck aboard the baggage car. Once the train got underway, they made their way to the engine compartment. They aimed their revolvers at the fireman, George Radliff, and the engineer, Joe Thorne, and ordered them to stop the train.

Clearly a rookie train robber, Bob wore a mask made of a white handkerchief that kept getting in his eyes, and to be able to see clearly, he pulled the mask down around his neck. As he did so, the fireman opened the door to the firebox and in the bright light was able to get a good look at Bob. Emmett smacked the fireman over the head with his revolver and ordered him to close the door, which he did.

The train came to a halt just fifty yards from where the robbers' horses were tied. Bob and Emmett marched the engineer and fireman down the side of the train to the express car. The expressman, C. C. Haswell, took a look out the door and could see the group coming. He quickly put out the car lights and locked the door and windows. Just then, the brakeman walked up with a lantern to see what was happening, and Bob took it from him.

With the light from the lantern, Emmett thought he could see a man through the glass window of the express car. He told Bob, who then began firing through the window. Immediately afterward, Haswell rested his revolver on the windowsill and fired the gun until it was empty. Then Bob resumed firing his reloaded pistol into the car. One of the bullets ricocheted off a steel bar by the window and grazed Haswell's forehead. As soon as Bob's gun emptied, Emmett began to shoot.

During all the firing, Radliff, the fireman, turned and ran. Emmett tried to shoot him and at first thought he had succeeded when Radliff stumbled and collapsed. He was indeed mortally wounded, but it would later be determined that he had been hit by one of Haswell's bullets. Unfortunately for the Daltons, they would be blamed in the subsequent newspaper accounts.

The expressman was not about to budge. He reloaded his gun, got down on the floor, and lay quiet. Bob and Emmett yelled and swore at him, but after several minutes, when there was no response, they concluded that Haswell was dead.* And for all that, they were not any closer to the inside of the pay car. The brothers hurried to their horses, untied them, and took off. As they did so, Bob fired at a deputy sheriff, who had taken his sweet time getting off the train to see what all the commotion was about.

As they rode away from the scene, Bob and Emmett accused each other of shooting the fireman. They headed west but soon became lost in the darkness and thick fog around Tulare Lake. After the sun rose and the fog lifted, the two were able to ride in the direction of the Estrella River and Bill's ranch, along the way using back roads and resting in secluded spots. When they finally arrived, they noticed that Bill's buckboard was gone and that there was a strange rig beside the corral. Afraid to go inside, they instead went to the ranch of Bill's father-in-law, Cyrus Bliven, where they learned that Bill had been out looking for them, having heard of the Alila incident.

Back in Alila, after the attempted robbery, the Tulare County sheriff, Eugene Kay, had been able to discern the horse tracks going west from where the train had stopped, but he lost them in the thick fog. After taking measurements and sketches of horse and boot tracks and finding a piece of wood that appeared to have broken off a stirrup, Kay, with his deputy, Jim Ford, set off in pursuit.

"The most remarkable exploit of Kay's whole career as sheriff was the pursuit of Bob and Emmett Dalton," declares Frank Latta. "It might also be stated with little fear of dispute that it was one of the most remarkable pursuits of criminals ever waged by a determined officer of the law. It began at Visalia, extended through seven western states and a portion of Old Mexico, blazed a trail six thousand miles

---

* The stubborn C. C. Haswell survived the attempted robbery. He was given a reward for protecting the express car. He was also indicted for manslaughter for killing Radliff. Haswell was eventually acquitted. Radliff's widow was given $2,500 by the Southern Pacific Railroad.

in length by every existing means of transportation, and lasted more than three months."

Days later, the two lawmen, driving a rig and having been guided by people who had spotted two horsemen, and with the sun soon to set, arrived at a farmhouse. They had not seen any tracks since leaving the hills and wondered if they had wandered off the route of the outlaws. Sheriff Kay knocked on the ranch door and was met by a woman with her two children. She told him that her husband wouldn't be home until late but that they would be welcome to stay the night. Kay and his deputy left their rig beside the corral and went inside for the dinner Jane Dalton offered them.

It was after dark when her husband, Bill Dalton, got to his father-in-law's ranch. He loaded Bob and Emmett into his rig and returned to his farm. Bill also had no idea who the buggy beside the corral belonged to, so he told the boys to sleep in the straw haystack next to the barn while he went inside alone. Bill did not know Kay or his deputy, who did not reveal themselves as officers, and that made him nervous.

They talked for an hour, and then, continuing to be calm under pressure, Bill offered them the spare bedroom. Moments after the visitors accepted and went to bed down for the night, Bill rushed out and warned his fugitive brothers to stay clear of the house.

The next morning, while getting their rig ready to ride, Sheriff Kay thought he would express his thanks to Bill and his wife by giving their barn a quick cleaning. As he began forking the manure pile out of the barn, he found the remnants of a saddle buried in it. The moisture from the manure had not penetrated the leather, so he knew it had been placed there recently. Kay saw that the saddle had a piece of wood broken from the stirrup. He took out the piece of hardwood they had found near Alila and noticed it was a perfect match. Kay then began to suspect that his host may in fact be associated with the robbers—and might even be one of the robbers himself. Kay put the saddle in his buggy, and he and his deputy left.

The suspicious sheriff spent the day learning what he could about the Daltons. He discovered that there were five brothers in the area, and three of them were regulars in the local saloons. Bill and Lit, however, seemed to have good reputations. Kay then received a telegram from Tulare and learned that three men had gambled from Traver to Delano for three days before the robbery following the Southern Pacific pay car. This was not unusual, but one of the gamblers was positively identified as Grat Dalton. The deputy, Jim Ford, now recalled that he had played cards with Grat and brothers Bob and Emmett while they were in Tulare.

While Kay was in Paso Robles, he was joined by a Southern Pacific Railroad detective, Will Smith, and the San Luis Obispo County sheriff, E. F. O'Neal. They discussed what Kay had learned, and it was decided to assemble a posse and that night surround and search Bill Dalton's farmhouse. Then there was a glitch: Anxious to collect the probable reward or simply impatient, Smith and O'Neal rode out to the Dalton place before sundown.

When the two lawmen arrived, Bill recognized both of them. This was when the trapdoor came in handy, because Bob and Emmett used it while their brother went outside to greet Smith and O'Neal. There was a bed in the attic, and both Bob and Emmett lay quiet with their six-shooters aimed at the trapdoor. Taxing Bill's fortitude as well as his hospitality, the sheriff asked if they could stay the night. While he and Bill put the horses in the barn, Will Smith immediately went in the house and began questioning Jane Dalton. She told him that Bob and Emmett had gone to Seattle.

When Bill entered, he and Smith got into an argument about the latter confronting his wife and children. O'Neal walked in during the middle of the shouting and tended to agree with Bill. The sheriff spotted a guitar, and trying to change the subject, he asked Bill if he would play for them. This suited Bill perfectly, as he was a skilled guitar player and needed to drown out any noise his brothers might make. Bill sang and played guitar until midnight, while Bob and

Emmett lay in the attic afraid to move and probably getting pretty sick of hearing their brother's voice.

According to Lit, "Bob told me afterward that if Will Smith had put his head through that trap door he would have stopped two .44-caliber bullets before he could have batted an eye."

Finally, the lawmen went to bed. That was good news, but the bad news was they didn't leave until after 10:00 a.m. Bob and Emmett had spent way more time in the small, stuffy attic than they cared to. Smith and O'Neal returned to Paso Robles and reported to Kay that there were no suspects at the Dalton farm and Bill had not been involved in the Alila incident.

CHAPTER 12

THE SEARCHERS

The lawman Will Smith was not done with the Daltons. A week later, he was in Fresno with another railroad detective named Hickey. They confronted Grat on the street and then tossed him into the Tulare County jail. Sheriff Kay was soon at the same calaboose to question Grat. He was not convinced that he had been involved in the robbery, but he believed that Grat could lead them to his brothers. Kay arranged to have the prisoner released.

Most likely, Grat surmised that he was no longer being accused of a crime he did not commit and maybe he could get a fresh start . . . but his troubles were just beginning. He did look for a job, but not finding one, he made a bad decision—he went to San Jose and its gaming tables. After he ended a midnight poker game, a man hired by Kay to follow Grat challenged him to a game of "Coon-can" for a dollar a game. Grat cleaned him out, and the deputy, by now embarrassed as well as broke, arrested Grat.

While Grat was cooling his heels in the jail in Visalia, Will Smith and Sheriff O'Neal returned to Bill's ranch, where his brother Cole Dalton was visiting. After questioning them awhile, both brothers were arrested and soon joined Grat in jail. Cole was released, but on

March 17, a Tulare County grand jury indicted brothers Bob, Emmett, Grat, and Bill Dalton for the Alila robbery. A $3,000 bounty was offered for the capture of Bob and Emmett. After a hearing, Grat was held for trial. Bill was able to secure a bondsman, and after his release, he hired attorneys to defend Grat.

Perhaps unaware that they were worth $3,000—which was $3,000 more than they had netted from the attempted robbery—Bob and Emmett had been hiding out in the mountains near Bill's ranch. Bill left out supplies and food, and there were several times the boys visited Bill's house at night. Clearly, with Bill's legal troubles, this could not last. Between the three of them, they did not have enough money to purchase a rail ticket from California to Indian Territory, so instead, with borrowed fresh horses, Bob and Emmett crossed the Tehachapis and began riding across the Mojave Desert. The ride almost cost them their lives, as they only saw water once in those seventy-five miles of arid desert.

What followed was as much a comedy of errors as an epic search. Sheriff Kay of Tulare County was relentless in trying to track down the two Dalton outlaws, but Bob and Emmett kept managing to escape handcuffs even when distracted. And the ever-loyal Bill was weaving in and out of the escape adventure, rushing around raising money for train fare and other expenses, and wondering if ultimately he would be the Dalton who would wind up in prison.

One close call for Bob and Emmett in the generally eastward meandering came in Ogden, Utah. Kay had received word that the brothers had been seen there, so he and his deputy, Jim Ford, jumped on a train. As luck would have it, soon after arriving, Ford spotted Emmett exiting a department store. Emmett had spotted Ford too, and he quickly ducked back inside the store. He alerted Bob, and the brothers ran through the back door and into a saloon across the alley. Ford drew his revolver and ran through another store to the alley to cut them off, but he was a tad too slow. Meanwhile, Kay notified the Ogden police to get them to begin searching the city. They must not have tried too hard because even with Kay and Ford checking out train and stage depots, the Dalton boys got away, having stolen a couple of horses.

Finally accepting the fact that Kay would stay hot on their trail, Bob and Emmett headed south into New Mexico. Even with Kay telegraphing ahead, lawmen elsewhere did not seem interested. Making another odd decision, the brothers boarded a train heading west. They stopped off in Kingman, Arizona, where they played poker all night and won a hundred dollars. Luck could not be credited because Bob pretended not to know Emmett, who then tipped him off to the hands of the others. With their earnings, the Daltons hopped a train to Phoenix.

Late again, Kay and Ford got to Kingman. They did not linger; the lawmen followed the Daltons by horse and stage from Kingman to Phoenix to Prescott, Gila Bend, Tucson, and then to Nogales, Mexico. There the American officers were offered assistance that even included a military escort. Still, they missed Bob and Emmett by only twelve hours in Cananea, then lost their trail completely in Fronteras.

Sheriff Kay assumed that the suspects were probably headed to El Paso, so he and Ford reentered the United States at Douglas. In El Paso, they were informed that Bob and Emmett had headed to Albuquerque instead and then had taken the train to Topeka, Kansas. From there, thinking they had lost the lawmen at last, Bob and Emmett headed to their mother's home.

They should have known Kay better by now. He and Ford tracked the Daltons to Kingfisher and kept watch on Adeline's house for a few days before learning that somehow Bob and Emmett had once more slipped through their fingers. Kay went ahead and knocked on the door anyway, and Adeline invited the weary and frustrated men in for breakfast. She denied any wrongdoing by her sons, stating that they were in fact lawmen too. Trying to be helpful, Adeline suggested that if Kay and Ford wanted to talk to her sons, they should head to Guthrie.

Okay, why not give that a try? When the lawmen arrived, they were told that indeed Bob and Emmett had been in Guthrie. They had gotten into a fight at one of the saloons there and badly beaten up two cowboys before leaving—back to Topeka.

This time, the brothers finally had lost the lawmen. They had to return to California because Grat's trial was soon to begin. Kay also accepted that the odds were stacked too high against them in that area.

"They had dozens of friends to furnish them with horses, guns, ammunition, and provisions," Kay lamented years later. "That country was crowded with desperados, and the few well-meaning, honorable people living there were entirely under subjugation, fearing to furnish any information whatever that might lead to the capture of an outlaw."

It had to have been a very long and fist-clenching train journey back to California.

After they realized they were no longer being pursued, Bob and Emmett could have counted their blessings at having survived both the Alila shoot-out and the pursuit by a determined sheriff and his sidekick. If they had used this opportunity to renounce any future criminal activity, the Daltons could have been only American frontier footnotes, if that . . . but at least they would have had longer, perhaps more satisfying lives.

Alas, they had a different thought: It was time to form what would become known as the Dalton Gang.

CHAPTER 13

THE WHARTON TRAIN

That Bob thought to create an actual gang as the Younger clan had done meant that the California adventures were just a prelude to becoming a full-fledged outlaw. Of course, that meant that Emmett had to become one too.

Bob had not gleaned from the experiences in California that thievery was an unsuccessful way to make a living, but they had taught him to stick to his own turf. Their only ally out west had been Bill, and now he had his own heap of troubles. Lit and Cole had expressed brotherly concern but otherwise had been downright discouraging. Grat was behind bars, and, furthering the Daltons' feelings about the injustice of the legal system, he might be convicted and sent to prison for a crime he did not commit. It was probably convenient to overlook that if he'd had a healthy horse, Grat would have been part of the Alila incident. It was even more convenient to ignore that a man had died during the attempted robbery, even though, specifically, it was not a bullet belonging to Bob or Emmett that had killed him.

No, the important takeaway here was to stick to the region and people you know, just as the Younger and James brothers had done. Going all the way to Minnesota had been their downfall. For the

Dalton Gang, Bob would find local men, and they would operate in the Oklahoma, Missouri, and Kansas nexus. They might even become folk heroes like Jesse and Frank James, striking blows against the railroad robber barons and other rich and contemptuous fancy folk.

There are varying accounts of how and when and where Bob recruited the gang members, but rather than sort them out, let us cut to who he gathered around him and Emmett in 1891. It is generally regarded that the first two were George Newcomb and Charlie Bryant.

The former was born in Fort Scott, Kansas, in 1866. His family was a poor one, so Newcomb was barely a teenager when he began working as a cowboy, including on the C. C. Slaughter Ranch in Texas before eventually working his way to Oklahoma where he met either Bob or Emmett Dalton. By then, being in a gang and stealing money had to seem more exciting than punching cows and fixing fences. He was known as "Bitter Creek" because his favorite drinking chant was, "I'm a bad wolf from Bitter Creek and it's my night to howl."

Charlie Bryant was from Wise County in Texas. He also worked at ranches and was in Oklahoma when he and the Daltons found each other. His nickname was "Blackfaced" because, like Bob, he unhappily sported a gunpowder burn on one cheek. According to the western historian Robert Barr Smith, Bryant "was a thorough-going hoodlum without, as the judges are fond of saying, redeeming social value." Making his appearance further disconcerting was that he "periodically shook and shuddered with an uncontrollable fever—probably malaria—which did nothing to improve his nasty disposition."

Joining the gang a few months later was the man who over time would become its most infamous member: Bill Doolin. Tall and slender with a red mustache, he was thirty-three when he became a member of the Dalton Gang. He had been born in Johnson County, Arkansas, and in 1881, he left his family and familiar surroundings to work as a cowboy in Indian Territory. While there, Doolin had made the acquaintance of Bitter Creek Newcomb and other men who would ride with the Dalton brothers. He was not necessarily looking to become an outlaw . . . but he got into trouble one day in Coffeyville (more about this a bit later).

Also attracted to the illegal ambitions of Bob and Emmett was Dick Broadwell, who was in his late twenties. He wanted money too but not because he came from a poor family. The Broadwells of Hutchinson, Kansas, were actually a prominent clan. Dick intended to chart his own course when the Oklahoma Territory was opened up, and he staked a claim in the Cowboy Flats area. Life there began well and got even better when he met a young woman who owned the homestead next to his. Soon after they married, she persuaded him to sell both claims and move with her to Fort Worth, Texas. One morning, Broadwell woke up and his wife was gone, with their money. He went from Texas to the Indian Territory and began working at ranches.* It was Bob or Emmett who invited him to join the expanding Dalton Gang.

It was Emmett, while working as a cowboy on the Bar X Bar Ranch near the Pawnee Agency, who met William Todd Power, mostly known as Bill Power, but he sometimes traveled under the name Tom Evans. Not much is known about Bill Power's background other than he was born in 1869. He drifted into Oklahoma from Texas with a trail herd from the Pecos, and maybe thought becoming an outlaw was a good career move. He was a stocky man of medium height with black hair and mustache and was known to enjoy a fight or similar fun.

That may have been true too for Charley Pierce, who before encountering the Daltons had been unsuccessfully racing horses in Pawnee, Oklahoma. He had relocated from Missouri rather than be

---

* Dick Broadwell was one of the scores of men on the frontier who was also known as "Texas Jack."

killed by the kin of a girl there whom he had impregnated. Pierce had an admiration for the men who had ridden with Quantrill and then the Younger and James brothers.

An unofficial member of the new gang was Eugenia Moore. She had waited dutifully for a summons from Bob Dalton, and when it came, she was off for Oklahoma. She could not have had any illusions about Bob being at least as enamored with crime as with her, yet perhaps, good or bad, she wanted more excitement in her life. In any case, poised for action, she rented a room in Guthrie. She was to become, according to Emmett, "a valuable ally. She was a girl of unusual tact and quick wit. Riding up and down on the railroad she was constantly on the alert for bits of information which might prove of value to us."

For a while, the gang was not yet fully formed and did not have a purpose. The members still worked ranch jobs and drank and gambled in the local saloons. But the latter activities wore out their wages. Instead of cutting back on the drinking and gambling, Bob thought it made sense to rob a train.

An initially reluctant Emmett pointed out that this had not worked well for them back in February. And not only had they barely escaped arrest, their brother Grat could spend years in prison for the botched Alila job. To Bob, that was not the problem—the problem was poor planning. And after all, what was the use of being in a gang if you were not outlaws? As usual, Emmett went along.

And so it was one night in May 1891 that a train was held up in Wharton, Oklahoma.* Much of the advance planning was assisted by Eugenia Moore. According to Emmett, she also was "an amateur

---

* After the opening of the Cherokee Outlet, also called the Cherokee Strip, two years later, Wharton would be renamed Perry. Another outlaw, Timothy McVeigh, was stopped on April 19, 1995, along Interstate 35 outside of Perry by Oklahoma Highway Patrol trooper Charlie Hanger. Hanger had passed McVeigh's yellow 1977 Mercury Marquis and noticed it had no license plate. He arrested McVeigh for carrying a loaded firearm. Three days later, while still in jail, McVeigh was identified as the subject of the nationwide manhunt for the recent Oklahoma City bombing.

telegrapher. Listening to casual bits of conversation at different times on the wires, Miss Moore learned that the Wells-Fargo Express Company was about to carry an unusually large sum of money from Kansas City."

Bob had bought her a horse, and once she had sufficient information, Moore got on it and rode out to "where we were," as Emmett cryptically put it. Where they were was the dugout camp four miles south of a ranch owned by Jim Riley, which in turn was sixty miles southwest of Kingfisher, where their mother lived. This seemed like too good an opportunity to pass up, so the brothers shared the information with Blackfaced Bryant and Bitter Creek Newcomb. The train station at Wharton, in the Cherokee Strip, looked like a promising place for a holdup.

At dusk on May 9, the gang rode toward Wharton. A quarter mile outside of the town were stockyards, and the men stopped there and hitched their horses. The plan called for Bob and Bitter Creek to walk to the Wharton station and wait for the train, which had begun its trip in Kansas City and was due to stop there at 10:30. When the conductor signaled to move out, the two men would leap into the engine cab and force the engineer and fireman to stop the train at the stockyards. Bryant and Emmett would be waiting there. The crew would be made to lie on the ground while the door to the express car was forced open and, hopefully, there would be access to the large haul of money.*

And that was how it worked out . . . well, pretty much. Bob and Newcomb, the lower halves of their faces masked, clambered onto the train. Bryant was nervously puffing on a cigarette when it stopped at the stockyards. While the rest of the gang stood guard over the confused members of the crew, Bob marched to the express

---

* In Emmett's version of events, he helped to procure horses and ammunition but did not participate in the robbery. His absence makes little sense, especially with the wealth of detail he offers, but it was a prudent position to take when the ex-prisoner wrote his memoirs.

car, accompanied by the engineer and the fireman. Whenever a passenger stuck his or her head out a window to see about the delay, they drew it right back in when a Colt pistol was aimed at them.

Bob pounded on the door of the express car. It opened, and the messenger stuck his head out: "What's the matter? What's up?"

He found out soon enough when Bob climbed up and pointed his pistol at him. The messenger, realizing he had no chance to get to his Winchester, chose not to be a hero and backed away.

In the car, Bob found two safes. The smaller one, he knew, was for packages taken in and dropped off at the stations along the train's route. The larger one, known as the "through safe," held the money. To reduce the risk of robberies, the railroad let it be known that the combination of this safe would be set at the point of origin—in this case, Kansas City—and was telegraphed to the train's final destination. Bob believed that was not the whole story.

He told the messenger to open the small safe. The terrified man did so immediately. As instructed by Bob, he plucked packages out of it and dropped them into the gunnysack Bob held out. When that safe was empty, Bob ordered, "Open the other safe."

"I don't know the combination," the messenger said. "Honest."

Bob stepped forward and stuck the barrel of his gun into the man's side. "Open it," he growled, "or it's the last chance to eat again."

The messenger slumped to his knees and said, "So help me God, I don't know the combination."

The two men might have volleyed words back and forth for a while longer, but suddenly, there were gunshots. The other gang members were firing their pistols in the air. The sound made the messenger either compliant or clairvoyant because he crawled quickly to the large safe.

According to Emmett: "In thirty seconds the safe was open and the messenger was throwing package after package, some bulky, some thin, but all valuable, into the gaping mouth of the sack. 'Guess that's all, young fellow,' Bob said as he turned toward the door and came out; we all got on our horses and rode back to our camp. There was a quick dismounting and tearing open of the packages."

The outcome was quite different from the Alila job—the Wharton train robbery netted the Dalton Gang around $9,000. In Emmett's perspective, "A train robbery in California had made the Dalton boys train robbers in name, and now they were train robbers in fact as well."*

The gang learned only later how close they had come to not getting away with it. On board the train they robbed was a U.S. deputy marshal, Ransom Payne. He was a fortyish, tall man who had lived in Iowa and Kentucky and then been a real estate salesman before accepting a commission as a lawman. But it was not as close a call as it could, or should, have been. Payne stayed safely on the train and did not display his badge or his guns until the thieves were escaping.†

Because they knew the back country so well, the members of the gang were able to evade a pursuit. *The Muskogee Phoenix* reported, "A large posse of well armed men left this city [Guthrie] early yesterday morning in pursuit of the Dalton gang. It is known that the men are carrying a large sum of money on their persons taken from cattlemen and settlers heretofore."

During the next year, the Dalton Gang would demonstrate a special talent for frustrating lawmen. But one member would prove to be an exception. Charlie "Blackfaced" Bryant would not be part of the Dalton Gang much longer, and not by his own choice.

---

* Two published reports had the take at less than $2,000, which may have been an attempt by railroad officials to minimize the enticement of robbing a train.
† Another account has Ransom Payne getting off the train and crouching in the bushes. While he did not distinguish himself here, he had a long lawman career that included having fired the first shot that started the Oklahoma Land Rush on April 22, 1889.

CHAPTER 14

"HE GOT ME TOO"

That summer, the Dalton Gang expanded to include its other members. The original outlaws managed to continue to elude lawmen and apparently spent the money they stole discreetly enough as to not attract much attention. They had friends in this part of Oklahoma, and even those who knew the location of the gang's hideout were not likely to give them up to the law.

Not so fortunate was Charlie Bryant. He had snuck off to visit his brother, and while in a town called Hennessey, he had been recognized by several men. Probably hoping for a reward, they found a deputy marshal, Ed Short, and told him about Bryant being in town.

Short was a well-liked and respected lawman. At age seventeen, the Indiana native had run off to become a cowboy in Kansas. He worked on ranches in Caldwell and Hunnewell and served as a peace officer in Woodsdale. The author Glenn Shirley described him as a "bad man" because "he was fearless. Like the dime-novel hero, he reveled in deeds of blood and valor, but there was little bravado about him. Short, despite his name, was a tall and robust man with blond hair and may have resembled the matinee-idol cowboy who appeared later in motion pictures."

He had done such a good job in Woodsdale that its citizens gave him an engraved Colt pistol. He married in 1887, but his young wife passed away after just five months into wedlock. That tragedy plus being on the losing side in the Stevens County Seat War prompted Short to give Oklahoma a try. He had participated in the 1889 Land Rush and settled in Hennessey in the Indian Territory. His lawing experience led to him being elected city marshal in that town's first municipal election. When the Oklahoma Territory was established in 1890, U.S. marshal William Grimes appointed him one of his first deputies.

It was during the first week in August that Short, two months shy of his twenty-seventh birthday, was told about Charlie Bryant. The outlaw was sick in bed at the Hennessey Hotel, recuperating from one of his mysterious fever attacks. After ascertaining the room number, Short took off his boots and quietly climbed the stairs, following an employee of the hotel who was bringing Bryant some food. When the outlaw opened his door to let her in, Short and his Winchester entered instead. A weak and startled Bryant was easily arrested.

It was a neat bit of policing, but then Short made two mistakes. The first was not notifying Marshal Grimes in Fort Smith about the arrest and his intention to bring Bryant to Wichita, meaning the marshal could not assign another deputy as backup. The second was transporting the prisoner over 140 miles without any help at all.

Short and Bryant boarded the train at the Hennessey station, and the journey began. It turned out to be a much shorter one than anticipated. The train was nearing the stop at Waukomis, still in Oklahoma, when the deputy marshal spotted a group of mounted men who looked as if they were trying to outrun the train. If that was the Dalton Gang looking to free their friend, this could be trouble.

Short hauled the handcuffed prisoner back through the passenger cars and sat him in the baggage car. Without realizing it, Short had made yet another mistake. Back in the passenger car, Bryant had complained that his arms ached from his hands being cuffed behind him, so the lawman had re-cuffed his prisoner with hands in front. Now, after putting the baggageman in charge of Bryant and giving him one of his revolvers, Short walked to the rear platform with his rifle. Though an understandably alert act, this was one last mistake.

The baggageman carelessly stuck the revolver into a pigeonhole message box and returned to work at the other end of the car, preparing the mail to be dropped off at Waukomis. Furtively, Bryant went to the message box and grabbed the revolver. He then ordered the baggageman to ignore him and to go back to his work. Bryant opened the door to the rear platform. The unaware deputy marshal was keeping his eyes on the riders. With his own pistol, Short was shot in the back. Though mortally wounded, the lawman managed to turn and fire his rifle. Both men died on the floor of the train.

Before Short died, however, the conductor, a man named Collins, hearing the gunshots, had rushed to the rear of the train. He heard the dying deputy say, "I got my man, but he got me too. I would like to see my mother."

His wish was not granted. However, Mrs. L. M. Short of Osgood, Indiana, was presented with a check for five hundred dollars, donated by the Santa Fe Railroad. The reward had been offered by the railway line for the arrest and conviction of any member of the Dalton Gang that had held up the train in Wharton back in May. Ed Short was buried in Osgood.

Bryant's body was claimed by relatives and transported to Decatur, Texas. He was probably buried in the cemetery there, but no tombstone marks his grave. Maybe the family could not afford one. "Although I know personally that Bryant had on his person about eighteen hundred dollars when he left our camp," Emmett contended, "yet when his brother Jim came to claim his body and effects at Hennessey they did not turn over to him anything but his brother's horse, saddle and Winchester."

Especially after hearing of the death of Blackfaced Bryant, the members of the Dalton Gang lay low. Some of their time was spent

digging a hideout in the steep hills in the cedar brakes on the Northern Canadian River outside of present-day Taloga. The deep canyons
of the area, covered with dwarf cedar and blackjack oak, made it an
ideal hiding place. It was at this location, despite their comrade's
fate, that Bob began planning the next train robbery.

According to Emmett, his brother wanted one more score before
getting away for good: "It was Bob's intention to have Miss Moore
take a train at Wagoner and go to Tampa, Florida where they were to
get married just before sailing for South America."

She played her part in preparing for this. Eugenia Moore, Emmett recounted, "was equipped with an excellent education and frequently interviewed officials of the railroads, posing as a magazine
writer gathering information for articles on the Oklahoma country.
Frequently, she was regaled with stories of the Daltons and the efforts being made to capture them."

Her queries finally resulted in a scoop—that a large sum of money
was soon to be shipped. "The plucky little woman saddled her horse
and started on a hazardous cross-country ride to bring us the information. Riding mostly by night through a country infested by
Indians and outlaws, she finally arrived at our camp with the news."

This next raid would take place at the small station of Lelietta,
four miles north of Wagoner. In this case, the safe in the express car
of the southbound Missouri, Kansas & Texas ("Katy") train contained money on its way to the Lehigh coal companies. How much,
Bob Dalton did not know, but he liked the plan's prospects.

CHAPTER 15

A DISPUTE WITH DOOLIN

The plan played out to perfection on the night of September 15. The train had just taken on water and was pulling out of the Lelietta station when two men appeared in the cab brandishing Winchesters. After hurriedly halting the steaming train, the engineer and fireman immediately hoisted their hands.

Recalling the robbery decades later, Emmett still harbored an amusing resentment that the fireman had yelled, "The Daltons!": "So it always was. The Daltons were always blamed even before anyone knew whether they really were the ones at the bottom or not. The fireman had never seen them and had he known them personally he had not had time to recognize Bob. But it was a robbery and the Daltons were to blame." Then Emmett conceded, "But this time he was right."

Four bandits stood outside to make sure no passengers made a run for it while the train crewmen were marched through to the express car. The company messenger, perhaps a family man, offered no resistance. The contents of at least one of the two safes were turned over.

The Indian Chieftain was to report in its September 17 edition,

"The train was not detained but a short time and very few persons knew what had happened." It added, "Two blood hounds were brought up from Atoka yesterday morning and an organized pursuit is being conducted." A day later, the *Fort Smith Elevator* informed readers, "So quietly did they do the job that passengers did not know the train had been robbed until after they pulled out and were nearly to Wagoner."

Just as they had hoped to do, the members of the Dalton Gang vanished into the night, with perhaps even their horses feeling proud of themselves.

A last scene of the raid that Emmett remembered was that one of the porters and another man had gotten off the train to see what the commotion was about, but both tried to climb back aboard after Bill Power fired several shots: "There was not enough room for two [on the stairs] and the fat man fell backward to the ground. Just then the train began to move and I could see him crawling on his hands and knees in the same direction the car was going as though he was trying to race the car. However, he got to his feet and managed to swing aboard the last car as it passed. He was angrily shaking his fist at us as the train was swallowed up by the night."

The good news for the gang was that this robbery resulted in their most profitable take yet, a shade over $19,000. But it seems that as a result of such success, the members began to argue over money. Bob doled out over $3,000 to each man, including his younger brother. One would think they would be happy enough with this payout given their previous shares. But the boys must have anticipated higher expenses during the time between robberies.*

And maybe it was also a lifestyle issue: Bill Doolin, especially, though no monk himself, complained that Bob was throwing away

---

* Another explanation for the discontent is that the total take was considerably less. As usual, the Katy officials downplayed the amount stolen, and the true take may have been somewhere in the middle.

too much money on gambling and women—presumably, ones in addition to the plucky Eugenia Moore. With Bob not promising to mend his profligate ways and that any extra money he kept was for the still-imprisoned Grat Dalton, a disgruntled Doolin quit the gang. Bitter Creek Newcomb and Charley Pierce followed him out the hideout door.

Doolin was not done with the gang for good, but as it was the first time he challenged its leadership, it's worth knowing more about the man who would come close to surpassing the Daltons as outlaws.

William Doolin was born in 1858 to Michael and Artemina Doolin. His father, a sharecropper who was known as Mack, had been a widower with four children from that marriage when he wed his second wife and had son William and daughter Tennessee with Artemina.

Mack Doolin was able to buy a forty-acre farm on the Big Piney River in Arkansas, and that was where his two youngest children grew up. During the Civil War, John Doolin, an older half brother of Bill's, enlisted in the Union army but soon kept trying to get out of it. He was finally sentenced to prison at Fort Smith, from which he escaped. By the time he felt it safe enough to return to the family farm, Mack Doolin had died. John took over and managed to avoid the notice of the law.

Bill Doolin grew up to be a tall man for the time at six feet, two inches. He was slender, and according to the biographer Bailey Hanes, he had "thick, unruly auburn hair above a high forehead. Penetrating pale-blue eyes, thin lips, and canine teeth were his trademark. And his nose was long and thin, with a pronounced hook at the end. He always wore a ragged brindled mustache that practically covered his straight mouth."

He was twenty-three when he left the farm, aiming west. After several itinerant jobs, Bill was hired by Oscar Halsell, who was from Texas and was establishing a new ranch in the Cowboy Flats area of Logan County, Oklahoma. Doolin worked there, and at times for nearby outfits, for the next decade. Among the other ranch hands who worked with him were Bitter Creek Newcomb, Dick Broadwell, Bill Power, and Emmett Dalton.

Doolin was not much of a go-to-town-and-get-rowdy sort of hand, so it was surprising that his trouble with the law began with beer. It was the Fourth of July, and he uncharacteristically decided to accompany several cowboys from the Bar X Bar Ranch across the state border into Coffeyville. Finding the holiday celebrations a tad understated, Doolin and the others appropriated several ash barrels, sawed them in two, and filled them with ice and bottles of beer. In case that would not be enough, they purchased two kegs of cold beer. Apparently, one could buy beer but not drink it there, so being careful, they put all the beer in a wagon and drove it out to a shady grove outside Coffeyville, inviting people to follow them for a drink.

Unfortunately for them, two deputy sheriffs could not leave well enough alone on that Independence Day. Perhaps there had been too many citizens wandering out of town and returning drunk. The two lawmen went out to the sudden saloon the ranch hands had created and asked who the beer belonged to. Doolin replied, "The beer doesn't belong to anybody. It's free, help yourselves."

Such generosity was not appreciated. The deputies said that because Kansas was a dry state, they would have to seize the suds. As one deputy began to roll a keg of beer away, someone fired a shot. There were more shots, and both deputies fell wounded. Doolin took off and kept going, eventually throwing in with the Dalton brothers.

Because the proceeds of the Lelietta train robbery were, after all, at least pretty good and probably because of the infighting and no doubt because of lawmen being more on the lookout than ever before, the Dalton Gang did not strike again until months later. But when they did, it was a doozy. And by then, the outlaw group had expanded to include a free and vengeful Grat Dalton.

CHAPTER 16

"CESSPOOL OF ABOMINATIONS"

Even though he did not attend a minute of it, Emmett Dalton declared that the trial of his brother Grat in California "was the most noted farce ever perpetrated on an innocent man." Thanks to not being able to afford a horse, Grat really had not participated in the Alila robbery and was indeed innocent. However, with the real perpetrators, especially two of his brothers, having gotten away, it was not likely the judicial system—especially one very much influenced by the railroad companies—would let another Dalton loose.

Both Bill and Grat were arraigned in April 1891. The judge presiding was Wheaton Andrew Gray. This was not good news for the Daltons. Gray had been a defense attorney—a recent client was C. C. Haswell—until the previous month when a telegram arrived from Governor Henry Markham informing him that he had been appointed to a judgeship. The grip of the railroad barons extended to Sacramento, and it was expected that Gray, who had campaigned for Markham's election the previous year, would represent those interests in court—such as making sure a couple of alleged train robbers were convicted.

Grat was to be tried first, in June. The pool of potential jurors had to be tainted by a story that appeared in *The San Francisco Chronicle* in May. It described a long bullet-riddled battle between the Dalton Gang and a high-powered posse that included ten U.S. marshals in addition to fifty U.S. Cavalry troopers. The firefight occurred near the Sac and Fox Reservation in Oklahoma's Indian Territory. During it, Bob Dalton had been killed and Emmett taken prisoner. The telegram on which the article was based turned out to be a hoax.

Despite the bad, if fabricated, publicity, Grat's trial got underway on the seventeenth. The defendant's attorney, J. W. Breckinridge, was not present, but Judge Gray did not order a delay.* The stated reason for the attorney's absence was he had a trial elsewhere to finish up, but the truth was Breckinridge had been drinking for a week and needed a few more days to sober up. It also did not impress the judge that the evidence to be presented had been held by railroad employees and not shared with the defense.

Jury selection was expected to be conducted swiftly, but there was a delay that first day because when the partial jury returned after the noon recess, one of its members was drunk. During the next couple of days, potential jurors did not return at all. Finally, on the fourth day, the full jury was seated. Judge Gray then denied a defense motion that a transcript of the trial would be recorded.

Literally, Grat was being railroaded.

The prosecution's presentation was that while two men had perpetrated the attempted robbery of the train at Alila, all four brothers were involved in the criminal conspiracy. Dozens of witnesses were paraded before the jurors, some of them contradicting each other. A few, apparently not adequately coached, admitted that they had not seen or heard anything that night, let alone knew anything about Grat Dalton. There was no doubt some coaching, though, as a few witnesses revealed that during breaks in the trial they had

---

* The defense attorney was the son of John C. Breckinridge, who had been vice president during the administration of James Buchanan, the fifteenth president.

been reminded by Southern Pacific detectives of details they had forgotten. Some witnesses admitted that the railroad companies were paying their expenses and they were traveling thanks to issued passes.

A dozen witnesses at the trial testified that the night of the Alila train robbery, Grat was playing cards and drinking—his two favorite occupations—in Fresno. And Breckinridge did provide a sturdy defense. Not only was the dated register showing Grat's signature at the Fresno hotel presented, so was the clerk and another witness who vouched that Grat had signed it that night. And not only did Bill and Lit Dalton testify on Grat's behalf, but the durable and loving Adeline had traveled from Oklahoma to support her son.

In his summation, the prosecutor kept citing the unfortunate George Radliff, trying to tie his death—though shot by Haswell—to Grat. It was surprising that the jury bothered to take twenty hours to announce a verdict.

Grat was convicted of complicity in the Alila robbery. Instead of walking out of the courtroom a free man, as he had hoped, he was returned to his jail cell. Grat would be there for a while because Judge Gray put off sentencing until July 29, and there would turn out to be several postponements.

Moments after the jail cell door clanged shut behind Grat, the well-traveled detective Will Smith appeared. Through the bars the exultant detective crowed, "I told you I would land you."

"That's all right," Grat responded. "It won't do you any good. I will beat this case yet."

His conviction actually benefited his brother Bill. In the wake of the verdict, his bail was reduced from $30,000 to $5,000, which allowed him to be released on bond. His trial would begin on October 5.

On September 3, a train was stopped near Ceres, but for whatever reason, the robbers took off without stealing anything. Because of the similarity to the Alila incident, and probably also because he was the only Dalton readily available, Bill was arrested again. He had a solid alibi, but an obsessed Sheriff Eugene Kay reintroduced him to the Tulare County jail anyway. Also nabbed was a friend, Riley Dean.

Some satisfaction for Bill was that a few newspapers, including *The San Francisco Examiner,* criticized the arrests and ridiculed the detectives who had conducted the Ceres investigation. As a result, the red-faced lawmen released Dalton and Dean. But Bill's liberty was short-lived because his bond was withdrawn. One compensation for this confusing series of events was his cell in the jail in Visalia was next to Grat's.

On September 17, the *Tulare County Times* published a jailhouse interview with a bitter Bill Dalton. He ridiculed the accusations against him and concluded, "The whole story is so absurd that no one but a Southern Pacific detective could ever conceive it." In the same newspaper a week later, Bill colorfully claimed about Will Smith that "this same man, whose mind seems only a cesspool of abominations, goes and attempts to coerce my wife into giving false testimony against me, something prohibited by law, in order to strew his path to fame and renown with one more rose."

While Bill was talking, Grat had been quietly planning. On the night of September 27, he and two other men escaped from the jail in Visalia while Sheriff Kay was in San Francisco. One story was that someone on the outside gave Grat a saw, and after some furtive work, the prisoners had squeezed through the bars and run off into the night. In the morning, when jailers found the cell empty, in the next cell Bill was strumming his guitar and singing, "You'll Never Miss My Brother Till He's Gone."

A more entertaining version of Grat's escape, promoted by a Daltons biographer known only as "An Eye Witness," continues to be told. Grat had been sentenced, and two deputy marshals were escorting him on the train taking him to prison. Though in leg irons as well as handcuffs, the convict managed to get loose. Grat threw himself through an open window. At that moment, the train was crossing a trestle above a stream. Grat landed in the water deep enough that he did not break his neck and clambered up onto the bank. A mysterious accomplice with a second horse waited for him there, and the two men rode off, beginning an unlikely journey from California to a Dalton reunion in Oklahoma.

Though this version is untrue, Grat's escape was daring and embarrassing enough. Sheriff Kay was on the trail again, and he managed to track down and arrest the two men who had broken out of jail with Grat. Kay was then informed that Grat and Riley Dean were hiding on the summit of a steep mountain three miles from the Kings River near Sanger.* The sheriff arranged for a holiday surprise.

On Christmas Eve 1891, a combined posse of men led by Kay and Sheriff John Hensley of Fresno County ascended the mountain to Grat's camp. They ambushed the two outlaws as they were on their way back from a boar hunt. Once again, Grat was able to escape, firing at the lawmen with a Winchester and running to a nearby ranch where he stole a horse. Dean was not so swift or lucky and was arrested once more. Grat lay low, then several weeks later, with the aid of his brother Cole, he left California altogether and made his way back to Oklahoma.

By the time he arrived, there had already been a Dalton brothers reunion. When Grat and the two other prisoners had escaped, by doing nothing, Bill had made the right move. At his trial the following month, the prosecution offered even flimsier testimony, and to counter it, thirteen prominent citizens—including a former supervisor of Merced County—testified as character witnesses for Bill. After just fifteen minutes, the jury returned to the courtroom and announced a not-guilty verdict.

---

* Dean had earlier been released because there was no evidence linking him to the Ceres job. In 1994, the Sanger Rotary Club erected a marker designating the site as Dalton Mountain.

Still, the entire experience had made Bill disgruntled about living on the ranch, so he sold the lease to it. He and Jane and their children moved in with her parents in Livingston. Maybe such crowded conditions did not work for Bill either or he felt the call of home in Oklahoma, because he soon left for Kingfisher.

However, he was not yet ready to become an outlaw, or at least not completely. Bill arrived in Kingfisher, and "equipped with the gift of gab and a burning hatred of banks and bankers," writes Robert Barr Smith, "Bill set up in the land-dealing business and prospered. On the side, Bill became intelligence gatherer and information broker for the gang."

Yes, a gang: Bob—and perhaps Emmett—may have still harbored thoughts of a fresh start in South America, but for now, there was more money to be harvested. What they had collected from the last heist, in Lelietta, was already running low. Food and liquor and women (perhaps Miss Moore was away gleaning information) to pay for and gifts made to local folk who kept their whereabouts a secret had drained the kitty.

Another reason why the Daltons stayed under the radar of the law was the amount of crime being committed around them, which gave the sheriffs and deputy marshals all the work they could handle. With the recent opening of Cheyenne Territory in Oklahoma, Emmett noted, "came a horde of wild, lawless characters beside whom we were meek and quiet as Presbyterian elders. Shooting scrapes and killings were the usual course of the day. Train robberies were not infrequent but we had no hand in them."

They had been waiting for Grat to arrive, having heard that he was working his way east, yet when he showed up, they did not have a plan for another robbery because "a suitable opportunity did not present itself."

As they got further into 1892, that would change. The brothers would get busy. "We were Daltons together," Emmett vowed, "and Daltons we would stay until the bitter end. And we did."

CHAPTER 17

RED ROCK ROBBERY

Early in 1892, Bill Dalton not only found himself back home in Adeline's humble house in Kingfisher but that there were now four Daltons together sharing feelings of resentment toward the law. "When Grat joined us the bitterness that had been burning within him burst forth and joined our flame of hatred directed toward the express company, toward Smith, the detective, and those who had taken part in the deal against us," Emmett wrote. "Then we believed ourselves the victims of a plot of persecution."

A reinvigorated gang was an appealing prospect to the three men who had left it after the last robbery the previous summer, and they fell back into the fold. A return to being ranch hands had convinced Bill Doolin, Bill Power, and Dick Broadwell that a workingman's life had not become any more interesting than before they left the gang.

With seven men waiting for instructions and the prospect of making easier money than wages, Bob Dalton devised the next train heist. He decided the target would be the Red Rock station on the Santa Fe line. Red Rock was a very small town consisting of loading pens, a store, a section house, a handful of residences, and of course a depot on the Otoe Indian Reservation forty miles south of Arkansas

City. On the night of June 1, the train was scheduled to arrive at 10:00.

It did, puffing furiously as though reluctant to stop, but the Dalton Gang stayed put in the darkness surrounding the depot. Bob's nerve endings were tingling; something was not right. Given the size of Red Rock, no passengers getting on or off by itself was not curious, but the nervous scurrying around of the station agent was. He hurried to the express car and appeared to be talking to someone inside it. Bob also noted that the interior of the train was dark. Sure, a few passengers might have been sleeping, but conductors would not go so far to accommodate them as to turn all the lights off.

"What are we waiting for?" muttered an impatient Grat.

Bob whispered, "I think it's a trap."

It was indeed. They would later learn that, first, the passengers had not been sleeping but waiting to witness quite a show, and second, the dark smoking car contained heavily armed deputy marshals and railroad detectives.

Somehow, word of the gang's plan had leaked to lawmen who had arranged the ambush with railroad officials. However, as the train chugged out of the Red Rock station, the other outlaws could only wonder why Bob was so skittish. They could contemplate this for only a very short time because another train was approaching. It was the regular express.

"This is the one we want," Bob said, becoming certain the first train had been a decoy.

As the train arrived at the station, the difference was obvious. This one was well lit up inside. Charley Pierce and Bitter Creek Newcomb jumped into the cab, startling and quickly disarming a guard who had been munching on a sandwich while sitting on a pile of wood. With the train stopped, the fireman and engineer were told to get down and walk to the express car. Waiting for them were Power, Broadwell, Grat, Bob, Emmett, and Doolin.

Just then, a young porter stepped off the train intending to help passengers disembark. He attracted the attention of the gang's guns. Just seeing them was enough; the porter jumped back on the train, and they could hear him telling the passengers that there was a holdup and to hide their valuables.

There were two men inside the express car—the messenger, E. C. Whitteny, and a guard, John Riehl. If they had been promised that the Dalton Gang would be dead or in handcuffs by the time their train pulled into Red Rock, they had to be mighty surprised now, but they had been quick enough to turn the inside lights off and lock the wooden door. An aggravated Bob Dalton gave the signal, and all the outlaws began shooting at the door with both pistols and rifles—it would later be estimated that sixty shots were fired.

Though terrified, the two men inside stubbornly refused to pull the door open. Bob gave the fireman, whose name was Rogers, a pick and ordered him to break the door down. He got to work, but only after begging Whitteny and Riehl not to shoot him. When enough whacks had opened a hole, Rogers crawled through it. The plan was he would then open the door, but the armed men within instead told him to go to the front of the car and lie down.

"I'll shoot the first man who pokes his head through that hole," Riehl declared.

The robbers expressed their displeasure by letting loose with another onslaught of lead. In the ensuing silence, they could hear petrified passengers screaming and crying.

Enough was enough. "Come on out," Bob called, "and no one gets hurt."

Figuring by now that the railroad could not fault their efforts, the three men dragged the door open and stepped out. Better prepared this time, the gang had brought along a sledgehammer and chisel, and Grat and Doolin made short work of the safes. They emptied what was inside; then, for having caused them so much trouble, they took Riehl's gold watch. A minute later, the gang was gone.

"The robbers are described by several of the passengers who talked to them as being well dressed and of gentlemanly appearance," reported *The Fort Smith Elevator* in its June 10, 1892, edition. "This is especially true of the leader, who apologized to the engineer for a rough remark made by one of the crowd, and promised him it should not occur again."

There was no apology for taking the money. Some reports claimed the bandits had made off with $70,000 that was being shipped to the agency office at the Sac and Fox Reservation. However, that had been on the heavily guarded first train. The second train carried considerably less, with estimates being anywhere between $3,000 and $11,000.

To be able to operate in the open and gather and feed information to his brothers, it was important that Bill Dalton be above suspicion. The night of the Red Rock robbery, he had taken care of that.

Bill entered the lobby of a hotel in Kingfisher before ten o'clock and, as he expected, found three men sitting there having a conversation about what cases were expected to be heard in court the next day. They were Judge John Burford; Horace Speed, who was the U.S. district attorney for Oklahoma; and George Yoes, who was a deputy marshal and son of the U.S. marshal Jacob Yoes. There could be no better alibi than to join these men for a spell, which Bill did.

At precisely 10:00 p.m., he looked at his watch and announced loudly to the three men that he was going to bed and that he looked forward to joining them for breakfast in the morning. After he left, Judge Burford asked Yoes who the man was, as he seemed educated and well informed. The deputy marshal replied that he was Bill Dalton, the brother of the notorious train robbers, and the judge asked him to introduce them when he came to breakfast.*

When Bill came down for breakfast, the three men were just arriving too, so they took a table together. At about eight, a messenger

---

* John Burford would have a long and distinguished career as a judge in Oklahoma but not so much in politics, losing the race for U.S. senator in 1914 and later relocating to Long Beach, California.

came into the room and handed Yoes a telegram, reporting the robbery at Red Rock by the Daltons the previous night. The deputy
handed the message to Judge Burford, who read it aloud to everyone
in the room. As soon as the judge had finished, Bill announced,
"Well, I can prove that I was not there, and not by accident either."

Bill was in the clear, but the other Daltons were not. With the
gang evidently resuming their criminal career, lawmen and bounty
hunters fanned out across the territory. A few days after the Red
Rock robbery, the gang had a close call. They were lounging in their
hideaway camp when two of them, Bill Doolin and Bill Power, noticed that their horses had wandered off. They walked up the creek,
figuring the horses would not stray far from water, and about a mile
away came upon another camp. This one was occupied by lawmen—
two marshals and two possemen.* And one of the horses tethered
belonged to Power.

The outlaws surprised the lawmen and displayed their Winchesters. Doolin and Power had no desire to harm them. As Emmett would explain, "Had we desired to kill officers, there was not a
month that passed but what we could have done so." But they could
not let them be either. They emptied the lawmen's guns and collected
all their backup cartridges and tossed the entire haul into the creek.
The four men pledged "to get out of that country and stay out," and
they apparently kept to it. Power got his horse back, but it was not
recorded if Doolin did too.

Even if as much as $11,000 had been netted from the Red Rock
robbery, that was not much spread over eight men, even if Bob did
not take a larger share for being the leader. Almost right away, the
gang had to get back to work.

---

* A couple of accounts claim that one deputy marshal was Chris Madsen, whom we
will meet in Act III.

CHAPTER 18

TWO HUNDRED SHOTS

Once again, the resourceful Eugenia Moore, or what Emmett referred to as "underground channels," informed them that there would be a big shipment of cash shipped on the Katy line. Bob's plan was to meet this train at the Adair station in Indian Territory.

With Charley Pierce just outside of town holding the gang's horses, the other seven men arrived early on July 14 for the targeted train, which was set to arrive before 10:00 p.m. First, they took what they could get their hands on in the express and baggage rooms. Then there was plenty of time to wait for the train on a bench on the platform, where they talked and smoked with their Winchesters across their knees.

When the train came in at 9:45 p.m., Bob and Bill Doolin were about to climb aboard when "it was easy to see that something was wrong," Emmett recalled.

What was wrong was that railroad officials were determined to stop being robbed, and many nighttime trains now often had armed lawmen, detectives, and hired guards aboard. On this particular train were thirteen of them, led by Sid Johnson, a marshal from Muskogee, and Charles LeFlore, a captain in the Choctaw Lighthorse Police.

There was also John Kinney, a veteran railroad detective. They were in the smoking car—which was, at least, dimly lit.

The gang members repeated what had become their usual routine. Once again, the express car door was closed and locked. As the familiar negotiations were taking place with the messenger inside, the officers and guards peered outside the smoker's windows. They could see several of the robbers standing on the station platform.

Marshal Johnson did not hesitate. "Those are the Daltons for sure!" he shouted. "Let's go!"

He hurried up the aisle of the car and down the steps. Johnson was followed by LeFlore and Kinney . . . and that was it. The other men—hired guns, and not very good ones—remained in their seats. The reality of actually squaring off with the vaunted Dalton Gang was too daunting. They hunkered down and avoided the windows in case bullets began to fly.

Fly they did, but it took a minute. When the three lawmen got off the train and ran for cover behind the station's coal shed, gang members assumed they were panicked passengers abandoning the train and let them go. Then, unwisely, the engineer remarked, "We expected you boys at Pryor Creek."

"We didn't want to disappoint you," Grat said, "so here we are."

Then it dawned on Emmett: if they were expected at all, that meant . . .

The three men behind the coal shed began firing their rifles. Train crewmen hurled themselves to the ground. "The boys were surprised and almost dumbfounded," reported Emmett. "This opposition was something new to them."

But the bandits did not stay stunned long. They returned fire, and it was later reported that as many as two hundred shots were exchanged. There may have been a handful contributed by the hired guards in the smoker, but otherwise they stayed put and probably prayed that the outlaws would not board the train.

"We heard from the time the train left Denison, some of these deputies swaggered up and down the train boasting loudly what they would do if the Daltons approached," Emmett reported. "To hear them tell it they were the bravest in the land. But with the first sound of shots there was a different story. They piled off the train with a whoop when Bob and the boys opened up on them, and they rushed pell-mell back into the cars or made a break for the town."

The three lawmen firing from the coal shed were wounded, but none seriously. The Daltons, partially protected by the hulking train, managed not to be hit. But two physicians were not so fortunate.

Drs. W. L. Goff and T. S. Youngblood were sitting on the porch of a drugstore near the depot. Both men, who were unarmed, were hit several times by stray shots. As *The Indian Chieftain* would detail it in the July 21 edition, "Both were shot in each leg and Dr. Goff fell forward exclaiming, 'I'm killed.' Dr. Youngblood started to run around the building when he was struck by another ball which brought him down."

In the case of the prescient Dr. Goff, his wound would indeed be fatal—a bullet severed an artery in his thigh, and he bled to death. Dr. Youngblood fared better, but he did have a portion of one foot amputated.

After Bob had jumped out of the express car, Doolin marched the engineer and fireman back to the engine compartment. The two men were told to get the train moving and not to stop. This they did, as Pierce arrived with the horses. The mounted outlaws watched the train go by. "They could see heads framed in the lights showing through the windows. A wild shot or two, a parting salute, and they wheeled their horses and were off."*

· · ·

---

* It is interesting to note how often Emmett switches to third person, as though he had witnessed but did not participate in events.

THE DALTON GANG had certainly won this battle, but there was no wisdom to standing around gloating. They rode off into the night with at least $10,000 in their saddlebags.

Railroad officials were apoplectic after hearing about the Adair robbery. Despite the bravery of Johnson, LeFlore, and Kinney, and thanks to the cowardice of the hired guns—*The Kingfisher Free Press* headlined that it was PUSILLANIMOUS CONDUCT—the Dalton Gang had once more slipped through the law's fingers.

"The fact that they had been able to dispose of a large guard sent with this train with but little trouble, angered the railroad and express company more than any of our previous exploits had done."*

They needed men with more sand to go up against these outlaws next time. The first step was to get such men interested. To that end, the Katy line offered a reward of $5,000 for each member of the gang, or an eye-popping total of $40,000 if they were all arrested or killed.

According to Robert Barr Smith, "The robbery of the Katy train at Adair, and especially the death of Doctor Goff, had generated massive public indignation and official energy. The public and the press saw Daltons behind every bush. The reward for the gang was now the biggest bounty yet offered for a single bunch of outlaws."

That might well help, but what the railroads needed most were lawmen who acted true to their badges. Luckily for them, joining the hunt for the Dalton Gang were men who would become famous on the remaining frontier as "the Three Guardsmen."

---

* There is a curious coda to Emmett's chapter (in his first memoir) on the Adair adventure. He claims that while the gang was hiding out afterward, Bob received a note conveying news about the death of Eugenia Moore. No details are offered. In 1918, she could very well have still been alive, and if Emmett knew this, he killed her off to protect her from being sought. On the other hand, Nancy B. Samuelson maintained that Eugenia Moore was a fictitious character, so it was simply easy enough to eliminate her with the stroke of a pen.

ACT III

THE LAWMEN

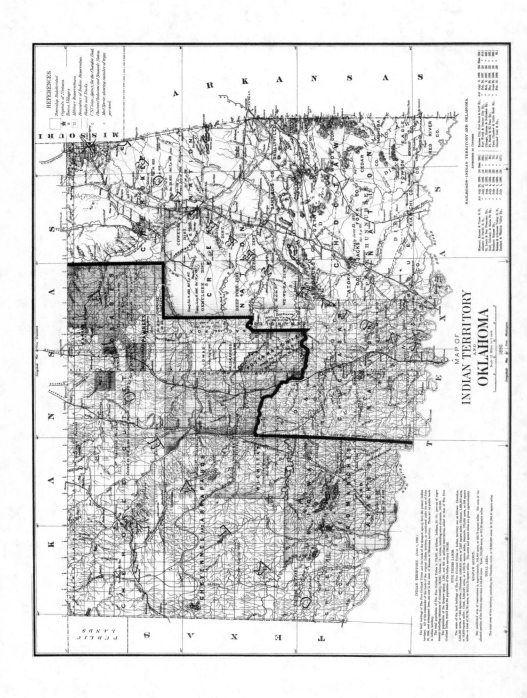

MAP OF
INDIAN TERRITORY
AND
OKLAHOMA

Scale 12 Miles to 1 inch

1890

CHAPTER 19

A KING'S RANSOM

If he could have testified to the events in Coffeyville in October and how they contributed to the end of an era, Bob Dalton would have stated that no lawman was more responsible for them than Heck Thomas.

By that summer in 1892 and after the audacity of the Adair train robbery, there was a whole array of sheriffs, deputy marshals, railroad detectives, and straight-out bounty hunters on the lookout for the Dalton Gang. A few of them were motivated by simply wanting to do their job and protect the public, but especially enticing was earning $5,000 to nab just one of the bandits. If the entire gang could be cornered, $40,000 was a king's ransom, a man would be set for life. And there was the fame that would come from capturing or gunning down the outlaws who were generating the kind of headlines once devoted to their Younger cousins and the James brothers.

By this time, according to Frank Latta, with just a bit of hyperbole, "Magazine and newspaper articles by the hundreds had been published about the exploits of the Daltons. Every schoolboy in the United States knew, or thought he knew, all about the Dalton Gang. They were the topic of conversation on street corners and park benches, in hotel lobbies and bar rooms and about the doors and steps of lodges, schools, and churches throughout the land."

Wild Bill Hickok, Wyatt Earp, Bat Masterson, Bass Reeves, and maybe a couple of others come to mind when listing the American West's most famous frontier lawmen, but in dedication and delivering results, Henry Andrew Thomas was right there too.

It was on January 6, 1850, when the youngest of as many as a dozen children of Lovick and Martha Ann Thomas came into the world, specifically in Oxford, Georgia, where the couple ran a hotel. (The number of children is not precise because Martha Ann had several from a previous marriage.) The youngest, Henry, would be able to boast of a proud pedigree, with his descendants in England including the Duke of Norfolk and a Lord Mayor of London. Members of the Thomas family had immigrated to America in 1632, and Francis Thomas had served as the governor of Maryland.

When the Civil War began, Lovick Thomas enlisted in the Confederate army and was assigned to Cobb's Legion, which later became known as the "Fighting Quartermaster" in the Thirty-Fifth Georgia Infantry. In the Battle of Mechanicsville in June 1862, Lovick was wounded seriously enough that he was sent home to recuperate. Two months later, he was ready to rejoin the fight, and when he did, he brought his twelve-year-old with him to serve as a Confederate army courier.

One would think that such a young boy would not be allowed near a battlefield, but something different about the Thirty-Fifth Georgia was it was commanded by Heck's uncle. Edward Lloyd Thomas was Lovick's brother who had served in the Mexican-American War and organized the Thirty-Fifth in October 1861. He would later be promoted to brigadier general and became one of the more effective brigade commanders in Robert E. Lee's Army of Northern Virginia. Apparently, the thought was that both his father and uncle would keep Heck out of harm's way.

As it was, the family had enough military men to go around. Two of Edward's sons, Scott and Edward Jr., were captains in the Thirty-Fifth Georgia. And one of Heck's older brothers was Lovick Thomas II, who as a lieutenant colonel commanded the Forty-Second Georgia Infantry. He fought in several major battles, including Vicksburg and the siege of Atlanta.

"Marbles, kites, leapfrog, and stilts had no appeal to him," the biographer Glenn Shirley wrote about Heck's abbreviated boyhood. "Reared amidst uniforms, sabers, guns, and cannon, pranks of his boyhood had been with these elements of warfare, and even before he entered his teens these accouterments had come into his hands for deadly work."

So much for Heck's safety: Lovick Sr. and his son returned to the front lines in time to participate in the Second Battle of Manassas, in late August 1862. Many years later, Heck would describe to his children how "a few bullets and lots of shells came over us." The adolescent standard-bearer and messenger was passing through a section of woods, hoping to avoid becoming a target, when "I came on a field hospital just abandoned by the Confederates, two dying soldiers in it. And a pile of legs and arms on the ground three or four feet high. It was a gruesome sight for a 12-year-old boy."

Heck's vividest memory of the time, however, involved one of the more celebrated Union generals. In the previous war, with Mexico, Philip Kearny had led men in several battles, including the Battle of Churubusco. In that engagement, Kearny led a rousing cavalry charge and suffered a grapeshot wound to his left arm that resulted in it being amputated. He soon returned to duty, and when the victorious U.S. Army entered Mexico City in September 1847, Kearny had the distinction of being in the forefront.

During the Civil War, General Kearny had led a division at what was also called the Second Battle of Bull Run, which saw the Union army routed and nearly destroyed by the Army of Northern Virginia.* The Union army retreated toward Washington and fought with the pursuing Confederate corps under Stonewall Jackson on September 1, 1862, at the Battle of Chantilly.

During a violent thunderstorm, Kearny decided to investigate a reported gap in the Union line. Responding to warnings of a subordinate, he said, "The Rebel bullet that can kill me has not yet been molded." He had been misinformed. When confronted by Confederate troops demanding his surrender, Kearny tried to escape on horseback. Shots were fired and one Minie ball entered his hip and came out his shoulder, killing him instantly. The Confederate general A. P. Hill, upon hearing the gunfire, ran up to the body and shone a lantern on it. He exclaimed, "You've killed Phil Kearny!" He added that the Union officer "deserved a better fate than to die in the mud."

It seems the rank-and-file Rebs did not agree. As Kearny's body was being borne to the rear, soldiers stripped him of his coat, boots, pocket watch, papers, and other items of value. However, after he learned who the deceased was, Robert E. Lee ordered that all of his belongings be returned despite the objections of soldiers who protested that a dead man no longer needed a warm coat and boots. Kearny's papers were given to Lee for examination, but they merely

---

* In the 1850s, Kearny had resigned his commission and traveled the world, including visiting France. In 1859, he was back, joining the Chasseurs d'Afrique, who were at the time fighting against Austrian forces in Italy. Later, he was with Napoleon III's Imperial Guard at the Battle of Solferino, where he headed a cavalry charge that penetrated the Austrian center and captured the key point of the battle. For this action, Kearny was awarded the French Légion d'honneur, becoming the first U.S. citizen to be thus honored. Back home to fight for the Union, Kearny is credited with devising the first unit insignia patches used in the U.S. Army. In the summer of 1862, he issued an order that his officers should wear a patch of red cloth on the front of their caps to identify themselves as members of his unit. The enlisted men quickly followed suit. Members of other units picked up on the idea, devising their own insignias, and these evolved over the years into the modern shoulder patch.

consisted of personal letters to his wife, which were burned. General Lee wrote a condolence note to her and ordered that the body be sent to the Union line.*

Major David Birney, commander of the Fifth Pennsylvania Volunteers, held a flag of truce as he crossed to the Confederate lines, escorting the wagon carrying General Kearny.†

Sometime later, there was another delivery. According to several accounts, including his own, the young Heck Thomas was chosen to cross the field to return Kearny's sword and horse. He recalled years later, "I carried them forward and it was the proudest moment of my life when I found myself under the observation of General Robert E. Lee." He was a bit sad too: "I had ridden [Kearny's] horse and cared for him up to that time and I hated to part with him."

His stay with the Army of Northern Virginia did not last the war. In the fall of 1863, Lovick Sr.'s health worsened—probably a lingering result from being wounded the previous year—and father and son left for Atlanta. The rest of the Thomas family was either already there or joined them there. They remained in Atlanta until General William Sherman's forces took it, when they relocated to Newton County in Georgia.

After the war, the Thomas family was back in Atlanta. Martha Ann, especially after her youngest child had witnessed the horrors of war at a tender age, wanted Heck to become a minister. He may or may not have attended Emory University to start down that path, but his father, Lovick, was selected to be the city marshal.

---

* At the time of Kearny's death, there were rumors in Washington that President Abraham Lincoln was contemplating replacing George B. McClellan with the man dubbed "Kearny the Magnificent" as commander in chief.

† Gen. Kearny's body first went to his home in East Newark, New Jersey, then was buried at Trinity Churchyard in New York City. In 1912, his remains were exhumed and re-interred at Arlington National Cemetery, where there is a statue by Edward Clark Potter in his honor. It is one of only two equestrian statues at Arlington.

When Heck turned eighteen, he was appointed a part-time deputy marshal.

The job did not begin easily, thanks to the Bush Arbor Riot in 1868. In this racial confrontation, the teenage officer received two bullet wounds. During another race-based conflict, Heck was slashed in the face, and the resulting scar would last a lifetime.

But he did not turn in his badge and seek a calmer occupation. Heck's career as a lawman that would span decades was already well underway.

More than any political or lawing event in Atlanta, it was the death of Heck's mother that prompted him to think more about his future. Martha Ann Thomas passed away in February 1869, and that was one less reason to stay put. Another was not being enamored with his full-time job, as a store clerk. A third reason was getting married.

The woman he wed, Isabella Gray, of Fulton County, was a cousin, and the date of the ceremony was June 22, 1871. Heck continued at his job, and the couple had two children, Henry and Belle. Probably in 1875, soon after his daughter was born, Heck decided he'd had enough selling store goods, and he and his family moved to Texas. Most likely, he had visited the Lone Star State before, but this time he went there for good.

Soon, Heck was working for the Texas Express Company as a messenger. Several accounts have Heck serving as a detective, and just one of his adventures was tracking down a gang headed by Sam Bass. However, as Nancy Samuelson points out, "In general, it appears that a lot of fancy embroidery work has been done by various writers on Heck's career in Texas." There were two connections to policing, though.

One involved Jim Thomas, another cousin of Heck's who also worked as a messenger for the same company. On February 22, 1878, a train carrying Jim was stopped by bandits, and their leader was indeed Sam Bass. The stubborn messenger took out his pistol and began firing. Shots were exchanged, and at least two of the robbers were wounded. The gang rode off with only their guns in their hands.

The second involved Heck himself. The next month, he was the messenger on a train stopped by the Bass gang at Hutchins, Texas. Acting fast, Heck turned off the lights in the express car, fastened the door, and concealed most of the cash. Not to be thwarted again, the bandits bashed through the car door with axes. When they appeared in the makeshift entrance, they held the engineer and two passengers in front of them, preventing Heck from using his pistol. One shot was fired, by the rear-car brakeman, which only wounded Heck slightly. The Bass boys grabbed what little cash they could find, which did not include the $4,000 Heck had hidden.*

Bass would go on to a more successful outlaw career, one that had him roaming far and wide. The following year, his gang stole gold from a Union Pacific Railroad train that had left San Francisco and from another train, in Big Springs, Nebraska. Combined, they collected $60,000, a very handsome heist, as that would be well over $1.5 million in today's money. Bass rode to Texas, where he formed a new gang and continued his lucrative career, with stagecoaches joining trains as targets.

Lawmen began to look for Sam Bass with more zeal, especially once the Pinkerton National Detective Agency became involved as well as Texas Rangers, including the captains Junius Peak and John B. Jones. The big break came in July 1878, when an informant inside the outlaw gang got word to lawmen that Bass planned to rob the Williamson County Bank in Round Rock.

On the nineteenth, Bass and others in the gang were scouting the town when they were approached by a Williamson County deputy sheriff, Ahijah Grimes, who requested that the strangers surrender

---

* For his "zeal and fidelity," Heck was given a $200 reward by the Texas Express Company.

their guns. Instead, they opened fire and killed the lawman. As Bass
rode off, two Texas Rangers shot him, but he kept riding out of
town. A posse was immediately formed, and it set out. It would have
probably ridden right by Bass, who was lying in a pasture, except he
called out, "Hey, I'm over here. I'm Sam Bass, the one you're looking
for." He was arrested but died two days later, on his twenty-seventh
birthday. He was buried in the Round Rock cemetery.*

Some years later, Heck and his family were living in Fort Worth.
He had apparently accumulated enough lawing experience by then
to run for city marshal in 1883. He lost but tried once more two
years later. He again came up short. Just as well, because not being
confined to Fort Worth allowed Heck to track down Jim and Pink
Lee. His lawman career was about to rise to a new level.

Bootlegging and rustling were just two of the activities that occupied the Lee brothers in northern Texas and Oklahoma. As if that
were not enough reason to put them before Judge Parker, they had
an accomplice, Dallas Humby, who was accused of murdering his
wife. He was hiding out at the Lee ranch in the Chickasaw Nation.
On May 1, 1885, a posse of five men headed by Jim Guy, a deputy
U.S. marshal, arrived to arrest him.

The posse cautiously approached the log main house, noting that
gun holes had been cut into the sides of the structure. Marshal Guy
called for those inside to come on out. A response came from Ed
Stein, a brother-in-law of the Lees, saying they were going out the
back door. When the posse walked around to that side to make the
arrests, they were met with a hail of gunfire. Two posse members died
immediately, both shot at least twice. A third was hit but managed to
stagger to a nearby tree, where he slid down to a sitting position . . .
and would be shot two more times, finally dying.

---

* Sam Bass's grave is marked with a replacement headstone because the original
one was gradually diminished by souvenir collectors. What remains of the original
headstone can be found at the Round Rock Public Library.

Guy and another man managed to escape. Sometime that day or night, the murderous occupants of the cabin left. They were wise to do so, because two days later, an angry mob arrived at the Lee ranch and put every structure on it to the torch. Two of the killers, the Dyer brothers, had not gotten far enough away—they were apprehended and lynched. A total reward of $7,000 was offered for the arrest of the Lee brothers and Ed Stein. Unlike the usual deputy marshals' compensation, this money would be paid if the killers were brought in dead or alive.

Remaining alive were Stein and Tom Lee. When found in Denison, they surrendered and were hauled to Judge Parker's domain in Fort Smith. They avoided a date with the executioner George Maledon by being acquitted. After walking free, Ed Stein resumed his bootlegging activities. He must have sampled more than he sold because he soon died of alcoholism. Perhaps thinking his luck would hold, Tom Lee surrendered again, to a different charge—larceny. But this time the jury found him guilty and he was sent off to prison.

Meanwhile, the gang's two leaders, Jim and Pink Lee, proved to be elusive . . . until September 7. On that day, Heck Thomas's relentless efforts to track them down finally paid off. He was not alone; with him was Jim Taylor, a deputy marshal out of Fort Smith, and several other men. The posse had received a tip that the Lee brothers were hiding out at the ranch of John Washington, a relative, on Lake Texoma.

When the bandit brothers spurned the suggestion that they surrender, a firefight of Winchesters and six-shooters began. Pink Lee, shot in the head, died right away, but it took a bunch of bullets to finish off Jim Lee. The bodies were tossed into a wagon and taken to Gainesville, where the posse headed by Heck and Taylor received the reward.*

---

* Heck did not forget about Dallas Humby, an associate of the Lee brothers. The deputy sheriff would arrest this outlaw and bring him to Fort Smith in January 1887.

Perhaps with some persuasion from Jim Taylor, Heck applied to be a Fort Smith deputy marshal and was hired. "Heck's record while serving in this district was outstanding," Nancy Samuelson declares. "Here he found his calling and his life's work."

CHAPTER 20

THE DANISH DEPUTY

Chris Madsen had as full a life, if not more so, than any lawman in the American West . . . according to Chris Madsen.

The man who would later be a member of the Three Guardsmen was born Christen Madsen Rormose in February 1851 in Denmark. His mother, who already had four children with a previous husband, was a postmaster, and her present husband was an overseer of postal roads after having fought in a war between Denmark and German states.

In a remarkable coincidence, as an adolescent, Chris was brought to war by his father. The Germans and Danes began a new war in 1864, and when his father reenlisted, the thirteen-year-old was assigned to be a messenger. During the conflict, in separate actions, a considerably older stepbrother was killed and Chris's father was wounded. The war did not last very long, ending before the year did, and Chris returned home and to school.

But the taste of war must have been intoxicating, because while still a teenager, he joined the French Foreign Legion, and after training, Chris was shipped out to Algeria. His unit was shipped back when the Franco-Prussian War began in July 1870. He was involved in the Battle of Sedan in September, which turned out rather badly for the French who were not only soundly defeated but Emperor Napoleon III was captured. Though on the winning side, Chris was a casualty, having been shot in the leg and sliced in the head by a saber. The war was over for him . . .

Or so we're told. Most of the information about Chris's early years comes from his memoir, *Under Three Flags*, which may not be the most reliable source. For example, it has been reported that no French Foreign Legion troops fought in the Battle of Sedan. If Madsen participated in that event at all, it may have been with a different unit. In 1995, Leif Ernst, a Dane and American West aficionado, claimed to have found records showing that instead of military service, Christen Madsen served several jail sentences for such crimes as fraud and forgery.

France had different ideas about Chris's alleged military service, but before he could be sent back to the front (or jail?), Chris slipped off to Copenhagen. The details in his memoir are murky, but eventually, he returned to his hometown in Denmark but was not welcomed there because of having fought for France. He moved on to Norway and found a job as a surveyor. He contended that he immigrated to the United States in 1876 because he wanted to fight Indians.

However, according to Nancy Samuelson, Madsen had never left Denmark at all because he was serving yet another prison sentence. After that: "It was a common practice to ship habitual criminals out of Denmark, a practice that American authorities had complained to Danish authorities about several times. Chris Madsen was actually deported from his native country to the United States."

More than a desire to fight Indians, Madsen probably joined the military in his new country because he had no other employment opportunities. He enlisted in the U.S. Army in January 1876, right after his boat docked in New York City. The enlistment was for five years, and after basic training, he began his tenure wearing a blue uniform with the Fifth Cavalry, stationed at Fort Hays in Kansas. It was soon ordered to join the campaign that General George Crook was waging against the Sioux on the Great Plains, with Sitting Bull and Gall as the recognized leaders. The Fifth Cavalry had not yet rendezvoused with Crook when, on June 17, the latter barely escaped annihilation at the hands of Crazy Horse and his warriors at the Battle of Rosebud. Eight days later, much of General George Custer's command was wiped out at the Battle of Little Bighorn.*

The Fifth Cavalry must not have made very good time in its trek across the plains because it would be August 4 when it joined Crook's forces in Montana. Madsen and his fellow troopers endured many hardships in the ensuing expedition during which the U.S. Army tried to round up the remnants of the Sioux and other tribes and force them onto reservations. Crook's men were plagued with repeated rainstorms and muddy conditions, and at times, the going got hard enough that the famished troops were forced to eat a few of their own horses.

What was dubbed the "Horsemeat March" pretty much concluded on the evening of September 8 when 150 troopers led by Captain Anson Mills surrounded the Indian village of Slim Buttes, and they attacked its thirty-seven lodges the next morning, shooting anyone who resisted. Taken by surprise, the Indians fled, with the Sioux leader, American Horse, mortally wounded and fifteen women and children hiding in a nearby ravine. They soon surrendered, and American Horse, having refused treatment by the army surgeons, died. The few Sioux who escaped spread the word of the slaughter to nearby villages. Crazy Horse was among the leaders of a newly formed war party.

The combined Sioux and Cheyenne force of some seven hundred warriors did not know that General Crook's main column of

---

* In his later years, Madsen claimed to have been a trooper in the Seventh Cavalry who was fortuitously reassigned to the Fifth Cavalry right before the event that became known as "Custer's Last Stand." There is no truth to this; however, coincidentally, a Christian Madsen did die in the Little Bighorn battle.

infantry, artillery, and other troopers had arrived at Slim Buttes. The warriors were understandably dismayed when they reached an overlook and saw much-larger-than-expected numbers of well-armed soldiers surrounding the village. From their positions atop the bluffs, the warriors opened fire, causing Crook to immediately form a defensive perimeter around his horses and mules. He also ordered the village to be burned.

Chris Madsen could have been a member of the line of skirmishers Crook sent forward. There were four companies of infantry in the lead, followed by dismounted troopers from three cavalry regiments. After a forty-five-minute steady firefight, the advancing soldiers drove most of the warriors from their hilltop positions. A few Sioux held their ground, even charging the perimeter at one point, but they were eventually killed or chased away.*

The Fifth Cavalry was next assigned to Fort David A. Russell in Wyoming, where it continued roundup activities. In July 1877, Company A, with Chris Madsen as a member, accompanied General Philip Sheridan on a tour of the Little Bighorn battlefield.

Madsen later contended that he personally escorted the general, but this was highly unlikely given that Madsen was only a private and had no real connection to that particular site in Montana.†

Madsen would remain in the U.S. Army until discharged in January 1891, when he was almost forty years old. His record was especially spotty for a future revered lawman. He had spent some time in the Wyoming Territorial Penitentiary in 1881, possibly for stealing sacks of grain. On the other hand, in subsequent years he kept his nose clean enough that in May 1886, he had been promoted to

---

* An outcome of the battle was that Crook's soldiers recovered a number of items taken by warriors after the Battle of Little Bighorn. They included a Seventh Cavalry guidon from Company I, the bloody gauntlets of the slain captain Myles Keough, guns and ammunition, and other related items, some of which were later presented to family members.

† He would also later claim, erroneously, that he escorted President Chester A. Arthur on a trip through Yellowstone Park in 1883.

regimental quartermaster sergeant. Afterward, and for the rest of his army career, Madsen was assigned to bases in Kansas and Oklahoma. It was at Fort Reno in Indian Territory that he was discharged. The army may not have been too sorry to see him go. Remarks in the Fifth Cavalry muster roll for January 10, 1891, include, "Character good but not suited for the position of quartermaster sergeant."

Out of uniform for the first time in fifteen years and middle-aged and married with two young children, what was Chris Madsen suited for? He apparently had done some forward thinking, because while still on active duty in 1889, he had acquired 160 acres during the first Oklahoma Land Rush. Farming, however, must not have appeared too appealing, because soon after his discharge, Madsen would go to work for Marshal William Grimes.

Originally from Ohio, Grimes had worked as a newspaperman in Nebraska and as the Johnson County sheriff. Like many others, he had followed the siren call of free land becoming available in Oklahoma, and in the land rush, he laid claim to what would become a farm near Kingfisher. In 1890, he was appointed a U.S. marshal, and he installed a fair and effective law-enforcement system—or as best he could, given the poor pay for deputy marshals.*

The poor pay did not dissuade Madsen from wearing a badge, or maybe it was the only steady employment the ex-trooper (and ex-con) could find. He would turn out to have a brilliant career. By the time of the Red Rock robbery in June 1892, Madsen had earned a promotion to chief deputy marshal.

After the Dalton Gang had made their getaway, at least five posses were hastily pulled together and sent out. One containing two dozen riders was headed by Madsen and John Hixon, who was sheriff of

---

* Grimes unhappily served as an example of another problem with the U.S. Marshals system: politics. He was a Republican, and in 1893, when the Democrat Grover Cleveland returned to the White House, Grimes was dismissed. He returned to farming and business interests, and several years later, he had a brief stint as the acting territorial governor of Oklahoma.

Logan County. They searched every nook and cranny they could until they were sixty miles west of Red Rock, where they concluded that the gang had either not come that way or were already gone.

Not to worry: Deputy Marshal Madsen would have another crack at the Dalton brothers.

CHAPTER 21

A DODGE CITY MAN

There are several conflicting accounts about the origins and occupations and military service of the father of one of the most famous lawmen of the American West. What seems to be reliable enough is that William Tilghman Sr. married Amanda Shepherd of Virginia in Lee County, Iowa, in November 1846. The couple moved several times, first to and then within Kansas, and were joined by two sons, Richard and William Jr., and a daughter, Mary. The father may have been a farmer, but probably not a productive one.

After the Civil War began, the elder Tilghman and his oldest son—who could at most have been fifteen—enlisted in the Thirteenth Kansas Infantry. William Sr. may or may not have seen combat; the only "wound" he suffered was a right eye ailment, which would cost him the sight in it. He received a discharge at Fort Leavenworth, Kansas, in July 1865. His son Richard had been discharged the previous month in Little Rock, Arkansas. During all this time, William Jr., despite being just eight years old when his father and brother enlisted, had to fend for his mother, another brother, Francis, and sisters Mary, Josephine, and Harriet as well as himself.

The Tilghman family returned to farming, but by 1880, they were operating a boardinghouse in Atchison City, Kansas. Before this, young Bill had struck out on his own. Eight years earlier, he and a friend, George Rust, had decided to become buffalo hunters. They set up a camp on the Arkansas River, east of Dodge City. They did well enough that they spent part of the winter selling hides in Colorado. There, Tilghman met Henry Born—not the sort of friend appropriate for a future lawman.

Born to German immigrant parents in Wisconsin in 1849, "Dutch" Henry would go on to become a legendary horse thief. By 1875, he was the leader of a ring of as many as three hundred bandits that operated from Kansas to Colorado and New Mexico and the Texas Panhandle.* They targeted Indian ponies and government mules because they had the best resale value. The only spread immune from the gang's activities was the JA Ranch because Born enjoyed drinks with its owner, Charles Goodnight.†

Henry Born was finally arrested in December 1878 in Trinidad, Colorado. He was to be tried for stealing mules, but a friend from his buffalo-hunting days, Bat Masterson, who was then the sheriff of Ford County in Kansas, showed up with a different warrant, supposedly for grand larceny, and escorted him to Dodge City, where he was immediately acquitted. Avoiding Colorado, Born moved on to New Mexico, where he further perfected his stealing expertise.

---

* Before fully focusing on a criminal career, Born was one of the twenty-eight buffalo hunters, including Bat Masterson, who had withstood the siege by hundreds of Comanche warriors led by Quanah Parker at the second Battle of the Adobe Walls in June 1874. Those interested in a detailed description of this fierce battle can find one in the book *Dodge City*, by yours truly.

† Among other distinctions, Goodnight cofounded the first Panhandle Stockmen's Association in 1880, which introduced purebred cattle, policed trails, and fought cattle thieves and outlaws. He and Oliver Loving were the ranchers who inspired the characters of Woodrow Call and Gus McCrae who undertook a long northbound cattle drive in *Lonesome Dove*.

One story has him selling a horse to a sheriff from whom Born had recently stolen it.*

Bill Tilghman was also flirting with criminality. When he returned to hunting, it was in the Indian Territory, and buffalo hunting there by white men had been banned in the Medicine Lodge Treaty signed in 1867. Such hunters with their powerful Sharps rifles were so effective in the territory and its surroundings that Comanche, Kiowa, Arapaho, and Cheyenne headmen, anticipating starvation otherwise, held a council and agreed to go to war. The subsequent "Buffalo War" in 1875 is better known as the Red River War.

An early casualty, even though it happened before hostilities began, was Dick Tilghman, Bill's older brother. A sad irony was his death was connected to a Cheyenne chief's desire to maintain the peace.

Little Robe, born about 1828, had earned distinction in battles with other tribes and became a headman in 1863. It was reported that he died in the Sand Creek Massacre the following year, but he was one of the few Cheyenne to have managed to escape Colonel John Chivington's rampage. In its aftermath, Little Robe led attacks against white forts and settlements. However, he became one of the early Plains Indian leaders to see the futility of resistance. In 1867, he aligned with Black Kettle to create and agree to the Medicine Lodge Treaty. Two years later, while camped in Sweetwater Creek, Texas, he met with Lieutenant Colonel George Custer to help secure the release of two captive white women. That spring, Little Robe surrendered at Fort Cobb and assumed the role of principal chief of the peace faction. He was a member of delegations that toured Washington, D.C., and other eastern cities in 1871 and 1873, meeting President Ulysses S. Grant during the second trip.

---

* Henry Born eventually went straight. He was fifty-one when he married. He and his wife had four children and farmed next to what would be called Borne's Lake in Colorado. He died in January 1921.

Then came the events of 1874. In March, some four dozen ponies were stolen from Little Robe. To keep the peace, he refused to go after the bandits, who were believed to be led by "Hurricane Bill" Martin. It was not a stretch to think this because Martin was a notorious horse thief whose day job was buffalo hunter with Bill Tilghman. The latter had to know about his friend's extracurricular activities, which also included gunrunning and selling whiskey to the tribes. Several younger Cheyenne, including Sitting Medicine, Little Robe's son, felt differently about the blatant theft, and they gave chase.

The posse did not catch up to Hurricane Bill and his accomplices—who may have included both Tilghman brothers. The Cheyenne instead stole horses and cattle from white settlers. Troopers of the Sixth Cavalry gave chase to the Indian bandits who had been chasing white bandits, and in a skirmish to recover the stock, Sitting Medicine was wounded. Sometime within these events, Dick Tilghman was killed. In her memoir written many years later, Zoe Tilghman, Bill's widow, contends he died near the buffalo camp on Kiowa Creek, possibly killed by "vigilantes" who had mistaken (or not) the Tilghman party for horse thieves.

In any case, the second Battle of the Adobe Walls in June 1874 was the true kickoff to the Red River War. The war lasted well into the following year, with army forces led by General Nelson Miles and Colonel Ranald Mackenzie taking on tribal forces led by Wild Horse and Quanah Parker. According to Nancy Samuelson, "Bill Tilghman may still have been involved in some questionable activities during the remaining months of the Buffalo War, which included being arrested for the killing and scalping of a 19-year-old man. But the lack of evidence and Tilghman's own strenuous denials resulted in his release."

He wandered about a bit, including in and out of Dodge City, and he participated in more hunting expeditions. It was while on his way to Big Wild Horse Lake in Oklahoma to rejoin Hurricane Bill Martin that Tilghman was chased by a band of unspecified

Indians. He later claimed to have outraced them all on his faithful horse named Chief, arriving at the Martin hunting camp after covering forty-two miles in just two hours. A tad more believable is that around this time, Tilghman and Hurricane Bill attended a dance in Sun City, and there he kicked up his heels with a fourteen-year-old named Flora, who two years later became his wife . . . though by then, she was already a widow.

Like Bat Masterson, Tilghman found the life of a buffalo hunter too arduous and dangerous and hoped that the booming Dodge City would offer other employment. He must have had some money in his pocket because he and another man, Henry Garris, opened a saloon called the Crystal Palace. *The Dodge City Times* predicted that the building's new front and awning "will tend to create a new attraction towards the never ceasing fountains of refreshment flowing within."

At this time, Dodge City was in the process of earning its reputation as the "wickedest city in the West," thanks to the cattle trade. Railroad tracks working their way west through Kansas had finally arrived in the area, and the town that had begun as a bar in a tent to serve soldiers at nearby Fort Dodge was almost overnight transformed into a bustling hub. Beeves brought up from ranches in Texas were loaded onto cattle cars for shipment to slaughterhouses to the north and east. The cowboys were paid off at the end of these trail drives and could not spend their money fast enough on women and whiskey. Saloons like the Crystal Palace popped up like prairie dogs to accommodate them.

But tending bar did not keep Tilghman out of trouble. In February 1878, he was one of several men arrested for trying to rob a train.* What makes this event especially remarkable is he was arrested by

---

* The supposed ringleader was Dave Rudabaugh. Known as "Dirty Dave" because of an aversion to good hygiene, he was already an experienced outlaw who would go on to be a member of the anti-Earp cowboy faction in Tombstone. He escaped from there unscathed, but an unhappy fate awaited him in Mexico: After a card game

Sheriff Bat Masterson, who the month before had hired Tilghman as a deputy. The charge, however, was dismissed for lack of evidence and probable mistaken identity. Soon, though, in April 1878, Tilghman was busted by his boss once more, this time for horse theft. Again, the charge was dropped, but Bat had to be wondering if Tilghman as a deputy was like the fox guarding the henhouse.

About young Flora: She was already married when she and Tilghman first met at the Sun City dance. When her husband died—one account is that a horse fell on him—Tilghman supposedly helped look after her and her child. Then he did more than that—he married her. Over time, the Tilghmans had a total of four children: Charles (a stepson), Dorothy, William, and Viona. Possibly because of the marriage or an offer too good to pass up, Tilghman and Garris sold the Crystal Palace Saloon.

He finally had an opportunity to be a good deputy to Masterson, and that was following the murder of Dora Hand in the fall of 1878. The married Dodge City mayor, James "Dog" Kelley, was smitten with the dance hall girl. She and a friend were staying at a house Kelley owned in town one night in October when James Kenedy, who had a jealous grudge against the mayor, let loose with a volley of gunshots. Hand was killed. Believing that he had murdered the mayor, Kenedy took off, bound for his wealthy father's ranch in Texas.

He was not fast enough. Sheriff Masterson took off after the killer, accompanied by Tilghman, Wyatt Earp, and others. The posse caught Kenedy, who was wounded by Masterson. Kenedy would weasel out of the murder charge but died months later in Texas from complications of the wound.

It does not appear that Tilghman was a lawman much if at all during the next few years. He pursued several business interests, apparently none of them very successful. In November 1883, he was

---

turned into a gunfight, Rudabaugh was decapitated with a machete and his head displayed atop a pole.

back with a badge in Ford County, having been appointed a deputy by Sheriff Patrick Sughrue. He also must have been serving drinks again because it was reported that Tilghman, "proprietor of the 'Oasis,' has sold out to his brother Frank, who will refit and fix up and make everything smooth and harmonious to the visitor."

Finally, Tilghman obtained an important lawman position. In April 1884, soon after selling the saloon, he became the city marshal of Dodge City. His appointment was a consequence of the Dodge City War the previous year. The gambler and saloon owner Luke Short had been run out of town by other saloon owners and prominent businessmen who wanted to control the city. Unwisely, they overlooked that Short counted among his good friends Wyatt Earp and Bat Masterson. They returned to their old haunts at the head of the tongue-in-cheek-titled Dodge City Peace Commission, which threw out the existing regime headed by A. B. Webster. Some of the fresh blood installed was Bill Tilghman.

He remained as marshal until 1886 dawned, when he devoted himself full-time to his new ranch. This turned out to be very bad timing because one of the worst blizzards of the nineteenth century in the plains struck that winter, and it wiped out the livestock on many ranches in the area, including the one Tilghman owned.* Not that it paid much, but he did still have a job as a Ford County deputy sheriff. In 1888, this role brought him up against Ed Prather in Farmer City. He and Prather were friendly enough, but the latter's behavior was seriously affected by alcohol.

On this July 4, Prather had been celebrating the holiday early, and when he encountered the lawman, he threatened and cursed

---

* That entire winter was particularly severe. A series of cold spells and heavy snowfalls culminated in the first week of January, when a huge snowstorm accompanied by high winds hit the central plains. Drifts of six feet or more were common, and the temperature dropped to 30 degrees below zero in some places. Many prairie homes had been quickly and cheaply built, leaving settlers ill prepared to protect themselves from such cold. The snow and wind were so fierce that people became lost after walking only a few yards from their homes.

him. Tilghman, according to a local newspaper account, "took all the abuse from the excited man without offering any retaliation. [Prather] became very abusive and threatened to put an end to him right there, and suiting action to his words, he threw his hand upon his revolver; but Mr. Tilghman was too quick for him and held a revolver in his face. Mr. T. ordered him three times to take his hand off his gun, and would have disarmed him if he had been near enough; but Prather sought a better position, but Tilghman pulled the trigger and Prather was a dead man."

After many years in Dodge City, it was time for Tilghman to move on. And from Kansas too, after the so-called Battle of Cimarron. Adjacent towns Cimarron and Ingalls were jostling over which would become the new county seat of Gray County. A referendum to decide that was in such dispute that the matter was handed to the Kansas Supreme Court. While the judges mulled things over, an Ingalls man, Newt Watson, declared himself the new county clerk and demanded that records be brought to him from the Cimarron courthouse. When Cimarron citizens refused, Ingalls hired a group of persuaders headed by Tilghman and Jim Masterson, one of Bat's younger brothers, who had also served as a Dodge City lawman. To give the mercenaries a semblance of legal status, Tilghman was appointed county sheriff by the self-appointed Watson.

A raid on the Cimarron courthouse to retrieve the disputed records took place on January 12, 1889. After pulling up to the courthouse in a wagon, Masterson and Watson and two others rushed into the building and began to grab documents. Realizing a raid was underway, armed Cimarron citizens moved in. Suddenly, shots were fired. Tilghman, on a horse, was hit in one leg, and three other raiders were wounded. They and the wagon rode off, leaving Jim Masterson and the other men inside the building.

They took up positions on the second floor to return fire. The Cimarron men attempted to storm the building by rushing the front door but were beaten back by the remaining raiders. Next, the attackers attempted to breach the building by raising a ladder to a window in the back. This plan was also thwarted when Masterson found the ladder and kicked it over. Eventually, the townsfolk made it into the first floor of the building, and from there, they fired up through the ceiling and into the second floor. The raiders climbed on top of filing cabinets, desks, and a steel safe to protect themselves.

Ultimately, the battle lasted for about six hours and finally came to an end when the Cimarron faction received a telegraph from Bat Masterson in Dodge City warning that unless his brother and his friends were allowed to leave town, he would "hire a train and come in with enough men to blow Cimarron off the face of Kansas." After that, Jim Masterson and the others put down their guns and were briefly taken prisoner. They were released even though one Cimarron man had been killed during the exchange of gunfire.*

Tilghman participated in the Oklahoma Land Rush that April. In Guthrie, the town created overnight, he built a cottage for Flora and their children. He kept horses and cattle and planted an orchard. As he had been in Dodge City, Tilghman was part of a group in Guthrie that developed a horse racing track.

Then the new U.S. marshal, William Grimes, invited Tilghman to become one of his deputies. Thus began a badge-wearing career that lasted twenty-one years. This was no easy feat considering politics. As his second wife and widow, Zoe, points out in her memoir, "Most of the administrations in that time were Republican, and Bill was an active Democrat. Nevertheless, his commission was renewed with each administration."

At that time, the organized western federal district was Oklahoma, and the eastern district was Indian Territory inhabited by the "Five Civilized Tribes"—Cherokee, Chickasaw, Choctaw, Creek, and Seminole. Tilghman worked in the western district, but he was one

---

* It would be another four years before the matter was settled, when Cimarron was designated the Gray County seat.

of the few deputies given a "courtesy commission," which allowed
him to also operate in the eastern district. This was due to his previous lawman experience and seeming aptitude for it. There was plenty
for the peace officers to do because horse- and cattle-thieving were
rampant. "In the untracked prairies, the woods and canyons, were
hiding places a-plenty for men and stock," wrote Zoe Tilghman. "It
was easy to round up a bunch and be off before they would be missed.
From Texas, northwest across the territory, ran the Horsethief Trail,
not a marked and trodden route, but a devious, changing way to
western Kansas and Colorado."

And: "The illicit trade in liquor for the Indians was a hydra that
constantly grew new heads." Because there were yet few banks in the
territory, money and valuables were often sent by horse-drawn mail
vehicles or railroad cars, and "they were in striking distance of towns
in four states. With these advantages, the reign of outlawry grew up
in Oklahoma, and the names of bandits filled the news dispatches
and won their sorry fame across the United States."

Well, not if Bill Tilghman and his colleagues could help it. He was
routinely sent to investigate mail- and horse-theft and cattle-rustling
cases. If he could, he caught the suspects and turned them over to the
jail keeper, and then the responsibility to convict them and send them
to prison fell to Horace Speed, the territory's district attorney.

It can be argued that next to Judge Isaac Parker, Speed was the
most instrumental law-enforcer in Oklahoma. The Kentucky native
had become an attorney and was hired by an Indiana law firm whose
senior partner was General Benjamin Harrison, who in 1888 was
elected president. The prospering firm would have been a good place
to stay, but Speed jumped aboard the 1889 Land Rush—apparently
with both feet, because on the very day of the chaotic event, April
22, he established a law practice in Guthrie. Once the Oklahoma
Territory became official, he was appointed its first U.S. district attorney.

Speed was an honest law-and-order advocate in a territory that was always on the edge of outlaw anarchy. He raked through the Land Office, weeding out the corrupt claims and winning back public confidence. He prosecuted thousands of suspects, with many of them being convicted (or persuaded to plead guilty) and put behind bars. One of the better examples of Speed's devotion to the rule of law took place after he had returned to private practice, in 1898. He was appointed a special prosecutor to investigate the lynching of two young Seminoles. They had been arrested for the rape of a white woman and the murder of her and her baby. Before they could go to trial, a mob took the two Seminoles from jail, hanged them from a tree with chains, and set them on fire. Speed's investigation resulted in the arrest and conviction of forty-five white men for the double homicide, purportedly the first time lynchers had been convicted in the Southwest.

It would seem one of the reasons that Speed was incorruptible was that he had no political ambitions. In 1905, he was offered the governorship of the Oklahoma Territory by President Theodore Roosevelt. The attorney turned it down, preferring his private practice and the occasional public service position. He was living in Tulsa when he died in December 1924.[*]

Bill Tilghman relished the opportunity to hunt down bad guys as a deputy to Grimes, E. D. Nix, and other U.S. marshals. And among the other deputies with whom he would ride trails were two kindred spirits—Chris Madsen and Heck Thomas.

---

[*] His son, Horace Speed Jr., would join the army, rise to the rank of colonel, and had the rare trifecta of fighting in World War I, World War II, and the Korean War.

CHAPTER 22

CLOSING IN

Heck Thomas did not pursue his calling as a lawman for the money. His compensation was no different from that of any other man riding for Judge Isaac Parker—fees and mileage. The fees included two dollars for an arrest, a dollar a day while tracking down a suspect to serve a warrant, and fifty cents for serving papers. There was also an allowance of seventy-five cents per day to feed each prisoner. If a deputy thought he might need help, he had to pay for his own possemen. Ten cents a mile was paid to bring in prisoners. And as the Dalton brothers had learned, a deputy marshal earning his pay and receiving it were often two different animals.

Sometimes, there was reward money, but a deputy could not collect one offered by the government because that arrest was considered part of his job as a federal officer. A solid deputy who did his job well enough could earn five hundred dollars a year, so rewards from private interests, such as the railroad companies, were most welcome.

But Heck enjoyed the lawman's life. This was even truer when he was given the opportunity to hone his detecting skills. In December 1887, a man named William Jones died in a boardinghouse in the Chickasaw Nation. After his burial, rumors persisted that this was not a natural death. Heck visited the boardinghouse and questioned the owner, Elsie James, and her daughter, Margaret. He became suspicious enough to have the body exhumed, and it was determined that Jones's skull had been crushed. Elsie and Margaret, along with two accomplices, were arrested for murdering Jones to steal sixty-five dollars he possessed. Judge Parker sentenced Elsie to hang, but her sentence was later commuted to life in prison.

"He was of exceptional caliber as a deputy," asserted Beth Thomas Meeks in her memoir, *Heck Thomas, My Papa.* "Often, those who volunteered for the job were as lawless as the men they sought. Inefficient and brutal, some had the habit of letting their prisoners escape if more money could be made that way. Others had a predominant taste for whiskey and a lack of scruples about taking human life."

However, as Heck's lawman career advanced, perhaps inevitably, his domestic life became troubled. His wife, Belle, was not fond of her husband being in such a dangerous profession, and especially one that had him away from home so often. And about home: She not only missed Fulton County in Georgia but did not care at all for Texas, coupled with having to raise four children on her own much of the time. The fourth one, Mary Joe, was born in Fort Worth in December 1883.

It did not get any better for Belle after another move, to Fort Smith. She did not like it any more than Fort Worth, and Heck could be off after outlaws for up to two months at a time. He was home often enough to help produce their fifth child, Lovick, who arrived in August 1888. To make matters worse, the family then moved out of Fort Smith to a place called White Bead Hill in the Indian Territory. They carried all their possessions in a covered wagon.

"We lived in a log house of four rooms and a kitchen," his daughter Mary Joe recollected in a letter to her children in 1966. "No front door, just wide open with a bedroom on either side of a sort of hall. Wide planks that were not even nailed down. Some one lifted one of the planks once and I saw a hen lay an egg."

White Bead Hill was a better location for Heck to be coming and going as a deputy marshal but not where a woman and five children should be left alone for long stretches of time. In a letter to her husband, Belle reports having "jerked the pistol from under my head" to fend off robbers who had entered the house one night. The letter concluded with a plea to Heck to "come home and stay with your darling all the time. Lovingly, Belle."

And she had very good reason to worry that before long she would wind up a widow. An article subtitled "Twelve Murderers, Rapists and Horse Thieves Captured" in the July 20, 1887, edition of *The Arkansas Gazette* reported that "Deputy United States Marshal Heck Thomas came in today from Chicasaw [*sic*] country" with the dozen shackled miscreants.* "The marshal was out about two months, killed one man in attempting to arrest him, engaged in a fight with three horse thieves, and he also killed two horses while exchanging shots with other outlaws."

Newspapers regularly reported on his lawing activities, sometimes in effusive ways. "Heck Thomas was one of the finest specimens of physical manhood one would want to see," gushed *The Vinita Republican.* "He was one of those dashing, intrepid officers who was always alert; of undaunted courage and who attracted the most dare-devil young men in the country as his possemen . . . to see him in the field was a sight never to be forgotten."

The closest Belle came to widowhood was in June 1887, when her husband and his posse went after the Purdy Gang in Oklahoma. The five men had held up a train six miles north of Muskogee and killed a cattleman riding on it. The gang also managed to steal $8,000 from a safe in the express car. They then jumped back on their horses and rode north toward the Cherokee Nation. The leader was Aaron

---

* This was not Heck's biggest haul by a long shot. A most impressive delivery of prisoners to the jail in Fort Smith was another occasion, in November 1887, when Heck arrived with forty-one prisoners, having transported them 275 miles in seven two-horse wagons.

Purdy, a moonshiner who had been arrested once before for selling whiskey in Indian Country.

Heck enlisted three men—Burrell Cox, Hank Childers, and Jim Wallace—to accompany him to track the Purdy Gang. The deputy marshal obtained information that Purdy had a still in a deep ravine at Snake Creek that was likely the bandits' hideout. Incautiously, Heck, arriving at the site, rode out front and called for the hidden men to surrender. Seconds later, Purdy and his four comrades opened fire with Winchesters. Heck was hit in the right arm and left side, knocking him from the saddle.

Eagerly, the outlaws emerged, ready to finish off the deputy marshal. Advancing quickly, Cox, Childers, and Wallace let loose with their own fusillade. Purdy, struck several times, fell to the ground. The rest of the gang threw their weapons aside and surrendered. They were loaded into a wagon with Purdy, who was somehow still alive. A bleeding Heck was lifted back on his horse, and the posse went in search of a doctor. They rode first to Red Fork, sixteen miles away, and when one was not available there, they pushed on to Tulsa, another fifteen miles away, with Heck at risk of bleeding out.

Dr. H. P. Newlin treated Heck's wounds (and Purdy's). Heck had to stay in Tulsa until he was well enough to travel. While there, he was introduced to the Reverend George Mowbray and his wife, Hannah, and their daughter Matie, who was a schoolteacher. As Glenn Shirley portentously put it: "She was of medium height, neither robust nor heavy, yet showing unusual strength and suppleness in her prim, simple dress. She was still in her teens, but a full-grown woman. Her large, dark eyes met his, and they gazed up from what Heck recalled 'the prettiest face I had ever seen.'"

It was at least awkward that Heck was a well-traveled and scarred thirty-seven years old and, of course, married with five children. He could not do much about the former, but the latter soon took care of itself: While Heck was away, Belle and the children had left. She was on her way home.

"Belle longed to return to Georgia," explained Heck's daughter Beth in her memoir, "and the culture of the old South. She wanted to rear her children as she had been raised. I am sure that Papa's long absences from home and his life of constant danger were factors in her feelings also."

For a time, Heck clung to the belief that Belle and the children had gone to Georgia just for a visit. But at Christmas 1888, he received a note from his wife stating she had enrolled the older children in school in Georgia and they would remain there. "In later years, Papa confided to my mother that he and Belle had never really gotten along well," Beth reported. "'Man hunting' had gotten into his blood, and she never had understood or accepted that part of his makeup."

Though he did not need much incentive, Heck became even more involved in being a lawman. His reputation rose with the number of outlaws he brought in. When he left on one expedition, the *Fort Smith Elevator* reported on Heck's departure and warned criminals that they "had better begin hunting their holes."

There were new holes to hide in after the land rush opened up more of the Oklahoma Territory. Heck was one of the many officers sent to try to block the sooners and then try to maintain some semblance of peace the first few days, which he described to Matie as "pandemonium." He and the young minister's daughter were now corresponding regularly. Heck was hoping to be assigned to the district that contained Tulsa, but Guthrie and the other towns created overnight as well as everywhere in between demanded too much attention.

That spring, Deputy Marshal Thomas was in the midst of trying to track down one murder suspect when he was directed to a small settlement fourteen miles north of Guthrie. A man named Stevens was squatting on a claim with two other men, who decided to eliminate Stevens with a bullet in the chest. He left a widow and four children. When Heck arrived, he arranged to have Stevens buried and by passing his hat around town managed to collect eleven dollars for Mrs. Stevens. But before he could embark on the trail of the two newer killers, another homicide was reported in Oklahoma City. And so it went.

Just riding and transporting took up time because Heck had a lot of territory to cover. He patrolled from Guthrie to Pauls Valley and Ardmore to Muskogee and at times transported prisoners via the Santa Fe and Texas Pacific lines. There also were still times when he had to take prisoners to Fort Smith if they had committed crimes in Judge Parker's jurisdiction.

A few of Heck's exploits made the newspapers. The August 29, 1889, edition of *The Indian Chieftain* told readers of the arrest of "the boyish murderer" Oscar Coulter. He had escaped a prison in Heck's native Georgia and was hiding in a camp on the Canadian River south of Muskogee. His freedom was abruptly curtailed when Heck found him. "The young desperado's hand flashed to his six-shooter as Heck stepped into view but upon looking squarely into the muzzle of the Winchester in the hands of the determined deputy, he changed his mind and gave up without further resistance."

In the summer of 1890, Heck was assigned to the northern division of the territory, headquartered in Vinita in the Cherokee Nation. This didn't necessarily mean less work, but it did place him closer to Matie Mowbray. There was no doubt the two were smitten with each other, age difference be damned. And it was also on one of his trips to Tulsa, that October, that Heck encountered Grat Dalton.

This was not the first time that he had crossed paths with the Dalton brothers. Heck had known Frank when he was a respected deputy marshal and occasionally had been invited to partake in one of the dinners Adeline prepared. Heck had been one of the officers trying to track down Frank's killer, which the Dalton family appreciated. About Bob, Heck later recalled that he was "a bit of a dandy, much given to fancy boots and guns and known to be utterly fearless."

When he met Grat Dalton in October 1890, Heck had arrest warrants for Bob and Emmett connected to their horse-stealing activities. Grat angrily told the deputy marshal that his brothers had done nothing wrong and warned him about lawmen having a vendetta against the Daltons, then stomped away. According to Glenn Shirley, "Heck watched him go with a deep feeling of regret. They were the only outlaws for whom he ever held any sentiment."

Heck's romance with Matie had to endure an awkward moment. Whenever he stopped by the Mowbray home in Tulsa, the reverend and his wife, Hannah, assumed the grizzled lawman was visiting them and that their daughter always just happened to be there. Finally, though, Matie announced that she had accepted Heck's proposal of marriage.

The Mowbrays were immediately opposed, citing Heck's age and dangerous occupation and, of course, low pay. Matie was undaunted, and the next time Heck got to Tulsa, they did not stay long, instead eloping to Arkansas City.

By this time, the Dalton brothers had had their California adventures and returned to the Oklahoma Territory to rob trains. Heck just missed his chance to confront them directly—he was one of the officers lying in wait on the first train that had pulled into Red Rock that June night, the one a suspicious Bob had let pass.

And then there was the next robbery, in July at Adair, that resulted in a dead doctor. For the rest of that summer and into the early fall of 1892, Heck and Fred Dodge were doggedly on the Dalton Gang's trail. The latter, who hailed from Butte County in California, was thirty-eight years old and already had a long and distinguished career as a crime fighter. He had been an undercover detective for Wells Fargo in California, Nevada, Arizona, and Kansas, including Dodge City, and served as a peace officer in Tombstone.

In December 1879, Dodge, still with Wells Fargo, had recommended that Wyatt Earp be hired as a guard and messenger for the stage line. The two quickly became good friends, and Dodge supported Wyatt and his brothers in their troubles in Tombstone that led up to the gunfight at the OK Corral and afterward. He remained friends with Wyatt and Virgil Earp for the rest of their lives. During the Earp Vendetta Ride, it was the double-barreled percussion shotgun borrowed from Dodge that Wyatt used to kill Curly Bill Brocius in a shoot-out at Iron Springs on March 24, 1882.*

With no lull in lawman responsibilities, Matie was now experiencing what her predecessor, Belle, had week after week. Writes Beth Thomas Meeks, "For the next twenty-four years, [Matie] was to wait at home, wondering when and if her husband would ever return. 'Home' would be wherever his work took him."

No doubt Heck missed his young bride, but he was certain he would find Bob and Emmett and their bandit companions. He even believed that because of his previous friendship with the family, the brothers, at least, would surrender without a fight. As he and Fred Dodge kept riding and reports of Dalton Gang sightings became more frequent, Heck knew they were closing in.

They were. Emmett would later write that Heck Thomas became the brothers' "nemesis" and that they could feel him "pressing close." September gave way to October, and the lawmen felt more confident. The Daltons still had many friends in the area but had begun to run out of safe havens, and even the staunchest friends were being tempted by the prospect of up to $40,000 in reward money.

Heck and Dodge believed they could be as close as only two days behind the outlaws. They had heard that the gang had been sighted some twenty miles from the Kansas border. It could be the Daltons

---

* Fred Dodge used the shotgun throughout his forty-year career, and then it passed through several owners. It was sold at auction in February 2020 for $375,000. Dodge also chronicled his experiences on the frontier, accumulating twenty-seven volumes of recollections by the time of his death. He used these detailed accounts to produce two books, *Life and Times of Wyatt Earp* and *Under Cover for Wells Fargo*.

would turn back, or they could be thinking of crossing the border to visit any remaining friends in Coffeyville. That looked like as good a place as any to confront the outlaws—if Heck and his fellow lawman could get there in time.

The legendary Missouri outlaw Jesse James
was a hero to the Dalton brothers.
Courtesy of Library of Congress

Frank James had a longer life than could be
expected of a famous frontier outlaw. *Courtesy of the
Western History Collections, University of Oklahoma*

Cole Younger was the leader of his gang of brothers who were related to the Daltons. *Courtesy of the Western History Collections, University of Oklahoma*

Captured after the Northfield robbery, Jim Younger spent many years in the Stillwater prison. *Courtesy of the Western History Collections, University of Oklahoma*

Of the three inmate brothers, Bob Younger did not survive his long stay behind bars in the Stillwater facility. *Courtesy of the Western History Collections, University of Oklahoma*

James Lewis Dalton spent much time away from home, yet he and his wife, Adeline, had fifteen children, including Bob and Grat.
Courtesy of the Library of Congress

Frank Dalton's life was cut short while serving as a deputy U.S. marshal. *Courtesy of the Western History Collections, University of Oklahoma*

Gratton Dalton pursued gambling and drinking as much as any occupation. *Courtesy of the Western History Collections, University of Oklahoma*

The charismatic Bob Dalton was the planner of the Dalton Gang's robberies. *Courtesy of the Western History Collections, University of Oklahoma*

Bill Dalton, though married with children, could not resist becoming an outlaw. *Courtesy of the Western History Collections, University of Oklahoma*

Isaac Parker presided in Fort
Smith, Arkansas, and was
known as the "Hanging Judge."
*Courtesy of the Western History
Collections, University of Oklahoma*

Judge Parker's hangman,
George Maledon, was
meticulous about preparations
for executions. *Courtesy of
the Western History Collections,
University of Oklahoma*

To outlaws, Heck Thomas was one of the most feared lawmen on the frontier. *Courtesy of the Western History Collections, University of Oklahoma*

Chris Madsen, originally from Denmark, had a long career wearing a badge. *Courtesy of the Western History Collections, University of Oklahoma*

Along with Thomas and Madsen, Bill Tilghman was one of "the Three Guardsmen" of Oklahoma. *Courtesy of the Western History Collections, University of Oklahoma*

Shown here are just a few of the U.S. deputy marshals who rode for Judge Parker out of Fort Smith, Arkansas. *Courtesy of the Western History Collections, University of Oklahoma*

The stubborn Ned Christie held out as long as he could, but the marshals got him in the end. *Courtesy of the Western History Collections, University of Oklahoma*

Belle Starr and Blue Duck were two of the more distinctive outlaw couples of the Old West. *Courtesy of the Western History Collections, University of Oklahoma*

Bob Dalton poses with a woman who may or may not be the elusive Eugenia Moore. *Courtesy of the Western History Collections, University of Oklahoma*

The Condon Bank displays a few of the many bullet holes created during the Coffeyville raid. *Courtesy of the Western History Collections, University of Oklahoma*

The "Death Alley" fence where the Dalton Gang tied their horses on October 5, 1892. *Courtesy of the Western History Collections, University of Oklahoma*

Dick Broadwell (above, left) and Bill Power (above, right) were two of the four Dalton Gang members who did not survive the raid on Coffeyville. *Courtesy of the Library of Congress*

Once the shooting stopped, the bodies of (L to R) Bill Power, Bob Dalton, Grat Dalton, and Dick Broadwell were put on display. *Courtesy of the Western History Collections, University of Oklahoma*

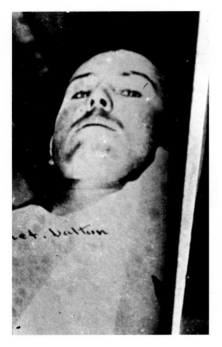

The only outlaw who survived the raid was Emmett Dalton, shown here being treated for the twenty-three wounds he suffered. *Courtesy of the Western History Collections, University of Oklahoma*

In a more bizarre display, the two dead Dalton brothers were stood up to be photographed. *Courtesy of the Western History Collections, University of Oklahoma*

The outlaw Henry Starr helped the Doolin-Dalton Gang get its start. *Courtesy of the Western History Collections, University of Oklahoma*

Al Jennings had a long career that ranged from outlaw to candidate for governor. *Courtesy of the Library of Congress*

For a time, the teenagers known as Cattle Annie and Little Breeches were members of the Doolin-Dalton Gang. *Courtesy of the Western History Collections, University of Oklahoma*

All the members of the gang met violent deaths, including Tulsa Jack Blake. *Courtesy of the Western History Collections, University of Oklahoma*

In 1894, two years after two brothers died in Coffeyville, Bill Dalton could not outrun a posse's bullets. *Courtesy of the Western History Collections, University of Oklahoma*

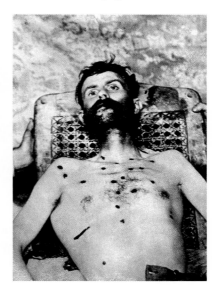

Bill Doolin was no match for Deputy Marshal Heck Thomas and his shotgun. *Courtesy of the Western History Collections, University of Oklahoma*

An older Emmett Dalton when he was an inmate at a Kansas prison. *Courtesy of the Kansas State Historical Society*

The marker at the Elmwood Cemetery in Coffeyville for Bob and Grat Dalton and the unclaimed Bill Power. *Courtesy of the Kansas State Historical Society*

THE SHOOT-OUT

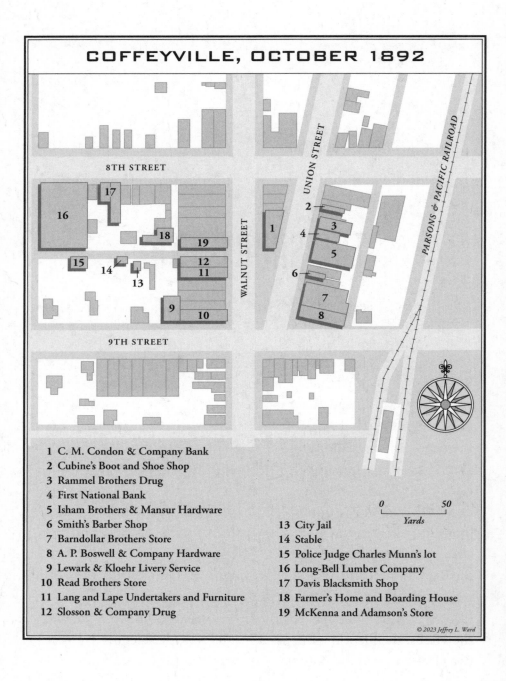

COFFEYVILLE, OCTOBER 1892

8TH STREET

UNION STREET

PARSONS & PACIFIC RAILROAD

WALNUT STREET

17
16
18
19
15
14
13
12
11
9
10

1
2
4
3
5
6
7
8

9TH STREET

1 C. M. Condon & Company Bank
2 Cubine's Boot and Shoe Shop
3 Rammel Brothers Drug
4 First National Bank
5 Isham Brothers & Mansur Hardware
6 Smith's Barber Shop
7 Barndollar Brothers Store
8 A. P. Boswell & Company Hardware
9 Lewark & Kloehr Livery Service
10 Read Brothers Store
11 Lang and Lape Undertakers and Furniture
12 Slosson & Company Drug

13 City Jail
14 Stable
15 Police Judge Charles Munn's lot
16 Long-Bell Lumber Company
17 Davis Blacksmith Shop
18 Farmer's Home and Boarding House
19 McKenna and Adamson's Store

0   50
Yards

© 2023 Jeffrey L. Ward

CHAPTER 23

A TOWN IN ITS TIME

Coffeyville may have been a fairly small city tucked away in the southeast corner of Kansas, but many of its citizens paid attention to events in the rest of the United States and in the world. In October 1892, Guglielmo Marconi was still five years away from founding his Wireless Telegraph Trading Signal Company (i.e., radio), so the most available sources of news remained what came across the telegraph lines and what was printed in the daily or weekly newspaper. *The Coffeyville Journal* had begun publishing in 1875, yet some citizens also had access to newspapers from Wichita and even as far north as Kansas City and St. Louis to the east.

In October 1892, a presidential election would be held the next month. The Democrat Grover Cleveland, from New York, who had already been president from 1885 to 1889, was back to challenge the Republican incumbent, Benjamin Harrison. This election would wind up being a historic one, with Harrison becoming the first president to lose the popular vote twice since John Quincy Adams in the 1820s, the first time that incumbents were defeated in consecutive elections, and the only time a Republican was voted out of the

White House after a single four-year term, a dubious achievement that would not be repeated until 1992.*

The residents of Coffeyville may have read or otherwise learned that Ellis Island in New York had begun accommodating immigrants to the U.S.; that in March in Springfield, Massachusetts, the first game of a new sport called basketball had been played, with the final score being five baskets to one; Abraham Lincoln's birthday was designated a national holiday; a device called the escalator made its debut at Coney Island Beach in New York; in Argentina, the world's first fingerprinting bureau opened; the Johnson County War in Wyoming, which pitted small farmers against large ranchers, was still raging, killing as many as thirty-eight men (including those who were lynched); in big business, the General Electric Company was created; Oil City in Pennsylvania caught on fire, killing 130 people; John Muir organized the Sierra Club in San Francisco; Chicago opened an elevated railway; the arrest of Homer Plessy for sitting in a whites-only railroad car in Louisiana led to an unsuccessful attempt in the U.S. Supreme Court to overturn the "separate but equal" doctrine; the "Great Fire of 1892" almost destroyed St. John's, Newfoundland; Lizzie Borden hacked her father and stepmother to death in their Massachusetts home (she was acquitted); William Gladstone became the prime minister of Great Britain; for the first time, the Pledge of Allegiance was recited in America; it was discovered that Jupiter had a third moon, and it was named Amalthea; and *The Baltimore Afro-American*, which would become the longest-running African American family-owned newspaper, published its first issue.

Since fixing its incorporation glitch in 1873, Coffeyville had steadily prospered. Surrounded by mostly successful farms, the city flourished as a trading destination along with becoming one of the most important grain and milling centers in the central west region.

---

* The only other time (so far) in American history that incumbent presidents lost twice in a row was Gerald Ford in 1976 and Jimmy Carter in 1980.

By 1885, the rudimentary Ayers banking house was transformed into the First National Bank of Coffeyville. The following year saw the creation of the Condon Bank.

A big boost for the city came in 1887 when the Missouri Pacific Railroad's tracks came to Coffeyville, further connecting it to not only the rest of Kansas but the country too. By then, the population had grown to two thousand citizens.

Five years later, Coffeyville was enjoying another growth spurt thanks to the discovery of plentiful natural gas and abundant clay. That May, the biggest well to date in the Mid-Continent field was brought in, and two months later, a gas well was drilled right in the center of the city. The population had doubled from 1887, and during the next two decades, the population of Coffeyville would increase sixfold. Its two banks were doing plenty of business.

By 1892, the "Wild West," as the dime-store novels kept calling it—and kept inventing it—was in the past. What some viewed as its last dramatic gasp, the so-called Vendetta Ride headed by Wyatt Earp and Doc Holliday in Arizona, had been ten years earlier. Earp's days as a lawman were long over, and now he and his wife, Josephine, lived in San Francisco; Holliday had died five years earlier.*

In 1890, the year after the first Oklahoma Land Rush, the director of the U.S. Census Bureau had announced that the frontier was closed. That year's census had shown that a frontier line, a point beyond which the population density was less than two persons per square mile, no longer existed. In 1893, Frederick Jackson Turner, a young historian at the University of Wisconsin, would present a paper to the American Historical Association titled "The Significance of the Frontier in American History." In it, he argued that the

---

* In her (justifiably) much-maligned memoir, Josephine claimed that it was in 1892 that she and Wyatt, whom she had met in Tombstone, were finally married. The ceremony supposedly was performed by the captain of a yacht owned by Lucky Baldwin, who also owned the Santa Anita racetrack, one of Wyatt's frequent haunts. However, to date, no public record of the marriage has been found.

experience of the frontier was what distinguished the United States from Europe—the frontier had shaped American history and had produced the practicality, energy, and individualism of the American character.

There were many in Coffeyville who would agree with that. Some of them had come to Kansas as young men and women before and after the Civil War when it was still very much the frontier. But in the 1860s, '70s, and '80s, that frontier had shifted steadily west until, according to the Census Bureau director, it no longer existed.

There was some nostalgia about that, but there was some relief too. While "frontier" had meant adventure and opportunity and the romance of wide-open spaces, it had also contained danger and violence and premature death. For a time, gunslinger was a real occupation and men like Wild Bill Hickok, John Wesley Hardin, and Billy the Kid had burnished their reputation by doing it better than other men. Gangs like those run by the James brothers and Younger brothers had struck terror in the hearts of common folk as well as bank clerks and train conductors.

But that was all over now, at least as far as the citizens in Coffeyville were concerned. As David Stewart Elliott, editor of *The Coffeyville Journal,* would describe his community, "The town of Coffeyville, Montgomery County, Kansas, is . . . made up of hardy men and noble women, who fearlessly braved the dangers and vicissitudes of life on the Western border in order that they might establish homes and build up a community wherein they and their children could win prosperity and live to enjoy the fruits of honest toil."

Because of the role he is about to play in the overall Coffeyville story, this is a good place to learn more about Mr. Elliott. His father, also David Stewart Elliott, was born in Pennsylvania and began a career in journalism and was married and settled with a son when the Civil War began. He had already served in the U.S. Army during the war with Mexico and could have easily begged off soldiering again, but devoted to the cause of preserving the Union, he enlisted in a Pennsylvania regiment of infantry.

He was in the service in Kansas in 1864, and the regiment was on its way to Fort Smith to assist in repelling the General Sterling Price invasion of Missouri and Kansas when he was killed by Quantrill's men at Baxter Springs. He and others of the command were captured by the Quantrill raiders, were lined up against a wall, and all were shot. The late Captain David Stewart Elliott left behind a widow and just the one son.

The younger David was born in December 1843 in Everett, Pennsylvania. When about fifteen years of age, he entered a newspaper office to learn the printing trade. He left that behind in April 1861 when he enlisted in Company G of the Thirteenth Pennsylvania Volunteer Infantry. That was a three-month regiment, and at the end of his term, he reenlisted in Company E of the Seventy-Sixth Pennsylvania Volunteers and was with that command for more than three years.

Elliott survived the war unscathed, and in 1868, he became editor of *The Bedford County Press* in Everett and continued in that capacity until 1873. He was also admitted to the bar of Bedford County, but after practicing a few years resumed his work as a newspaper editor. In the mid-1880s, he relocated to Coffeyville and became the energetic editor of the city's newspaper. Elliott was so energetic that early in 1892 he established *The Coffeyville Daily Journal.*

He also established a marriage, by wedding Clara Barndollar, who also had an impressive lineage. One of her ancestors was John Williams, who served in the First Battalion of Bedford County during the Revolutionary War. Another was Richard Dunlap, who was captain of the Bedford Company in the First Battalion of Militia and was killed while fighting at Frankstown, Pennsylvania, in June 1781. And a third was Captain James Martin, who married his bride in the home of Benjamin Franklin.

There were still plenty of troubles in Oklahoma to keep hundreds of deputies doing their duty, but that was on the other side of the border and felt almost like a world away. Coffeyville was a safe city, so much so that its citizens did not carry firearms, and even its marshal, Charles Connelly, made his rounds without a gun. The local people, feeling safe and secure, were not looking back but were confidently anticipating the twentieth century less than eight years away.

There was the Dalton Gang still on the loose, sure enough. But few in Coffeyville fretted about them. The Dalton family had lived in and around the area for a time, so one would think it was the last place those boys would show up to cause mischief, being so easily recognized. And with regular reports of Heck Thomas and other lawmen and detectives closing in, the Daltons would soon be behind bars or under mounds of dirt.

However, the Wild West was not as over as the people of Coffeyville thought. They would not have to look for it; it was coming to them. During that first week of October 1892, the Dalton Gang was indeed on their way. The three brothers and their accomplices were not conscious of the fact that, like the official designation of the frontier, outlaws belonged in the past. They were about to be rudely awakened.

CHAPTER 24

"THE LAST TRICK"

As usual, it was Bob's idea. He was contemplating both the past and the future to figure out the present. The past, to him, was not the larger picture of the Wild West but a family history that prominently included the raid by the James brothers and his Younger cousins on the bank up in Minnesota. That the escapade up north had failed miserably did not deter Bob. Instead, he saw a Coffeyville caper as a golden opportunity to erase that stain on his mother's side of the family with an even more audacious raid. As a bonus, a successful adventure would elevate the Dalton Gang into the realm of legend.

He would be proved right, but not the way he had envisioned.

What the immediate future held for the gang was not glory but an inability to get away with daring heists. There were fewer loyal friends to help hide them and more lawmen than ever. Bob kept hearing that Heck Thomas and his posse were right behind them. Everyone in Oklahoma knew that Heck was fearless and sure not a quitter. What made sense to Bob was one quick, profitable score and it was adios.

Emmett noted, "For a day or so Bob was unusually quiet and taciturn. I knew he was studying out some problem. Finally he turned suddenly one afternoon and said to all of us: 'Come on, we're going to Coffeyville.'"

He explained to Grat and Emmett and the others that trains were now too risky and the brothers needed a big enough score to get away and stay away, wherever that might be—though he did mention South America. A disadvantage of Coffeyville was the Dalton family members were known there. However, an overriding advantage was that there was not one but two banks in the prosperous town. Bob's bold plan: "We can take the C. M. Condon and the First National Bank at the same time. That ought to give us enough to get out all right."

He added: "No one is going to get hurt."

Speaking more to Grat and Emmett than Bill Power and Dick Broadwell, Bob reminded them of the family connection to the Younger brothers. According to him, the Coffeyville raid would be at least as dramatic as the Northfield strike, and a good outcome would ease the pain of that 1876 debacle—although Bob was the only member of the Dalton gang who felt any pain at all. Perhaps Grat and Emmett would allow that with the Younger brothers still in prison, hearing about a successful Coffeyville raid committed by their literally younger cousins might give them some comfort.

And apparently, by this time, the Dalton brothers had bought into the myth that they were sort of Robin Hoods, stealing from the rich railroad robber barons and distributing the proceeds—well, some of them—to the local folks who needed it most. As Emmett described, "It was nothing for me to go into a country store, get a few things which probably called for thirty or forty dollars and leave one hundred dollars or two hundred dollars with the store-keeper. Lots of these poor fellows scratching out a meager existence needed the money. I only hope it did them more good than it would have done the express company."

Just imagine what the profits from busting two banks could do.

A mystery has endured for over 130 years as to why the Dalton

Gang by early October had dwindled to the three Dalton brothers and Power and Broadwell. Left behind when this quintet took to the trail were Bitter Creek Newcomb, Charley Pierce, and Bill Doolin. What happened to them?

Over time, there have been as many theories as gang members. To the Doolin biographer Bailey Hanes, the huge reward offered for the gang's capture was a factor: "In view of this development, the Daltons felt the gang should be streamlined for the sake of mobility. Furthermore, some of the members were dissatisfied with their share of the loot. They also felt that Bill Doolin was headstrong and unruly at times, and of late he, too, was dissatisfied with the cut the Daltons gave him."

Another possibility was the three men thought Bob's plan was daft. Did it make a whole lot of sense to be among people who might recognize you, rob *two* banks, and commit the crime in broad daylight?

"And why not Bill Doolin?" Robert Barr Smith speculates. "By all accounts Doolin was a cool hand in a tight place, a smart, tough gunman who, as the saying went, 'would do to take along' on any raid." But, he adds, "Doolin may have been left behind simply because Bob did not trust him."

As far back as the Lelietta robbery, Doolin had ridden into Wagoner to have a photograph taken—one for him, and a copy sent to a girl he liked in Ingalls. It was passed around there until finding its way into the hands of the lawman Charles LeFlore, who now had confirmation that Doolin was a member of the Dalton Gang. Who knows what kind of loose end Doolin could be in Coffeyville?

Or, as Barr further muses, "Although others describe Doolin as reckless and foolhardy, even he might have been daunted by the prospect of invading a populous town where three of the gang members were well known. Doolin may or may not have been 'levelheaded,' but he was far from stupid. And so, when the gang was cut down to five, Doolin may already have decided he wanted no part of Coffeyville."

According to Emmett's curious explanation, Bob made the decision to leave the three other members of the gang behind because "they had seemingly gotten so they did not like to ride too long at a time and were too prone to lie around their friends, after they had made a little raise."

Perhaps Bob was being sensible that the gang be streamlined to five members who could strike fast, ride out faster, hide out well, and keep their mouths shut until it was time to leave the region altogether. Still, given how big this job looked to be, why not spend a little more time casing Coffeyville, and the banks in particular?

That was what Emmett suggested. But Bob nixed that idea, fearing Emmett would be recognized and that would tip off too many people in town—most notably, the marshal—that the Daltons were near and could be up to something.

The rumors of lawmen closing in were certainly accurate. Deputy Marshal Chris Madsen was heading his own posse, one of perhaps a dozen stalking the Daltons from all directions. But Heck Thomas was indeed the most troubling. As Fred Dodge would write in his *Under Cover for Wells Fargo* memoir, Heck "was a man that was known to always get his man—sometimes dead but he got him." Emmett routinely referred to Heck as the gang's "nemesis," so if he and his posse were nearby, there was no time for a deliberate reconnaissance.

Indeed, according to Dodge's recollections, he and Heck may have been only a day behind the Dalton Gang. He reported that they had found where the Dalton brothers and their two comrades had camped the night of October 3. They did not know that Coffeyville was their destination, but they believed if they pushed on in the direction the gang appeared to be going, they would catch up.

The Daltons knew there could be no delay. That first week in October, they steered their horses toward southeast Kansas. "Soon we found ourselves back in familiar neighborhoods," Emmett reported. "We came near to Kingfisher where our mother was. I know

I wanted to take a chance and see her again." However, he was out-voted by Grat and Bob.

Stick to the back trail: "It was a case of ride about all day and night just as we saw fit and as the weather and country indicated. We kept away from all settlements, dropping in on some friend now and then for a meal. Out on the plains or in the hills and moun-tains when worried by the suspected proximity of a posse, a few long draws of a pipe or cigarette was often more consoling than anything else we could think of."

Bob had also devised an escape plan. It involved paying Amos Burton, who the Daltons knew as "a typical Texas negro cowboy," to find and purchase a sturdy wagon and good horses, then fill it with food and ammunition. Burton was to drive it out to a desig-nated location in the Cherokee Strip and wait for the gang there. "We figured that we would be able to lose, in the Osage hills, any posse which followed us out of Coffeyville after the raid, then we would get in our covered wagon." The less recognizable Broadwell and Power would sit up front and say they were on a horse-trading trip while the three brothers stayed hidden in the wagon.

By this point, Bob had concluded that he and Grat and Emmett would winter in a secure hiding spot, then in the spring head north-west, eventually to Seattle. From there, they would sail to South America. What Power and Broadwell did was up to them.

On the morning of October 4, the bandits mounted their horses and set off for Coffeyville. They wanted to enter the city in the morn-ing, so later that day, they stopped to make camp in timber at the headwaters of Hickory Creek some twelve miles from Coffeyville. Then Bob decided this was too far away from the target, so they packed up and rode closer, making camp at the Onion Creek bot-toms. This site was about a mile and a half southwest of Coffeyville.

The Daltons knew the land they set a dry camp up on belonged to a family named Davis and was as secure a location as any other, with lawmen not welcome. As their horses munched on the corn they had "borrowed" from a nearby farm, the men noted that the air was turning cooler. Soon enough, there would be the first frost of the season in southeast Kansas.

That evening, after a no-frills supper of hard-boiled eggs and biscuits, and while sipping whiskey and hoping to become drowsy enough to sleep, Bob and the four other men went over the bold plan one more time. The target for Bob and Emmett would be the First National Bank, and Grat, Power, and Broadwell would go across the street and enter the Condon Bank. Bob knew of a hitching post in front of the C. M. Condon building where their horses could be kept close by.

Inside the banks, the thieves would make short work of guards or any other resistance, get the vaults open—presumably, rifle muzzles inches from faces would be as persuasive in a bank as they had been on the trains—stuff as much loot as they could into sacks, hustle out to their horses, and gallop off before the first alarm sounded. By the time a posse was put together, the gang would be long gone.

They slept fitfully and were up with the sun. They fed their horses again and ate what they could keep down, then at 8:45, they saddled and mounted up. Bob and Grat each held empty sacks they expected to fill with cash.

"On to Coffeyville!" Bob called out with a laugh. "This is the last trick!"

With less enthusiasm, Emmett echoed, "The last trick." But then, seeing Bob turn his coat collar up against the chill of the October morning, he joked, "Just wait till we get to Coffeyville, Bob. You won't need any coat 'cause it's going to be hotter than hell."

Emmett would later comment, "Both of us were unwittingly telling the tragic truth."

CHAPTER 25

"A FLASH OF LIGHTNING"

The five men followed one of the main roads into Coffeyville, one that the Daltons recalled became Eighth Street when it entered the town. As they neared Coffeyville, they were noticed by several people riding to and from it. Perversely, to reduce the risk of being recognized, the Daltons had clumsily disguised themselves with false beards, mustaches, and sideburns. Long cloaks concealed their weapons—heavy Colt revolvers as well as Winchesters. As they intended, they appeared to be a party of deputy United States marshals on official business.

The ruse seems to have worked. However: "Even in frontier country where any man might wear a gun without arousing comment, five heavily weaponed men riding together should have caused some interest," writes Robert Barr Smith. "Perhaps it was the day; bright and bracing, a clear, wonderful morning, the kind that makes people eager to work and achieve. Still: Somebody should have wondered."

As they rode up Eighth Street—the three brothers side by side, the two other men trailing behind—many eyes were turned upon them, but, they hoped, without the slightest suspicion. In a history of Coffeyville published for its centennial, one citizen was colorfully quoted, "Indian Summer was here, with its mild sunshine and purple haze. The bandits, like young Lochinvars, came out of the West."

The gang's plan included tying their horses on the north side of Eighth Street, in front of the opera house, diagonally across the street and behind the Condon Bank. There, the horses would be readily accessible when the need to flee came. But right away, they encountered their first complication: A municipal project requiring that the street be torn up to install curbs and gutters was underway, and the old hitching post had become history.

So instead, after Bob scanned their surroundings, he led the gang to an alley that ran directly off the street. They tied their horses to a wooden fence at the rear of a lot owned by Charles Munn, who was a city police judge. Apparently, not one of them realized this was an unwise decision. True, the hitching post near the banks had been removed, but there had to have been other options to tie their horses than a fence down an alley that was a good three hundred feet—meaning, a long run—from the banks.

Perhaps they were too focused on the next step in the plan. According to David Stewart Elliott's account, "Quietly forming in lines as they had been riding, three in front and two following, the men walked at an ordinary pace down one alley, in an easterly direction toward the Plaza." They carried their Winchesters at their sides.

An opportunity to sound an alarm was lost. A stonecutter who was working on the Eighth Street project had been in the alley to examine a pile of rocks. He was not a resident of Coffeyville, and he must have assumed that a group of heavily armed men was a common sight there. The stonecutter emerged from the alley after the outlaws and simply turned to go back to work on the street.

Most likely, no one in the gang saw that, moments after they left the alley, an oil wagon pulled by two horses turned in to it. There it came to a halt and stayed put, partially blocking the entrance to the alley and access to where the outlaws had left their horses.

With the exception of the hitching post disappearance, downtown

Coffeyville was as Bob, Grat, and Emmett remembered it. Facing south, the Condon Bank sat on a triangular space of ground in the center of what was the main plaza. To the east, directly across the street, was the First National Bank. It was in the center of a row of stores that faced west. The Isham Brothers' Hardware Store was the first store south of the First National, and on the other side of it was the Rammel Brothers' Drugstore.

From Ninth Street to the alley on the west side of the plaza were six shops in a row: Slosson & Co. drugstore, Lang and Lang's General Store, A. P. Boswell's General Store, Wilhalf's General Store, the Coffeyville Post Office, and the Reed Brothers' General Store. And across from the alley were Mitchell and Ulms' Restaurant, Wells' Dry Good Store, and McKenna's Dry Good Store. It would appear that the city was prosperous indeed, given the overlap of some of the stores, and of course the two thriving banks facing each other on the plaza.

Everyone seemed to be going about their business . . . but that was not quite true. A few people here and there noticed the group of men bearing rifles sauntering through the plaza. However, no strong suspicion was aroused. It was the time of year when men hunted, so by itself, carrying rifles was not ominous. If anything caused some curiosity, it was the fake facial hair the Dalton brothers sported.

In close order, the five gang members crossed Walnut Street from the alley to the Condon Bank, Winchesters held snug against their legs. Grat, Dick Broadwell, and Bill Power entered the Condon Bank, and Emmett and Bob strode across Union Street to the First National Bank.

But not fast enough: They had also been noticed by a man named Aleck McKenna, who was sweeping the sidewalk in front of his dry goods store. Unlike the oblivious stonecutter, McKenna, instead of retreating inside his shop, took a second and closer look. His eyes followed the three men who had entered the Condon Bank. He thought, despite the disguise, that he recognized one of the men as Grat Dalton. Then, with an unobstructed view through a large plate glass window, he could see a man pointing a Winchester at the cashier's counter.

McKenna called out, "There go the Daltons!" Then one of the street workers shouted to the people inside a store, "The Daltons are robbing the bank!" The advantage of surprise had barely lasted a minute.

Very soon, half the businessmen around the plaza knew what was going on, and the message quickly passed throughout the town. As Emmett recalled, "From then on things went so rapidly" that the action blurred at times.

Right after Grat entered the Condon Bank, he had indeed pointed his Winchester at the cashier while Power and Broadwell took positions at the door. The stunned employees staring at Grat—and no doubt noticing his incongruous facial hair—were Charles Carpenter, a bank officer, and Thomas Babb, a bookkeeper. It was Carpenter who had the Winchester pointed at him after the three thieves entered.

"We have got you, goddamn you," Grat said. "Hold up your hands!"

Carpenter raised his hands. But the bandits had not noticed Babb, who was sitting at a desk near the vault. The bookkeeper was not so shocked that he didn't have the presence of mind to furtively slip into the vault—or, as David Stewart Elliott would later put it, Babb "discovered the character of the men before they discovered him." Not so fortunate was a customer, John Levan, who picked the wrong time to transact business at the Condon Bank. As soon as he entered, Power and Broadwell had him lie on the floor.

Another cashier, Charles Ball, heard sounds coming from the lobby. When he walked out from the back to investigate, he encountered the gun-toting gang members and Carpenter. Grat stepped behind the counter and gave Ball the grain sack. He instructed the cashier to hold it open while Carpenter—reluctantly, but without risking a bullet—gathered the money on the counter and in the cash drawer and dropped it all into the sack.

Another surprised citizen was Luther Perkins. He had an office above the Condon Bank, and out his window, he'd happened to see Bob and Emmett enter the First National. Suspecting the two men were up to no good and wanting to warn the Condon employees, Perkins had gone down the back stairs to Walnut Street behind the bank and come in by the back door. He got far enough to see Carpenter covered by a Winchester, and he immediately backed out, shutting the door behind him. Perkins hurried back upstairs to join two coworkers, Joe Uncapher and J. H. Wilcox, who were at the window waiting to see what transpired.

Back downstairs, Babb's few minutes of being undetected ended. Having put everything they had swiped up into the sack, Carpenter and Ball were ordered into the vault. As he followed them behind the iron screen that partitioned the vault from the lobby, Grat found the trembling bookkeeper cowering behind a rack of books. Grat "gave the young man a terrible cursing," according to Elliott, and had him emerge with his hands up.

Things looked promising in the vault area: The doors of the safe were open, revealing three canvas bags. Grat told Carpenter to empty them into the sack the cashier carried. He watched with satisfaction as silver coins flowed from the bags.* That done, there was one other target—a bulletproof chest, with a combination lock. Grat told Ball to open it.

"I can't," replied the cashier. "The time lock is on a setting."

"What time will it open?"

"Nine thirty."

---

* It has often been reported that the coins added up to $3,000, and with their addition, the grain sack's contents now weighed two hundred pounds. This is unlikely, though there is the possibility that by then Ball, the cashier, could only drag the sack along the floor and Grat was not aware of its heaviness until it was time to hurry out of the bank.

Grat demanded, "What time is it now?"

The cashier made a point of looking at his watch and responded, "It's nine twenty."

As Robert Barr Smith put it, "Charley Ball was an immensely courageous man, or an immensely foolish one, depending on your point of view. He blandly laid his life on the line for his employer's property, in spite of all the threats and curses and the leveled Winchesters." Ball was also aware that there "was no FDIC to cover his friends and neighbors"—whatever thieves made off with would not be replaced.

A quick-thinking Carpenter reached out and pretended to be unable to turn the chest handle, indicating it was locked. Convinced, Grat announced, "We'll wait."

In the space of only a few seconds, Grat had made several serious mistakes. First, he believed Ball, who had the presence of mind to lie. Yes, the combination lock was on a time setting, but it had opened at 8:00 a.m., one hundred minutes earlier. Grat could have simply swung the door open. Second, apparently not having a watch, he accepted that it was 9:20 when a glance at a clock on the wall would have told him it was 9:40. And third was the decision to wait. This could have turned out well, because inside the chest was at least $40,000 and presumably Ball would have run out of excuses.

But a shock wave of violence was about to strike an unsuspecting city. As David Stewart Elliott put it a tad floridly, "The people of Coffeyville were never in the enjoyment of more peaceful and comfortable surroundings than on the eventful morning of October 5, 1892. People came and went and vehicles moved about in ordinary numbers until about fifteen minutes before 10 o'clock, when the most remarkable occurrence that has ever taken place in the history of our country came upon the peaceful city like a flash of lightning from a clear sky."

"After the initial alarm, it's certain that people at different points of the plaza excitedly passed the news around," reports Lue Diver Barndollar in *What Really Happened on October 5, 1892.**

And then they started moving, fast. With a bank robbery underway—as they were soon to learn, *two* bank robberies—the first priority was to get hold of guns. This they did with amazing alacrity.

---

* Barndollar wrote her book for the centennial anniversary of the Dalton raid in 1992. Her husband's grandfather James Judson Barndollar had settled in Coffeyville in 1871 and owned the Barndollar Brothers shop on the town plaza.

CHAPTER 26

BLOODY WORK BEGINS

While the duped Grat, Bill Power, and Dick Broadwell waited for the safe to open, across the plaza, Bob and Emmett had entered the First National Bank. Displaying their Winchesters froze everyone in place. There were two bank employees and three customers who now stared back at them, astonished and fearful. Bob "with a horrid oath," reported Elliott, "called upon every one present to hold up their hands."

He then ordered the cashier, Thomas Ayers, to open the safe, and when he did, the brothers grabbed the cash and gold pieces within and dropped them into the sack. So far, so good. Still, Bob "kept those present in a state of nervous excitement by his dreadful profanity and the reckless manner in which he flourished his gun."

The brothers could not see what was happening outside and did not know an alarm had been raised. "A 'call to arms' came simultaneously with the alarm," recalled Elliott, "and in less time than it takes to relate the fact a dozen men with Winchesters and revolvers in their hands were ready to resist the escape of the unwelcome visitors."

As news had spread of a robbery in progress—and more amazingly, perhaps two robberies—people had dashed through the plaza to the two hardware stores. A. P. Boswell & Co. was housed in a two-story brick building at the southeast corner of the plaza, and just south of the First National Bank was the one-story brick building containing the Isham Brothers store. Both businesses sold firearms, but on that dangerous morning, employees were freely passing out guns and ammunition.

But why did people have to go to the hardware stores? As Elliott explains, "When the robbers were first discovered in the banks, there was not an armed man any where upon the square or in the immediate neighborhood." Even the city marshal, Charles Connelly, "had laid his pistol aside and was totally unarmed when the crisis came."

Some citizens already had weapons at their disposal. One was George Cubine, proprietor of the Boot and Shoe Shop, three doors down from the First National. He had a Winchester hanging on the wall. He grabbed it and hurried out the door. The co-owner of a Coffeyville livery service, John Kloehr, was one of those who armed himself thanks to A. P. Boswell & Co. He took what ammunition he needed from behind the counter, and by the time he was back on the street, his Winchester was loaded and ready.

Kloehr found that Boswell's was turning into an epicenter of armed resistance. By this time, at least a dozen men holding rifles and shotguns had collected there. They in turn had moved several wagons closer together to form a barricade. From this position, the men could clearly see the front of the Condon Bank. Taking up a solitary position on the awning atop the Barndollar Brothers store was Parker Williams, who had picked out a Colt .44 pistol from Boswell's. He too had a clear view.

Inside the Isham hardware store, the co-owner, Henry Isham, and his two clerks had been casually serving customers when men began running into the shop. One was Charles Gump. After excitedly telling those inside what was happening, he was handed a double-barreled shotgun. He exited and placed himself behind one of the shop's iron awning posts. Isham himself, after shutting the shop's

safe, plucked a rifle from his inventory and stood behind a large steel
stove near the front door. Soon joining him was one of his clerks,
Lewis Dietz, who held a revolver.

Moments later, Lucius Baldwin entered the shop. He was a clerk
at Reed Brothers, and after hearing about the rumored robbery, he
crossed the street and chose one of Isham's pistols.

"No one waited for the selection of a commander or the authority
of a leader," Elliott wrote. "Each individual formed himself into an
independent commander. The volunteer defenders of law were not
impelled by sentiment; they were inspired by a high sense of duty to
their neighbors and the community."

For Bob and Emmett, things were going a bit smoother inside
the First National Bank. They had corralled four customers to hold
as hostages—three who had already been in the bank, and a fourth
when he had stepped in a minute afterward and tried without success
to step back out after spotting the two bandits with Winchesters. In
addition to Ayers, the other employee was W. H. Shepard, a teller
sitting at a desk near the vault.

Leaving Emmett to guard the six men, Bob strode down a hall to
a private office in the back of the bank. There he found Bert Ayers, a
bookkeeper who was the son of the cashier, sitting at his desk. "Get
out front," Bob told him.

He did, with Bob prodding him with the rifle. A few seconds
later, the situation became obvious to the bookkeeper when he saw
the second armed man and his father and the others looking helpless
and frightened. Bob then ordered the younger Ayers into the vault
and to remove whatever money was in it. When Ayers hesitated, he
was persuaded to move fast when the Dalton brothers declared they
were about to shoot him. He first put the contents of the cash drawer
and whatever was on the counter into the sack Bob carried.

Next was the money in the safe. This time, it was Ayers the cashier
who, hoping to divert attention from his son, withdrew its contents
and dropped them into the grain sack. To be of further assistance,

he informed the thieves that there was some gold in the vault, if they wanted that too.

"Yes," Bob told him. "We want every damn cent."

Thomas Ayers complied, then declared that was all there was. Bob was suddenly suspicious of such easy cooperation. Brushing past Ayers, he walked into the vault and yanked the safe door open. Sure enough, there were two more packages of money, totaling $5,000. Once they were in the sack, Bob roughly estimated the First National had yielded at least $20,000.

It could have been more. Bob had picked up a box belonging to a bank customer, which contained gold watches. However, he was assured by Thomas Ayers and Shepard that the box contained nothing but papers. Bob put it back down on the counter.

It was time to get while the going was good. To be on the safe side, as Bob and Emmett went out the front door, they were preceded by the four customers and the three bank employees. But there would be no escape that way.

"Look out there at the left," Emmett warned.

From the doorway of Rammel Brothers' Drugstore, George Cubine fired his borrowed Winchester. He was joined by C. S. Cox, an American Express agent, who squeezed the trigger of his revolver.

No one was hit, but there was an immediate reaction. Bob and Emmett moved quickly back into the bank. So did Bert Ayers and Shepard. Thomas Ayers ran away from the bank and right into Isham's Hardware. After plucking a rifle off the rack and clutching a fistful of ammunition, the cashier went back outside and took a position with a clear view of the First National.

The unlucky bank employees had made the wrong snap decision. Bert Ayers and Shepard were once again hostages. They were dragged along as the Dalton brothers, with the sack in Bob's grip, ran through the bank to the back door. The plan to meet with Grat, Power, and Broadwell and cross the plaza to the alley, where they could make their escape, was immediately scrapped.

Back at the Condon Bank, the thieves had heard the gunshots. Grat realized that the full grain sack was too heavy to carry and ordered the silver taken out. He then stashed what cash he could fit into his coat pockets and vest. Forget the time lock—it was time instead to get out of there.

Meanwhile, the citizen defenders of Coffeyville had gone out on the tops of buildings and spread to alleys and back lots while others stood boldly out in the street. As they waited for Bob and Emmett to make another appearance, they targeted the Condon Bank. Bullets from pistols, rifles, and shotguns blew holes in the plate glass windows. Power and Broadwell got busy, each firing their rifles at citizens outside the bank. It would later be estimated that just the men behind the barricade in front of Boswell's fired about eighty shots into the building.

That firepower was hard to avoid. The customers and bank employees on the floor managed to do so, but Power did not. He cried out that he'd been hit and couldn't use his arm to shoot any longer. Broadwell was not going to just stand there and take it. The plate glass on the southeast door was still intact until he put his rifle against it and began firing. He was aiming for Parker Williams on the Barndollar awning. He missed, but it dawned on Williams that he would have a longer life span if he got off the awning.

Grat was done with robbing. Now he had to focus on getting his two companions and himself out of there.

Bob had to be having similar thoughts as the gunfire became more intense. He made his way back to the First National's front door while Emmett, holding his Winchester under one arm, tied a string around the opening of the money sack. Bob peeked out the door and spotted Charles Gump and his shotgun standing by Isham's awning post. Bob took aim with his Winchester and fired. The bullet struck Gump on his gun hand and then the gun itself, shattering the shotgun. Several men appeared and helped the wounded man into the shop.

Gump soon had company in the hardware store. An employee, T. Arthur Reynolds, with one of the shop's rifles, rather rashly stepped out onto the sidewalk and began shooting at the southeast door of the Condon Bank. A bullet sent by one of the outlaws found Reynolds's foot. He too was hauled into Isham's.

It was obvious now that going out the front door was a very bad idea. Bob and Emmett ordered Shepard to open the back door of the First National for them, and they headed in that direction. At about the same time, carrying a pistol, Lucius Baldwin, the twenty-three-year-old from the Reed Brothers store, ran out the back door of Isham's into the alley running behind the bank. Bob and Emmett saw him as they stepped out of the First National. They leveled their rifles at him and told him to stop.

The bold Baldwin did not. His pistol held at his side, he continued his approach in the alley. But before he could get off a shot, Bob, aiming his rifle from the hip, fired. The bullet hit Baldwin in the left side of his chest and came out his back.

"I was told that before he died he admitted that Bob had called to him to stop but that he was too overcome by fear and surprise to either stop or shoot," Emmett wrote. "That momentary spasm of fear cost him his life."*

As the Dalton brothers ran to the north entrance of the alley, Emmett carried the heavy grain sack. He struggled to keep up with his older brother. "You hold the bag," Bob had told him, "and I'll do the fighting." They had to reach the horses. With luck, Grat and the two other gang members were doing the same thing.

In any case, as Elliott intoned in his narrative, "It was then that the bloody work of the dread desperadoes began."

---

* Indeed, *The Coffeyville Journal*'s commemorative issue would include an interview conducted years earlier with Jack Long, a young man at the time of the raid. "I heard Bob Dalton tell him two or three times, 'Boy, throw that gun down. I don't want to hurt you.' But Baldwin stood there like he was froze, and Bob shot him."

CHAPTER 27

SAYING THEIR PRAYERS

Leaving the mortally wounded Lucius Baldwin behind, Bob and Emmett began to make their way toward the end of the alley. Immediately after the Dalton brothers took off, several people appeared in the alley and carried Baldwin to join the other wounded men at Isham's. There he regained consciousness, but, according to David Stewart Elliott, three hours later, "his young life went out in triumph and he died, the first martyr in the battle against the unholy designs of his wicked slayers."

Spurred by desperation, Emmett now ran ahead of his brother. Bob called out to him, "Go slow, I can whip the whole damn town." He breathlessly added, "Let's get to the horses. The rest ought to be through by this time."

Suddenly, they stopped short. According to Emmett, a fourteen-year-old named Bobbie Wells "ran out of a back door toward us. He had a small .22 revolver in his hands and, pointing it at us, he boyishly said, 'What are you fellers doin' here?'"

Laughing, Bob said, "Run home, boy, or you'll get hurt."

"Then taking the butt of his Winchester he gave little Wells a paddle, and that youngster, yelling as though he was killed, ran away back into the alley."*

The brothers resumed running. When they emerged onto Eighth Street, Bob looked to the south and fired his Winchester twice. There was no particular target in sight; he mostly wanted to discourage others from shooting at him and Emmett. Both were disappointed to see no sign of the rest of their gang.

The reason for their absence was Grat, Dick Broadwell, and the wounded Bill Power were still pinned down by torrents of gunfire. Inside the Condon Bank, bullets continued to infiltrate the interior walls and pockmark the desks. The three thieves were returning fire as best they could without exposing themselves. Obviously, this situation could not continue, as there could now be little doubt that all of Coffeyville had been alerted and its citizens had a lot more guns and ammunition than the bandits possessed.

Finally, as Robert Barr Smith caustically put it, "At last the dimwitted Grat reluctantly decided the time had come to run for it, loot or no loot. And it finally dawned on him that a hasty retreat carrying two hundred pounds of silver was not an encouraging prospect."

When Grat asked if there was a back door, he was told—falsely— that there was not. It would have to be a quick burst out the front door, then. After Grat felt the full weight of the grain sack, he told Carpenter and Ball to carry it to the street door. But they did not get far. There were so many bullets streaming through the Condon Bank windows that the robbers and the employees retreated and joined together behind the counter. The customers, still facedown on the floor, were no doubt reciting every prayer they had ever memorized and probably inventing some new ones.

Bob and Emmett, at least, were not trapped inside a building.

---

* Years later, Emmett confided about the Wells boy that he "is now one of the most prominent attorneys in Washington, D.C., and a good friend of mine."

With a new hope that the other gang members had already reached the horses, the brothers began working their way west on Eighth Street. When they reached the intersection with Union Street, Bob spotted George Cubine. The thirty-six-year-old boot shop employee, carrying a Winchester, was standing in the doorway of the Rammels' drugstore, with a southern view of the First National Bank. Bob and Emmett took aim and fired their rifles.* Of the four shots, one hit the plate glass window of the shop while three hit Cubine—one in the ankle, one in the thigh, and one through his heart, killing him instantly.

Then Charles Brown made a poor decision. The shoemaker, who was old enough to have fought in the Civil War, saw Cubine fall next to him. Brown bent to pick up the dead man's rifle. When he swung it toward the Dalton brothers, their Winchesters fired four more times, striking Brown. He fell beside Cubine. Elliott tells us that the "brave old veteran . . . lived three hours in dreadful agony, and then peacefully passed away."

The brothers did not pause to consider their handiwork. Bob and Emmett completed their run across the intersection of Eighth and Union and started up the steps to the raised sidewalk at the corner. They had to feel by now that every armed man in Coffeyville was after them. Reaching the horses was the only way to get out alive.

Bullets continued to fly fast and furious inside the Condon Bank. One of them struck Broadwell, who, like Power had done minutes earlier, cried out that he could no longer use his shooting arm. That forced Grat to make a decision. He ordered the employees to join the customers lying on the floor. He then announced to Power and Broadwell that it was time to leave.

They found a side door and used it to make a mad dash out of the bank and across Walnut Street. Their immediate destination

---

* Emmett would unconvincingly claim in his memoirs that he did not fire a shot at anyone at any time that day.

was the alley where they had hitched their horses. To discourage any interference, Grat fired off a couple of shots. This did not do much good, because the three thieves were suddenly caught in a cross fire between the shooters in front of Boswell's and those at Isham's. The interior of that hardware store was by now stained with the blood of the wounded.

Bob and Emmett were giving the three other members of the gang what covering fire they could, but it must have felt like spitting into a strong wind. Still, a bullet was about to locate another Coffeyville citizen.

After the two Dalton brothers had exited the First National Bank, Thomas Ayers had hurried to Isham's and gotten a Winchester. He now stood with it at the shop's northeast door. His initiative would cost him dearly.

Spotting Ayers some seventy-five yards away, Bob Dalton stopped, aimed his Winchester, and squeezed the trigger. The bullet found the cashier's face, entering right below the left eye and exiting at the base of his skull. Miraculously, he survived—thanks in no small measure to the quick thinking of George Picker, an English-born mason. Without hesitating, he applied a thumb to the entrance wound to stop the spray of blood. Ayers would survive but be paralyzed.

Just then, Grat, Power, and Broadwell reached the alley opening. Before going farther, Grat and Broadwell fired at least nine shots into Isham's. Then the three men were on their way again.

But during the fusillade of fire, Grat and the already wounded Power had been hit, apparently more than once, because dust was seen to be flying off their clothes. They were not knocked down, but they were staggering as they got deep enough into the alley to be clear of the shooters at Boswell's. But the men at Isham's could still see them, and they poured it on. "The town echoed with the ceaseless hammer of the rifle fire," writes Robert Barr Smith, "and above the roar rose the screams of wounded horses, thrashing wildly, dying."

Broadwell was responsible for two of the horses. Because their plunging disturbed his aim, he shot the two horses hitched to the oil wagon.

Power sought the shelter of a doorway, but it was not enough. He frantically tried to open the shop's rear door, but it would not budge.

Knowing he was still too exposed, Power began to run down the alley, hoping his horse was where he had left it. It was, and Power was closing in on it when yet another bullet hit him, this time in the back. Seconds later, Elliott informs, Power "fell dead at the feet of the animal that had carried him on his errand of robbery."

That he would not be the last of the Dalton Gang to die is why, to this day in Coffeyville, the corridor leading to where the outlaws' horses were hitched is known as "Death Alley."

CHAPTER 28

"DEATH ALLEY"

The four fleeing members of the Dalton gang were probably unaware of what direction they were going—all that mattered was that it was toward the fence where they had left the horses. But in Grat's case, he was heading west down the alley. Here the oil tank, anchored by the dead horses, gave him some respite, because it shielded him from the cascade of bullets coming from Isham's.

Grat was able to reach a stable on the south side of the alley, two hundred feet from Walnut Street, still out of sight of the relentless shooters. He paused there to fire his Winchester. He was not shooting at anyone in particular; most likely, Grat was furious and his rifle represented that.

At this time, three men were on the south side of the plaza, determined to intercept the bandits before they could reach their horses, and they began walking west on Ninth Street. One man was Carey Seaman, a barber; another was John Kloehr, the livery owner; and the third was Charles Connelly, the city marshal. The latter, realizing he was still unarmed, peeled off to hurry into Swisher Brothers Machine Shop. Connelly borrowed a rifle from the proprietor and ran back out.

The marshal's bravery in going after the outlaws cost him his life. Connelly moved quickly through a vacant lot on the north side of Ninth Street. Thanks to an opening in the fence there, he was able to enter the alley. With luck, he would surprise the gang members.

But the only luck he had was bad. Connelly looked west, where the gang's horses were. He was unaware that Grat was standing some twenty feet behind him. Now he had a target to shoot at. Without giving the marshal a warning, Grat lifted his Winchester and fired. The .38–56 bullet struck Connelly in the back of the head, and he died as he fell.

There were now five men dead or on their way to it in Coffeyville.

It did not take long before there was a sixth. By this time, Kloehr had also entered the alley. Grat had walked past the marshal's body to finally get to the horses—where he hoped his brothers were, and maybe Broadwell too.

"Here he stood for a few moments," reported Elliott, "waiting for Bob and Emmett to join him, or else because he was unable to go any farther. Here he fired several wild shots from where he stood."

When Grat paused, he must have heard or sensed motion behind him. He turned and lifted his Winchester again. But Kloehr did not hesitate. His rifle blazed first, and the .44–40 bullet entered Grat's throat and broke his neck. As he had done to Connelly, Grat Dalton was dead by the time he hit the ground.

The wounded Broadwell had not yet made it to the horses . . . but he was close. He found some safety in the yard of the Long-Bell Lumber Company and looked for someone to shoot who might try to prevent him from reaching the horses. Suddenly, though, it was quiet, or at least only a few random shots were heard. Seeing this as an opportunity, Broadwell hustled out of his hiding spot and became the first member of the gang to get to his horse.

And he became the third member of the gang to die. As Broadwell began to ride away, gaining twenty feet and some confidence, Kloehr and Seaman jumped out. The combination of the bullet from the livery owner's rifle and a blast from the barber's shotgun mortally wounded the outlaw. Even while blood spurted from his mouth, Broadwell somehow managed to continue riding, reeling in the saddle, and was soon out of sight.

However, minutes later, his body was found on the side of the road a half mile west of Coffeyville.

During all this in "Death Alley," Bob and Emmett had been running south from Eighth Street through a different alley. Their prospects, they thought, had brightened after not encountering anyone and the citizens' firepower being directed elsewhere. They did spot a man climbing out the back window of the Slosson & Co. drugstore some thirty feet away, and he was armed with a pistol. Bob fired off a shot. It was a rare miss: The bullet hit the window, smashing it instead of the man, F. D. Benson, who quickly climbed back in and would later tell everyone about his narrow escape.

"Just how many shots were fired in that battle I do not know," Emmett wrote. "It seemed to me like one wild roar. From all parts of the city came a continuous popping, directed to no place in particular but adding to the general din."

At the intersection of the two alleys, Bob stepped out. He looked up to scan the rooftops. If no one was up there firing down at them, they might now have a clear path to the horses. And if they got away, they would at least have the $21,000 in the grain sack that was clutched in Emmett's hand.

Bob was apparently unaware that he had made himself visible to the shooters in Isham's store. According to Elliott, "As he did so, the men at Isham's took deliberate aim from their positions in the store and fired at him. The notorious leader of the Dalton gang evidently received a severe if not fatal wound at this time. He staggered across the alley and sat down on a pile of dressed curbstones near the city jail. Still true to his desperate nature, he kept his rifle in action and fired several shots from where he was sitting. His aim, though, was unsteady and the bullets went wild. While sitting on the rocks"—which, Elliott noted, were covered with blood—"he espied John Kloehr on the inside of the fence near Slosson's store."

While Kloehr's subsequently published newspaper account contains some falsifications—or more kindly, inaccuracies—he was right to point out that he and Bob Dalton knew each other from when they had competed in sharpshooting matches. Kloehr contended that when Bob noticed him, he exclaimed, "Hell, there's Kloehr. I hate to do it but he's got to fall."

The outlaw tried to raise his rifle, but he was by then too weak from the loss of blood, and he managed only a wild shot. Then he tried again, even managing to stand and stagger a few steps.

According to Kloehr's colorful account, "For a moment I was transfixed, watching his face intently as the bird watches the snake about to seize it. Then instinctively my own rifle came to my shoulder. I fired just as Bob pulled the trigger. His bullet went wild, striking the side of the alley, taking a tangent course and entering my barn, where it demolished a buggy wheel."

The bullet from Kloehr's rifle was true, striking Bob in the chest. A moment later, he crumpled to the ground.

Meanwhile, his younger brother had separated from Bob and miraculously was still unhurt. Emmett had kept running until he attempted to mount his horse . . . and that made him an easy target. A half dozen rifles were then fired in his direction as he undertook to get into the saddle. The two intervening horses belonging to Bob Dalton and Bill Power were killed by some of the shots intended for Emmett.

Somehow, Emmett succeeded in getting into the saddle, but not until he had received a shot through the right arm and another through the left hip and groin. "There was no pain, just a numbness that seemed particularly aggravating as I tried to untie my horse. I finally got the rope loosened and swung up. The dull pop, pop, bang, bang, was the only sound I heard as I started to ride away."

During all this time, Emmett had clung to the sack containing the money he and Bob had stolen from the First National Bank. Now his only chance to survive was to ride and ride fast. But glancing around, he saw his brother on the ground in the alley. He chose what had to be almost certain death. "Whatever his other failings might have been, Emmett Dalton was long on courage," writes Robert Barr Smith.

As Emmett recalled, "Right into the face of that rain of lead I rode. How I escaped is something no one can explain. Not a single bullet touched me. Up to where Bob was, I went. I saw at a glance he was not dead. There was a convulsive shiver as he opened his eyes and muttered, 'Good-bye, Emmett. Don't surrender; die game.'"*

It was at that moment that Bob Dalton died. Even so, Emmett would not abandon his brother. He leaned down and kept attempting to clutch Bob's hand and haul him up atop his horse. But he was out of time and luck. Coming up behind him was Carey Seaman, who emptied both barrels of his shotgun.

Emmett recalled that "suddenly above all the other noises came a loud detonation. Then I felt myself falling. I had been shot again with buck-shot. I fought back the feeling. I was there to save Bob. Maybe I was just getting sleepy. But the numbness was growing and, try as I did, I was unable to keep from slipping to the ground. Finally I gave up and with a loud thud I fell alongside of Bob."

"The youthful desperado dropped from his horse and the last of the Dalton gang was helpless," Elliott reported. "In falling, the sack containing the twenty thousand dollars he had periled his soul and body to get went down with him, and he landed at the feet of his brother."

---

* David Stewart Elliott recorded that Bob's final words were, "It's no use," but if Bob did indeed say anything at all, Emmett was the only person who could have heard him.

For Emmett, "then came the darkness and quiet. The popping of guns died away. The brightness of the sun ceased and all was still. I sank back on the ground."

There was silence for a few seconds. Then a man cried out, "They're all down!"

CHAPTER 29

A GHASTLY SCENE

A hush fell with the last shotgun blast," writes Lue Diver Barndollar. "The entire gunfight had lasted less than fifteen minutes, but bodies, dead horses, and smoking rifles seemed to be everywhere. Then some of the defending citizens hurried to those who had fallen."

According to David Stewart Elliott, "The scene that was presented in the 'alley of death' was ghastly beyond human conception."

As Bob's body was searched, they found that the pistol in his belt had not been fired but his Winchester had been emptied. Two more pistols were found, one in his vest pocket and one in his boot.*

Grat's two revolvers had not been fired either. Searchers found the cash stuffed inside his vest and pockets. Somehow, despite all the frantic activity, the fake hair was still stuck to his face.

Bill Power's Winchester was also empty. No one knew who he was, as he was unrecognized and he was not carrying any identification.

To the astonishment of those who first hurried to him, despite suffering twenty-three bullet and pellet wounds, Emmett Dalton

---

* In September 2021, one of Bob's pistols, a black-powder Colt single-action Army revolver, was sold at auction for $322,000.

was still alive. While some Coffeyville residents poured into the alley and surrounded the bodies there, Emmett responded to the command to hold up his hands by raising one arm and, according to Elliott, "making a pathetic appeal for mercy." The editor wrote that he was the first man to reach the youngest Dalton and he took his two handguns, which also had not been fired. Another citizen, H. W. Read, picked up the grain sack and walked away, toward the First National Bank.

At first, Emmett's appeal for mercy was rejected. Instead, several men suggested that the surviving outlaw be finished off. A man ran up carrying a rope. The sight of it, Barndollar wrote, "aroused the crowd, and soon there were many who wanted to lynch Emmett." Protesting this was the first physician on the scene, Walter Wells, whose reasoning was that the young bandit was so badly wounded they would be hanging a dead man.

Here some mercy was offered. Dr. Wells prevailed, and he had Emmett, by now in great pain, lifted up and carried to the physician's office above Slosson's drugstore. The doctor counted as he removed each of the bullets and pellets in Emmett's writhing body. It was another miracle that the outlaw survived the procedure. He was then lifted up and carried again, this time to the Farmer's Home Boarding House. Though its occupant was hovering near death, several men guarded the room.

Elsewhere, Elliott reported, "excited and indignant men, weeping women and screaming children thronged the Plaza and crowded the alley in which the last scenes of the fight had taken place. A few cool-headed citizens kept disorder from ensuing. [T]he city sat down in sackcloth and ashes to mourn for the heroic men who had given their lives."

He added: "The country is rid of the desperate gang, but the riddance cost Coffeyville some of its most precious blood."

Was even more blood about to be spilled? Rumors ran rampant that there would be a new raid on Coffeyville, this one not to steal money but to avenge the shot-to-pieces Daltons and their accomplices. "Coffeyville citizens were worrying about rebuttal from outlaws who might have worked with the Dalton gang," notes Barndollar. A message given to the grieving mother of Lucius Baldwin assured her, "We have been warned of another raid by the Dalton gang and the people are armed and try to be ready. There are over fifty Winchesters in readiness [but] I am frightened all the time."*

WHILE SOME CITIZENS would be kept busy brandishing rifles, shotguns, and revolvers in anticipation of a vengeance raid, others participated in a bizarre yet commonplace ritual. On the south side of Death Alley, a rack for loose hay was pressed against a stable. The Long-Bell Lumber Company donated boards, which were propped against the rack. The bodies of Bob and Grat Dalton and Bill Power were propped on the boards. Dick Broadwell's would soon join them.

It was noted that some articles of the dead outlaws' clothing were missing. When citizens had first crowded into the alley, a few had torn off pieces to keep as souvenirs. Later, after a sufficient amount of ogling and picture-taking, the boards bearing the bodies were taken to the city jail, which became an impromptu morgue.†

Some people were in shock over not just this grisly scene but what had just happened on what had been a typical, quiet morning in early October. It still seemed unreal, a collective dream, or nightmare. Yet, according to Elliott, "While the people of Coffeyville wiped out the outlaw gang at a terrible cost of valuable lives, they insured their city against any more such visitations during the lifetime of the present

---

* A week after the shoot-out, John Kloehr would receive a note that informed, "I take the time to tell the citizens of Coffeyville that all of the gang ain't dead yet by a damn sight, and we will come and see you." It concluded: "[Y]our time will soon come when you will go into the grave and pass in your checks. So take warning."
† Even more bizarre, for at least a couple of photographs, the bodies of Bob and Grat were displayed standing up next to several local men.

generation, and conferred a service upon the state and upon society by demonstrating how risky and unprofitable such raids are likely to prove."

Elliott may have had a different kind of profit in mind. At some point, he had helped himself to Emmett's guns, probably realizing that they would be especially valuable souvenirs. Two months later, however, under the threat of legal action by the Dalton family, the editor handed the guns over to the constable, defiantly contending that Emmett had "surrendered" the guns to him while lying in Death Alley.*

Word of the bullet-riddled gun battle spread quickly beyond the confines of the city. In fact, during the shoot-out itself, telegrams had been sent out stating that the Dalton Gang was attacking Coffeyville and to send help. A train from Parsons carrying fifty armed men collected by the Katy line had taken less than forty minutes to travel the forty-two miles. Other telegrams arrived offering assistance, but by then, as the fifty men learned when they arrived, the battle was over. Still, they fanned out, keeping their eyes peeled for approaching riders.

Elliott found himself especially busy in addition to gun collecting. In the two hours after the last shot was fired, he received seventeen telegrams from other newspapers requesting information. One of them was from as far away as *The New York Herald.* The Coffeyville editor began to write a detailed account for *The Daily Journal,* which would also be a primary source for other news outlets, such as the next day's edition of *The Galveston Daily News*:

---

* With some evident glee, *The Independence Reporter,* after accusing the editor of outright theft, intoned, "We do not believe that [the] ravings of D. Stewart Elliott represent the feelings of the citizens of Coffeyville, and the sooner they have their wind shut off the better."

The Daltons Wiped Out

A BLOODY DAY AT COFFEYVILLE FOR BOTH SIDES

The Place Strewed With Corpses of Robbers, Officers
and Citizens—The Plot and the Battle Described.

COFFEYVILLE, Kan., Oct. 5.—The Dalton gang has
been exterminated—wiped off the face of the earth. They
were to-day shot down, but not until four citizens of this
place yielded up their lives in the work of extermination.
Six of the gang rode into town this morning and robbed
two banks. The raid became known to the officers of the
law, and when the bandits attempted to escape they were
attacked by the marshal's posse. In the battle which ensued four of the desperadoes were killed outright, and one
so fatally wounded that he has since died. The other escaped but is being hotly pursued.[*]

Other topics which attracted universal comment were
the fulfillment of a prophesy that the Daltons would "die
with their boots on," the peculiar fate which had decreed
that they should die by the hands of their old friends in
the vicinity of the place of their birth, and the excellent
marksmanship of Liveryman Spears, who with three
shots sent death to as many bandits.

A TALK WITH EMMETT DALTON

Late tonight an Associated Press representative had a
talk with Emmett Dalton. He declared the stories of hidden treasures all nonsense. "If there had been a hidden

---

* It is a curious juxtaposition that the newspaper declared Emmett dead and then
printed an interview with him—but probably one eagerly eaten up by readers. Also,
the "other escaped" bandit refers to the rumor that would persist for decades that
there was a sixth member of the Dalton Gang involved in the raid, but he had arrived too late to participate and had remained on the outskirts of Coffeyville during
the gun battle. The candidate most often cited was Bill Dalton or Bill Doolin. However, the "sixth man" myth has been debunked repeatedly.

treasure," he said, "we would all be alive today. It was because we were all broke that we planned the Coffeyville raid. We were being hard pressed by the officers down in the Territory, and Bob decided that we would have to get out of the country. He planned the robbery about two weeks ago while we were camped in the Osage country. We tried to persuade him not to do the job then. He called us cowards. That settled it. We started."

It was with great difficulty the bandit told the story, as he was suffering terribly from wounds in the side. The physician says he cannot possibly survive.

With Emmett not expected to live, it might become moot, but the legal machine began to turn its wheels. On the next day, Thursday, October 6, the city's justice of the peace, C. L. Long, approved two complaints. One charged Emmett with the murder of Lucius Baldwin, and the other was for the murder of George Cubine. With Marshal Connelly dead, it fell to William Kime, the Coffeyville constable, to go to Dr. Wells's office and arrest the remaining Dalton Gang member. A hearing on the charges was scheduled.

"Then the city went into mourning over the death of Marshal Connelly, George Cubine, Charley Brown and Lucius Baldwin," reports David Stewart Elliott. "Stalwart men wept great tears of grief, whilst the women and children cried and wrung their hands in agony."

And, inevitably, there would be funerals. Cubine was put into the ground first, at the Elmwood Cemetery. He left behind a wife and seven-year-old son. Mrs. Cubine had already suffered misery enough, with two children having died in infancy.

After the one night in jail, the bodies of the Dalton Gang had been transferred to the building owned by Lang and Lape Undertakers. Grat and Bob Dalton and Bill Power were placed in black-varnished coffins, and the Dalton brothers were buried in the Elmwood Cemetery soon after the Cubine funeral.

The next day was Friday. During it, Dick Broadwell's brother and brother-in-law—Lue Barndollar notes that "both [were] from good families in Hutchinson"—arrived in Coffeyville. In anticipation of bringing him back to Hutchinson, Broadwell's body was placed in a sealed can. When no one showed up or even inquired about Bill Power, he was buried next to Grat and Bob.

Friday was a busy day. It included the burial of the forty-six-year-old Charles Connelly, at a cemetery in Independence. The marshal left behind a son and daughter from his first marriage and a widow and daughter from his second.* There was also a memorial service for Lucius Baldwin in Burlington. The twenty-three-year-old's only survivor was his mother.†

And Friday also included the arrival of a grieving Adeline Dalton, accompanied by two sons, Ben and Bill, and a daughter, Eva Whipple. For the former, it had been a trip full of sorrow from Kingfisher. The only silver lining was that at least one son, still only twenty-one years old, had survived. That he had made it to Friday under Dr. Wells's care was encouraging.

The shoot-out had not been good for the dead and wounded (and a handful of horses), but it turned out to be a boon for some local businesses. According to Barndollar, "At least 2,000 people had visited Coffeyville by Friday evening. During the next few days, trains brought hundreds more visitors. Souvenir hunters cut portions from the manes and tails of the Dalton horses and cut all the strings from their saddles."

Incredibly, there were those expressing sympathy for Emmett and praising his brave struggle to live. And there were even some who excused his actions. A Kansas congressman, Jeremiah "Sockless Jerry"

---

* Adding poignancy to the marshal's death was that it was known locally that Connelly, a teacher by profession, was about to turn in his badge to become principal of the West Side School in Coffeyville.
† The fifty-nine-year-old Charles Brown would be buried in Coffeyville on Saturday. In his obituary, it was stated that he left behind "an aged widow in dependent circumstances."

Simpson, even opined in a letter to *The Kansas City Journal,* "The Dalton Boys were no worse than the national bankers and thousands of others who are engaged in pretended lawful pursuits, while really they are robbing the people. They are to be no more condemned for their acts than the bankers they robbed."*

Bob Dalton may not have achieved his goal of outdoing his Younger relations in bank robbing, but to those who agreed with Sockless Jerry, the Dalton Gang had indeed achieved Robin Hood status.

Bill Dalton remained in Coffeyville after his mother, brother, and sister left. He was more a cranky presence than a mourning one, telling everyone who would listen—with justification—that souvenir hunters had taken all the personal possessions that his brothers had on them and "passed them around or sold like tokens from a county fair." Bill also asserted that Emmett had nine hundred dollars on him when he came to Coffeyville and it was now missing. Few people paid him any mind other than to wonder if he had had anything to do with planning the raid with his brothers.

There was another arrival of a person of some note in Coffeyville that week: Heck Thomas. Bob Dalton had been right that their "nemesis," as Emmett labeled him, and his posse were hot on their trail. On that previous Monday, October 3, the deputy marshal, Fred Dodge, and their men found where the Daltons had camped soon after the outlaws had ridden out to the north. Then on Tuesday, they located a second camp. Another day or two and the lawmen would likely have caught up.

They still had a job to do in Coffeyville. Wells Fargo wanted Heck and Dodge to "make proof" that the Daltons were indeed dead, so the lawmen hopped the train there. With dozens of witnesses, there

---

* In his 1889 campaign, Simpson had run against James R. Hallowell, a Republican attorney who Simpson derided as a wearer of "fine silk hosiery." Hallowell responded by stating that fine hosiery was better than being sockless. The derisive nickname stuck, but Simpson won the election and would serve three terms in the House of Representatives.

was no doubt who had been killed when and how. Heck would later receive a letter from Wells Fargo, which included a check for $1,500. While Heck did not wind up arresting or killing the gang, Wells Fargo officials "feel that your work more than anything brought about the extermination of this gang."

Heck was ready to deposit the check and close this chapter. It probably never occurred to him that he—and Chris Madsen and Bill Tilghman—would have more work to do because the gang had not been completely "exterminated."

The explosion of violence in the small southeast Kansas city became national news, with some newspapers not just praising the Coffeyville defenders but seeing a heroic example. "What this country needs is a multiplication of Coffeyvilles," blustered *The Washington Post*. "Towns of that caliber should be distributed freely all over this glorious and happy land. Wherever robbers, murderers, incendiaries, and bandits congregate, some new Coffeyville should spring up in the night, populated by Browns, Connellys, Kloehrs, Baldwins and Cubines, and filled with a spirit of emulation in marksmanship. No county in any State should be without its Coffeyville."

Emmett, meanwhile, remained in the Farmer's Home room for six days, not only to recover from what should have been fatal wounds but the Montgomery County sheriff, John Callahan, feared the young bandit would be lynched if moved too soon to Independence. Finally, on October 11, lying on a cot, Emmett was transported the twenty-two miles north to the county courthouse. Elliott commented, "He recovered with the quick elasticity of youth."

"Although I never fired a shot," Emmett continued to claim in *Beyond the Law*, he was officially charged with the murders of George Cubine and Lucius Baldwin as well as robbing the First National Bank. Attorney Joe Fritch represented him.

The deal Emmett finally agreed to was to plead guilty to a second-degree murder charge in the killing of Cubine for which he would receive a sentence of between fifteen and twenty years. "I flatly refused, knowing that I had actually killed no one and they had no proof of it." But he was finally pressured into agreeing rather than take his chances in a trial.

On the following March 8, 1893, Emmett, hobbling on crutches to stand before the judge, pleaded as he had agreed to do. The court imposed a sentence of ninety-nine years. He had been betrayed by the legal system. "Had I not been well balanced, and knew the self-ishness, shams and deceits of human nature, there, that day, I would have been born an anarchist," he later recorded.

An hour later, he was on a train taking him to the state prison in Lansing. Upon arrival, Emmett was greeted by the deputy warden, John Higgins, who suggested the new inmate "try to make the best of it." Then, after a bath, "I was taken to a cell where I was doomed to sleep for fourteen years, five months, and twenty-eight days."

During that time, he would learn about the violent death of an-other outlaw brother. For Bill, Coffeyville was not the end of the Dalton Gang but a fresh beginning.

ACT V

THE DESPERADOES

CHAPTER 30

BROKEN BROTHER

The events in Coffeyville on that October morning that included the deaths of his brothers and the wounding and arrest of Emmett may well have signaled the end of an era, but for Bill Dalton, they were the inspiration to completely cross over the line to being an outlaw. Plus, he had few options: As Littleton Dalton reflected, "[Bill] never broke with the boys, but they sure broke him. When Bob and Emmett and Grat finally finished with him he was a bum; his stock and farming equipment were gone, he was broke."

Or possibly, Bill just could not escape being a Dalton who lived a life outside the law. Years later, Sheriff Eugene Kay commented, "Although Bill occupied the respectable position of family man, politician, and rancher, he kept all doors open all the time and I had the feeling that he might disappear through any of them, any time. Bill was a great actor. He posed until the last as a harmless wag and clown, but there was more than that under the surface."

Before giving serious thought to forming a new gang, Bill might have done well to visit his brother Emmett and learn about the unpleasant rigors of prison life. Such knowledge might have persuaded

Bill, before it was too late, to not take up an occupation that had become more hazardous than ever.

"The prison cells are an abomination," Emmett would recall. His new home was four-and-a-half by eight-and-a-half feet with one dim light and a small air hole. There was, of course, in 1893, nothing in the way of climate control, so his cell was quite cold in the Kansas winters and quite hot in the summers. Even though in such an environment "more insanity is produced than anywhere else," Emmett vowed to be a model inmate. He traded in the roaming outlaw life for working in the prison's tailor shop. He learned how to cut and fit men's clothes so well that, he boasted, four months after becoming an inmate, "I took charge of the shop and worked from twenty-five to forty men for fourteen years."

But probably nothing would have deterred a grieving and bitter Bill. As with bold bandits before him, like Jesse James, he not only felt aggrieved, he enjoyed the effect the Dalton notoriety could have on people. Being feared was intoxicating. Most likely, it was Bill who had written the threatening letter to Coffeyville signed "Dalton Gang." And he had to be aware of the telegram—or, at least, its impact—sent by a railroad agent at the Wharton station to Fred Dodge.

According to this missive, as many as forty white men and "half-breeds under the command of one of the survivors of the Dalton gang" were riding hard, and when they arrived, "no mercy would be given" to Coffeyville. Once this information was passed along, it was time for the town to load up their rifles again.

Telegrams were sent to communities as far away as Kansas City to request help, and the Coffeyville railroad station was turned into a fortress manned by rotating squads of men with Winchesters and shotguns. "The town was blacked out," reports Robert Barr Smith, "and armed citizens mounted guard at bridges and other strategic spots. The citizens also built an enormous bonfire in the plaza, to be touched off to provide shooting light if the raiders threatened the town after dark. Then the people loaded their weapons and waited, tense and alert."

Hours went by, then days. The impromptu Coffeyville militia became less tense and alert. Their ears pricked up again, though, on October 14 when the news arrived that the night before in Caney, Kansas, eighteen miles away, a train had been robbed. The report contended that the four bandits were Bill Doolin, Bitter Creek Newcomb, Bill Dalton, and a man who might be named Yantis.* There was relief that Coffeyville had apparently been spared, but a new gang on the prowl was not at all consoling.

Where did this gang come from all of a sudden? After being left out of the plans for the Coffeyville raid, Doolin, Newcomb, and Charley Pierce had not been idle. By accident or design, the trio was about seventy-five miles northeast of Kingfisher conducting robberies. There, they threw in with Henry Starr, who was related to Sam Starr, the husband of Belle Starr. Henry was busy carrying on the family's outlaw tradition, and despite that occupation, he would have a surprisingly long life.

Born in 1873, Henry Starr had grown up in the Indian Territory. Inevitably, as a boy, he encountered gangs of cutthroats riding along the back roads and he became enamored of them. Still, he stayed at home on the farm until he was twenty-three, when his father passed away and his mother took up with a man Henry did not like. It was time to find a life other than that of a farmer. Starr was working as a cowboy on a ranch when he was arrested for the first time, for selling whiskey in the territory. Somehow, this encouraged him to make the leap to robbing banks.

It was in the months after the Coffeyville raid and into 1893

---

* There was indeed a farmer-turned-bandit in the area known as Ol' Yantis, but it was also possible that this fourth thief was Charley Pierce.

that Doolin, Newcomb, and Pierce rode with Starr, and it was that year when he was tracked down and arrested for murder. Judge Isaac Parker presided over the trial, and after the verdict of guilty, he sentenced Starr to die by hanging. The fastidious Mr. Maledon awaited him at the scaffold. But after a series of appeals, the sentence was reduced. Not long after, for some head-scratcher of a reason, Starr received a presidential pardon and was released from prison.

Understandably unimpressed with the legal system, Starr resumed his outlaw ways. He formed a new gang and led it on a crime spree in Arkansas. A reward of $5,000 for his capture went unpaid for many years. It was not until 1915 that Starr was once more in prison, this time in Arizona. While there, he composed an autobiography that was titled *Thrilling Events, Life of Henry Starr*. Whatever its literary merits, the parole board must have liked the book, because Starr was again released. In 1919, he went from writer to actor, portraying himself in the film *A Debtor to the Law*.

But Starr's star was not to shine in Hollywood. Two years later, the forty-seven-year-old was back to robbing banks in Arkansas. In one of them, in Harrison, he was shot by the bank president, W. J. Myers, and later died of his wounds.

In between jobs with Starr, Doolin and his two criminal companions traveled to Kingfisher to console Adeline Dalton on the death of two of her sons. As it happened, Bill was there, as was Lit, from California. Doolin suggested that Bill and Lit join forces with him, Pierce, and Newcomb and avenge the deaths of Grat and Bob. Lit wanted nothing to do with this scheme, but Bill was all for it.

As Lit Dalton later told Frank Latta, "I talked to Mason and tried to get him to go back to California with me. I also put Mother on his trail and she did all she could toward the same end. Mason would listen to us and laugh and tell us he wouldn't have anything to do with any outlaw gang. I knew better. But I had to come back to California without him."

Thus was born what became known as the Doolin-Dalton Gang.*
With various comings and goings, the gang would include eleven
men. In addition to Bill Doolin, Bill Dalton, Bitter Creek Newcomb, and Charley Pierce, there was William "Tulsa Jack" Blake,
Dan "Dynamite Dick" Clifton, "Arkansas Tom" Jones, William "Little Bill" Raidler, George "Red Buck" Waightman, Richard "Little
Dick" West, and the former farmer Ol' Yantis, who apparently was
not worth a colorful nickname. These bandits caused lots of havoc
but did not have lasting power—only two of them survived into the
twentieth century, and all died in gun battles with lawmen.

Ol' Yantis should have stayed put behind a plow because he
had only a brief tenure with the new gang. One afternoon, he and
Doolin and Newcomb robbed a bank in Spearville, Kansas. With
the $1,700 taken, the trio rode south toward the Oklahoma border.
Once across, they thought they were safe and they split up.

Yantis was on his way to the home of a sister, Mrs. Hugh McGinn,
when his horse gave out. He stole another one, killing a farmer for
it, then rode on, arriving at his sister's house. He was unaware that
a posse was on his trail and gaining on him. It was led by Chalkley
Beeson.

The forty-five-year-old had once been the co-owner of the famous
Long Branch Saloon in Dodge City when Wyatt Earp and Bat Masterson were still lawmen there. In 1884, he had formed the Dodge
City Cowboy Band. The group was well received wherever it played.
Its members cut dashing figures in full "cowboy" regalia—enormous
white Stetsons, blue flannel shirts, and boots festooned with orna-
mental spurs. Their fame finally spread far enough that they were
featured performers in the March 4, 1889, inaugural parade of President Benjamin Harrison. This was the band's finest hour, but soon

---

* The gang members were also sometimes referred to as the Oklahoma Long Riders
because of the long dusters that they wore.

after their return to Dodge City, Beeson sold the ownership of the band to a man from Colorado for $750.

Now Beeson was the sheriff of Ford County in Kansas, and he was accompanied by three Oklahoma peace officers. Acting on a tip, they arrived at the McGinn house and confronted Yantis. Unwisely, the thief grabbed a pistol from a shoulder holster and squeezed the trigger. The four lawmen fired faster and true, perforating the former farmer with bullets. He died shortly after the shoot-out.

Beeson and his comrades were not done with him, however. After Yantis was laid out in a coffin, a photo was taken and given to Deputy Marshal Chris Madsen in Guthrie. This allowed the lawmen to collect the $450 that had been offered for the capture or death of any of the bank robbers.[*]

As Eugenia Moore had been to the Dalton Gang, there was for a short time a female member of the Doolin-Dalton Gang. Actually, there were two of them, who were known as Cattle Annie and Little Breeches.[†]

According to Nancy B. Samuelson, Anna Emmaline McDoulet, who became known as "Cattle Annie," and her sidekick, "Little Breeches," whose real name was Jennie Stevenson Midkiff, were spies for the Doolin-Dalton Gang and later with Doolin's smaller circle. Born in Kansas on November 29, 1882, Anna was the daughter of J. C. McDoulet, who served as a justice of the peace in Red Rock, Indian Territory, as well as an attorney for Indians living nearby.

---

[*] Subsequently, the McGinn family filed a $20,000 lawsuit for damages to their property caused by the officers' bullets that did not wind up in Ol' Yantis. The suit was dismissed because of a technicality, then after it was refiled, all the paperwork and supposed evidence was lost when the courthouse in Stillwater burned down.

[†] The movie version based on the novel *Cattle Annie and Little Britches* by Robert Ward and starring Amanda Plummer and Diane Lane—with Burt Lancaster as Bill Doolin, Scott Glenn as Bill Dalton, and Rod Steiger as Bill Tilghman—is a highly fictionalized but entertaining ode to the last days of the Wild West.

For Anna, working in restaurants and as a domestic paled in comparison to dreams of freedom. Still an adolescent, she bought a pony and saddle, left home, and teamed up with her friend Jennie Midkiff to roam the territory. It would have been during this time that they were spies and lookouts for Bill Doolin and the other outlaws. Supposedly, both girls became crack shots with rifles, and they stole horses to earn their keep. To better blend in, the teenagers wore men's clothing and packed pistols on their hips.

They were living on the Otoe Reservation when they were arrested for selling liquor to Indians. Numerous reports attribute the girls' capture to deputy U.S. marshal Bill Tilghman, though newspapers at the time credited the arrests to Sheriff Frank Lake and deputy U.S. marshals Steve Burke and Frank Canton.

Next to nothing is known about the rest of Jennie Midkiff's life other than after being released from prison, she may have moved to Tulsa and married there. More is known about Anna's long and full life. After her release on April 18, 1898, she obtained a job, probably again as a domestic, with a Mrs. Mary Daniels, in Sherborn, Massachusetts. However, Anna was drawn back to Oklahoma, where she married Earl Frost. The couple lived in Perry and had two children. In October 1909, however, the couple divorced, probably because Anna had joined a Wild West show. Later she married Whitmore R. Roach, a general contractor, and they lived in Oklahoma City.

The former Cattle Annie lived out her life as a quiet, respectable bookkeeper. She was an active member of the American Legion Auxiliary and the Olivet Baptist Church. Anna McDoulet Frost Roach died on November 7, 1978, age ninety-five, and was buried in Rose Hill Burial Park in Oklahoma City.

The Doolin-Dalton Gang quickly gained a reputation as the dominant outlaw group in Oklahoma and southeast Kansas. They hit banks and trains and then vanished, and well into 1893, Yantis was the only casualty. Bill Dalton could always find a hideout in the

Kingfisher area, and the other gang members had their secure spots where lawmen were not welcome.

The summer of 1893 found the gang members in Ingalls, Oklahoma. One of them was Bill Doolin, and he was there because he had fallen in love—and this almost got him killed.

CHAPTER 31

LEAD FLIES IN INGALLS

For much of the year, Bill Doolin had not been a stranger in Ingalls, which was ten miles east of Stillwater. Nor were members of his gang. "It was known as their holdout," wrote Zoe Tilghman in her memoir about her husband. "Here they came openly. There was always some one to give warning if a marshal were approaching. Only a few miles distant were wild and unsettled parts of the Pawnee country [with] hills and timber along the Cimarron, where escape was easy."

Ingalls was one of the towns that sprang up overnight thanks to the April 1889 Land Rush. It was named for one of Kansas's U.S. senators, John J. Ingalls.* The following January, the new community was awarded its own post office, but the population would peak at only a paltry 150 citizens. A big reason for the lack of growth and prosperity was four years after its founding, it was the setting of a particularly deadly day for lawmen.

Edith Ellsworth was one of thirteen children sired by a Methodist preacher who had also served for a time as the postmaster of the new

---

* A second cousin of the senator was Charles Ingalls, whose daughter Laura Ingalls Wilder was author of the *Little House on the Prairie* series of books.

post office in Ingalls. She was working in a general store owned by her father as well as in the OK Hotel when, sometime in 1892, she met Bill Doolin. His biographer, Bailey Hanes, describes Edith as "tall and dark, with thin, prominent teeth, dark hair, and a wholesome complexion, but she was very plain in appearance. She had dark, penetrating eyes and moved with a decisive step—with the air of one who knew what she was about."

She was about to become Mrs. Doolin. His outlaw reputation was well known in the Ingalls area, of course, and it is unlikely that her minister father was thrilled when the two began courting. Probably to save the family embarrassment, when the two married on March 15, 1893—Edith's twentieth birthday—they did so by eloping, taking the train to Kingfisher. And when they returned, they told no one about the marriage and quietly rented a small house between the OK Hotel and Wagoner's Blacksmith Shop.

Also seeking some domestic bliss was Bitter Creek Newcomb. The object of his affections was a rather odd choice—Sadie Conley, the widow of John Conley, a deputy U.S. marshal who had been gunned down in a saloon in Cushing, Oklahoma. Apparently, Sadie did not hold Newcomb's occupation too much against him. In fact, as Zoe Tilghman indicated, Bitter Creek and the other gang members were at least tolerated in Ingalls. The inhabitants, especially saloon owners, were glad for their business, wherever the money came from.

Doolin did not let marriage get in the way of his chosen career. With his coleader, Bill Dalton, robberies were planned and committed. One involved stopping the Santa Fe Railroad's California Express just west of Cimarron, Kansas, in June. The messenger, a man named Whittlesey, had been wounded when the gang fired into the express car to persuade him to open it. After grabbing about $1,000, Doolin set up a cot and laid the wounded messenger on it, then he jumped on his horse and dashed off with the others. In Guthrie, Deputy Marshal Chris Madsen was assigned to pull together a posse and catch up to the bandits.

He and his "deputies"—who were actually Indian scouts—almost did. By figuring out where the bandits were going to enter Oklahoma and some hard riding, the posse was able to intercept Doolin and his fleeing comrades. Shots were exchanged, and a bullet fired by Madsen from a new .30–30 Winchester found Bill Doolin's right foot. He would later learn that the steel-jacketed bullet entered his heel and traveled to the ball of the foot, where it shattered the bone. For the rest of his days, Doolin would be in pain.

The gang members rode off in different directions, frustrating Madsen and his posse, who soon lost track of them as the sun set. Arkansas Tom Jones had stayed alongside the bleeding Bill Doolin and took him to the ranch of a familiar friend to bandits, Jim Riley. The wound was treated, but the next morning, the right foot was so swollen that the outlaws knew they had to get to the doctor in Ingalls. The lone physician there was away, not returning until the next day. That resulted in a painful night's stay at the OK Hotel. When the doctor was finally back in Ingalls, he removed pieces of shattered bone and the bullet, which Doolin kept in a pocket from then on. In an odd way, maybe he thought it would bring him good luck.

During the summer, the other gang members made their way to the friendly surroundings of Ingalls. Bill Dalton was the only one who did not spend nights there, as he preferred the farm of a friend just outside of town. During the day, writes Bailey Hanes, "All the men were heavily armed with Winchesters and Colts and were on guard at all times—and they generally traveled in pairs. Most of them boarded at the O.K. Hotel and played cards and did their drinking in old man Ransom's saloon."

The establishment did not put too much of a dent in their robbery earnings because whiskey "sold for a dime a shot, and if you wished, you could have a large glass of cold beer for the same price."*

---

* A common practice of Ransom and other bar owners with some sympathy for thirsty men was to keep a bottle with a funnel in it behind the bar. Into it were

This kind of life of raiding banks and trains and almost flaunting their ill-gotten gains in Ingalls was not sustainable. The law-enforcement authorities were catching heat from the more upstanding citizens in Oklahoma. Finally, the man who vowed to end the crime spree of the Doolin-Dalton Gang—and with it, put an end to what represented the last lawless remnants of the Wild West—was Evett Dumas Nix.

Nix was the new U.S. marshal in charge. He was born in September 1861, in Kentucky. With an uncle serving as county sheriff and father as a deputy sheriff, becoming a peace officer was almost ordained. However, it took Nix a while to get to it. He first worked in his father's factory, then operated a grocery, hardware, and furniture business in Coldwater. Moving to Paducah, he became a traveling sales representative. In 1885, he married Ellen Felts, who had been a childhood sweetheart.

Nix was one of the many men who participated in the Oklahoma Land Rush of April 1889. He and his wife settled in the instantly formed Guthrie, where he became a prosperous businessman. He was viewed as a bright and ambitious young man, and he courted influential friends, including the rancher Oscar Halsell. These friends promoted Nix to the right people in law-enforcement circles, and when the position of U.S. marshal for the Oklahoma Territory opened up, the thirty-two-year-old Nix became the youngest one thus far appointed.*

Right off the bat, he believed the best duty he could perform was to kill, capture, or run off the way-too-many outlaws in Oklahoma. To that end, he assembled a formidable force of deputies,

---

poured the dregs of whiskey left behind in glasses used by paying customers. When a man down on his luck came in, he was given a drink on the house from the hidden bottle.

* Nix's tenure as U.S. marshal would come to an unhappy end. He was accused of mismanaging public funds, and an audit resulted in his dismissal from office in January 1896. Many historians believe that Nix was a victim of the ongoing inefficient—to say the least—fee system for payment of U.S. Marshals Service officers.

many of whom already had lawing experience. The force included Heck Thomas, Bill Tilghman, Madsen (who certainly wanted another shot at Doolin), and John Hixon. The latter was a forty-three-year-old Ohio native who had lived in Indiana before trying his luck in Oklahoma. Nix put him in charge of a special mission: Confront and capture the members of the Doolin-Dalton Gang in Ingalls.

Without delay, Hixon headed there. Officially, he was to serve a warrant for the murder of Marshal Charles Connelly in Coffeyville ten months earlier. Accompanied by the deputy marshals Thomas Hueston and Bill Masterson (one of Bat's brothers) and two dozen other deputies and Indian police officers, Hixon closed in on Ingalls. As the posse camped out beside a creek on the night of August 31, a young boy discovered them. They held him overnight, but at dawn, the boy snuck out and ran into Ingalls.

"The marshals are coming!" he announced as he rushed into Ransom's saloon.

The Doolin-Dalton Gang members getting an early start on a day of playing cards and drinking and smoking did not completely believe the youngster. There was always someone claiming to see lawmen lurking behind every tree, and that would be especially true of an impressionable boy. But to be on the safe side, they ambled to the livery stable next door and saddled their horses. That was the extent of their escape preparations, and they returned to their leisurely activities in the saloon. The only member of the gang not present was Arkansas Tom Jones, who was still in bed at the hotel, probably thanks to a bad hangover.*

· · ·

---

* Jones, whose real name was Roy Daugherty, was actually from Missouri. There really isn't an explanation as to why he adopted "Arkansas Tom" as a nickname other than he did not want people to know he was from Missouri, where both his brothers were somewhat prominent preachers.

THAT MORNING, HIX and his posse quietly entered Ingalls. Not noticing them, Bitter Creek Newcomb stepped outside and got on his
horse. As he began to ride, there was rifle fire. The outlaw fired back,
but after being hit twice, Newcomb spurred his horse, and it carried
him out of town.

According to the account later prepared by Marshal Evett Nix, after Newcomb fled, other members of the gang in the saloon opened
fire out the windows. The deputy marshals returned fire, but the
only casualty was a horse, which happened to be at the wrong hitching post at the wrong time. Still, the officers' fusillade was furious
enough that the cornered criminals ran out a side door to take refuge
in the stable.

During this short escape, the saloon's bartender, a man named
Murray, did a foolish thing. Perhaps because the gang members had
proven to be such good consumers of his whiskey, he grabbed a rifle
and provided some covering fire. But he did so from the saloon's
front doorway. He was shot in the side and one arm and was soon
arrested.*

His boss, George Ransom, who had been napping on a pool table,
was also wounded, in the leg. Wisely, he did not become involved in
the gunfight. He instead hid out in the saloon's icehouse and would
recover from his wound. Not so lucky was a saloon customer named
N. A. Walker. When the firing began, he ran out the front door.
Thinking he was a Doolin-Dalton Gang member, the peace officers
shot him.†

Another casualty of the shoot-out (not counting the horse) was

---

* Two years later, despite having fought on the side of outlaws, Murray sued the federal government for damages to the saloon as well as himself. The case was quickly
dismissed.

† Poor Mr. Walker lay sprawled in the dusty street until the shooting stopped. The
bullet had passed through his liver, and a doctor determined only a physician in
Stillwater could save his life. In an effort to keep him cool until he could be taken
there, Walker was stripped naked and placed in the window of a restaurant. The display made an impression on the local children, who kept having to be herded away.

Deputy Marshal Thomas Hueston, a thirty-eight-year-old widower. He had been one of the possemen who had been with Chalkley Beeson the previous November when Ol' Yantis was killed. Arkansas Tom Jones, awakened by the sudden eruption of gunfire, grabbed his Winchester and ran to his hotel room's window. Seeing the lawmen arrayed in the street, he fired his rifle repeatedly. The officers scattered for cover from this unanticipated assault from above, but a bullet found Hueston. The unfortunate deputy would die the next day.

Moments later, there was another man mortally wounded. A bystander named Young Simmons was struck by a stray round as he attempted to take cover inside a different saloon. He died within a few minutes.

The death of another of the deputies, Richard Speed, just twenty-five years old, came about when Bill Doolin shot him. And Bill Dalton shot Deputy Marshal Lafayette Shadley. Seeing Dalton get atop his horse, the lawman had fired, but his aim was off, and he succeeded only in breaking the horse's leg. Dalton toppled to the ground but jumped up again, firing. His aim was true, and Shadley succumbed to his wound the next day.

Dan "Dynamite Dick" Clifton was then hit in the neck, though not a mortal wound. But when a bullet found one of his hands, he lost three fingers. He was still able to climb on his horse and ride, leaving Ingalls at a gallop.

Because of his outlaw activities that included exploits with the Doolin-Dalton Gang, Clifton would have a $3,500 bounty placed on his head . . . and because of that, he would be dubbed the "most killed outlaw in America." People would repeatedly turn in a corpse claiming the body as Clifton's, despite the fact the bodies had all ten fingers, while other men, who would randomly cut off three fingers, would often remove the wrong ones. He would finally be killed for sure in 1896 by Chris Madsen, who knew which fingers were missing.

Despite the numbers and firepower of the posse, all the members of the gang managed to escape—except Arkansas Tom Jones.* His firing from upstairs had been effective, but when Ingalls was emptied of outlaws, he found himself trapped and surrounded. He shouted down that he was prepared to fight on but changed his mind when Jim Masterson displayed the banded sticks of dynamite that he was about to light and toss in the hotel window.

One would think that by surrendering, Jones avoided the violent end that was in the cards for the other members of the gang. Not true . . . but it took a while. He was convicted of manslaughter and given a prison term of fifty years. After a few years, his preacher brothers began advocating for his release, and their prayers were finally answered in 1910. Out on parole, Jones ran a restaurant in Drumright, Oklahoma.

But slinging hamburgers and clearing tables held his interest for only two years. Jones quit the eatery and headed west, to Los Angeles, hoping to land roles in Hollywood westerns. Unable to gain a foothold in the acting game, Jones returned to robbery. In 1917, he and several other men hit a bank in Neosho, Missouri, and unfortunately for him, he hadn't gotten any better at eluding the police. Jones spent four more years behind bars.

A free man in 1921, he chose the outlaw path again, robbing another bank in Missouri, this one in Asbury. Somehow, this time, he managed not to be caught. Arkansas Tom Jones remained a wanted man, though, and finally, in August 1924, peace officers located him. The distinction of being the last member of the Doolin-Dalton Gang still alive ended when he was shot to death as he tried to get away.

Though Bitter Creek Newcomb was seriously wounded, he was able to join up with Charley Pierce, who was slightly wounded, and get to the Dunn ranch, where they were cared for by Rose Dunn, Newcomb's girlfriend.

---

* Doolin had to leave his wife, Edith, behind in the hotel. She escaped injury during the shoot-out, which was especially fortunate, because she was five months' pregnant.

Bill Dalton, along with Red Buck Waightman and Tulsa Jack Blake, barely got away. Dalton burst from the livery stable astride another horse in full gallop. Alas, this one was also not swift enough to outrun a bullet and was struck in the jaw by Marshal Hixon. A bullet from another gun broke one of the horse's legs. With the two others providing covering fire, Dalton found a third horse, and the three outlaws rode off. Bill Doolin, spurring his horse in another direction, also escaped.

"The acrid smell of gunpowder was everywhere, and a blue haze of gunsmoke drifted lazily in the warm September breeze," relates Bailey Hanes. "All was quiet now. The gun battle had taken less than thirty minutes. Six men had been killed or wounded in the streets of Ingalls that day. It was a deadlier fight than the one at the O.K. Corral at Tombstone, Arizona Territory."* A rough count revealed there were at least a hundred bullet holes in Ransom's saloon; no one thought to check the livery stable too.

Some years later, a stone marker was placed in the town to commemorate the shoot-out. But Ingalls did not have much of a future. Over the years, it became almost a ghost town, featuring several old, deserted buildings. Its post office closed in 1907. Every September 1, there had been a reenactment of the gun battle, but that ended in 2012. In the 2020 Census, only 192 people were listed as living there.

---

* In that shoot-out, as detailed in the book *Tombstone,* three men were killed and three were wounded. Of the six people mortally wounded in Ingalls, N. A. Walker was the last to succumb. After being transported from the restaurant window to Stillwater, he lingered two weeks until he died on September 15.

CHAPTER 32

MORE BADGES THAN BANDITS

There was no time for the lawmen working for Evett Nix to recover from the explosion of gunfire in Ingalls. Only two weeks later, the fourth of the Oklahoma Land Rushes took place, this one opening the Cherokee Strip to mostly white settlement. Because of this—the largest of the four land rushes—and the ongoing activities of the Doolin-Dalton Gang, men wearing badges were going to have their hands full for the rest of 1893 and beyond.

The Treaty of New Echota in 1835 had given the resettled Cherokee Nation three areas in which to live in Oklahoma Territory. Previous land deals and rushes had pretty much taken two of those areas. By late summer 1893, with Grover Cleveland back in the White House and the country reeling from an economic panic, it was the turn of the Cherokee Outlet, or Strip, to be flooded with newcomers. Its role as grazing land for the tribe's animal stock was coming to an end.

The land rush event began at noon on September 16 with as many as a hundred thousand participants vying to carve out homesteads on six million acres. Land offices to record claims had already been established in Alva, Enid, Woodward, and Perry. Also in these towns, U.S. Army infantry troops had been stationed, and cavalry units were roaming the Strip. Officials knew, however, that the military presence would not be enough. Marshal Nix expanded his force of deputy marshals to 150 men, and among them were Chris Madsen, Bill Tilghman, and Heck Thomas.

During that year, Madsen had been steadily employed as a lawman. Tilghman had not, spending his time building up his ranch and livestock. Thomas had also gone about his badge-wearing business, and he and Matie were living in Guthrie. All three men attended a conference of deputy marshals arranged by Nix to prepare for the land rush. He "ordered his men to safeguard their own lives and the lives of others by always getting the drop on the other fellow before they commanded him to hold up his hands," reported Beth Thomas Meeks. "No doubt the Three Guardsmen smiled at this sage suggestion."

The land rush got underway, and the expected chaos ensued. Even with the vigilance of the military and marshals, sooners once more slipped in and laid claim to some of the best locations, especially in the eastern third of the Outlet and at many of the townsites. With demand for the land far outstripping that which was available, many of the participants were unable to secure a claim for themselves.

That unhappy consequence was not Marshal Nix's concern. He had to have his marshals pivot to providing law and order in the brand-new communities as well as the ones already established. Perry, for example, became so racked with violence that Nix appointed Bill Tilghman as its new city marshal and Heck Thomas as his deputy. The latter's daughter wrote with evident satisfaction, "The two soon cleaned out the vicious element in town and reduced the number of saloons from one hundred ten to fifty two."

On November 23, 1893, the *Daily Times* newspaper commented about Tilghman and Thomas, "These are wonderful men, and their appointment had a wonderful effect. The most notorious characters skipped out at the first intimation that they were not wanted. Others are going."*

But both Bill Doolin and Bill Dalton and their gang members remained at large. They committed at least two more train robberies and were credited with other bank and railroad raids.† Heck Thomas jotted in his personal journal that "the people of the territory appealed to Nix for relief of the terrible suspense hanging over them by reason of this vicious band's depredations."

What had to be frustrating for Nix was that other outlaws as well as members of the Doolin-Dalton Gang continued to escape capture. With the expansion in the number of lawmen in Oklahoma, the territory was at a tipping point where there were more badges than bandits. Still, deputy marshals, despite their best efforts, sometimes came up empty-handed, and there was still plenty of lawlessness to go around.

One of Chris Madsen's missions was to track down Zip Wyatt, who was born Nathaniel Ellsworth Wyatt in Indiana and was also known as "Wild Charlie" and Dick Yeager. His family was one of the settlers of Guthrie in 1889, and he had begun his bandit ways with the influence of his father and his older brother, known respectively as "Old Six-Shooter Bill" and "Six-Shooter Bill." Probably because he could, the younger Wyatt, who had for no discernible reason acquired the "Zip" nickname, shot up Mulhall, Oklahoma, wounding two people in the process, then fled to Kansas. A deputy sheriff, Andrew Balfour, found Wyatt in Pryor's Grove and was killed trying to arrest him.

Wyatt was eventually caught and convicted, but, on his second

---

* In the No-Good-Deed-Goes-Unpunished Department, the following spring, while Tilghman was on leave tending to his farm, the Perry City Council dismissed Thomas and told Tilghman not to return, because the two lawmen had done too fine a job and a community that was so law-abiding was not good for business.
† As had happened with the original Dalton Gang, almost every robbery of a train or bank was being blamed on the Doolin-Dalton Gang. This exaggeration made for better, blaring headlines in the nation's newspapers.

attempt, he broke out of an Oklahoma prison. And so it was that Chris Madsen was on his trail in 1893. That trail kept going cold, even after the reward for Wyatt's arrest reached $5,000. It would not be until August 1895 when a posse of lawmen, minus Madsen, cornered and shot Zip Wyatt, wounding him seriously enough that he would perish. Before he did, though, he conducted interviews in his jail cell while groggy from morphine. Finally, reduced to skeletal form, Wyatt died on September 7.*

One of Heck Thomas's missions in 1893 was to bring Earnest Lewis from the Osage Nation to the jail in Guthrie. Born in Kansas City, Lewis began a life of crime early, having been convicted of robbery by the age of sixteen and serving a year at the Kansas State Penitentiary. Afterward, while a member of Henry Starr's gang, he was suspected of murder and train robbery. In June of 1893, having been deposited there by Heck Thomas, Lewis was sitting in jail when he became acquainted with Tom King—the aforementioned Flora Quick Mundis—and was part of her bold escape.

Lewis would stay busy and evade peace officers until September 1895, when he was found guilty of train robbery in Colorado and was sentenced to ten years in prison. He served only six years and was released in 1901, returning to Oklahoma Territory. There he married Julia Johnson Gilstrap, and they opened a saloon, called the Uno Joint, in Bartlesville. Six years later, inside this establishment, Lewis killed a deputy marshal named Williams and was in turn shot to death by Deputy Marshal Fred Keeler. His widow, Julia, grieved for about a year, then in September 1908, at age thirty-eight, she married the recently paroled Emmett Dalton.†

And another mission involved Bill Tilghman, according to the

---

* Wyatt was buried in an unmarked grave in a pauper's field outside Sheridan, Oklahoma. Presumably, his bones still lie under the residential development that was eventually constructed there.
† Before Earnest Lewis was her husband, Julia had been married twice before, to Albert Whiteturkey and Robert Gilstrap.

memoir of his widow, Zoe. It turned out to be both an aggravating and humorous close call with members of the Doolin-Dalton Gang.

Urging a spring wagon through snow, Tilghman stumbled upon a dugout. Though believing it was empty, he went to check it out anyway . . . leaving his rifle in the wagon. He descended a few steps to a door and knocked. He was surprised when a gruff voice called out, "Come in."

Once his eyes had adjusted to the dark interior, Tilghman saw double bunks screened by sheets against the earthen walls. The deputy marshal now suspected they were occupied by the missing outlaws. One man with a beard, a rifle across his knees, sat before a small fireplace.

Tilghman stepped close to warm his hands and said, "A cold day."

That was greeted with only a grunt. When he turned away from the fire, he could see the muzzles of Winchesters poking out from the curtained bunks. Tilghman knew they could open fire at any moment, but remaining calm, he said, "Guess I better be going. How does a fellow get out of here?"

The man rasped, "The same damned way you got in."

The lawman lifted the latch on the door and stepped out. He would later tell his wife, "I could feel the bullets in my back at every step." By then, he would have learned that in the dugout were Bill Doolin, Red Buck Waightman, Dynamite Dick Clifton, Tulsa Jack Blake, Charley Pierce, and Little Bill Raidler. Once Tilghman left, Waightman wanted to go after and kill him, but Doolin said, "Tilghman's too good a man to shoot in the back."

That might seem a bit too honorable for a bandit. What Doolin also reportedly said makes more sense: "If you kill Bill Tilghman there'll be a hundred men here and they'd dynamite this place off the face of the earth."

There had to be a better way to find the outlaws than doing so accidentally. Chris Madsen had a brother-in-law named Morris who agreed to go undercover to learn the whereabouts of the gang. He and two other men hired by Madsen rode a "cow-man's cook-wagon" in the region around Ingalls and Jennings and asked people they encountered about any possible hideouts. They were told of one on the Dunn farm, a dugout that opened into a ravine, and men had been seen going to and from it. This seemed like good intelligence. It was, but . . .

Madsen and Heck Thomas met at Tilghman's farm near Chandler, and from there, the trio went to the camp established by Morris and the two other men near the farm. During the night, the three deputy marshals took up positions to stop anyone from leaving the dugout. At dawn, they shouted for whoever was inside to come out and surrender.

The initial response from inside the dugout was to refuse that invitation. There was a second response after Thomas tossed two sticks of dynamite on the roof. Eight men hurried out with their hands in the air. As the lawmen handcuffed them, they glumly noted that none of them were Doolin-Dalton Gang members. Most likely, the eight guilty-looking men were wanted for something, so the cuffs remained, and they were kept under guard by the cook-wagon crew while Thomas, Tilghman, and Madsen rode away.

Apparently, one of the men had offered a tip about Doolin and four others being warned about the posse and heading off a few hours earlier. The three deputy marshals set off in that direction. When they stopped at an isolated cabin, the owner of it greeted them with a grin.

"The others said you would be along," the man said. "We got dinner ready."

Earlier, Doolin and his companions had eaten breakfast at the cabin and told the accommodating owner that the rest of their party would be along soon and would pay for all the food. The red-faced Three Guardsmen did—after, at least, wolfing down their dinner.

With the outlaws evidently knowing they were being pursued, the chances of finding them were considerably lower, so the posse returned to the Dunn farm to pick up the prisoners.*

Perhaps a reflection of the U.S. Marshals' office in Oklahoma having its hands full were the newspaper reports late in the year that Nix was trying to negotiate a lenient deal with Bill Doolin and Bill Dalton. At first, Nix told one reporter, "That's the worst rot I've seen lately. Such a thing as a compromise with an outlaw never entered my mind. Let Bill Dalton, Bill Doolin, Dynamite Dick and the others roam. They will soon be brought up with a short turn."

However, some officials, possibly with Nix's knowledge, were trying to work something out. One of them, W. L. Norman, who was a deputy clerk at the District Court of Stillwater, wrote the Oklahoma attorney general, Richard Olney, that he had recently "seen Bill Doolin and talked with him. He is anxious to drop the business he is in and will willingly come in and give up, provided he can have fair treatment and not too long a term in the Pen."

Concurring was Frank Dale, the territory's chief justice. As he wrote to Olney, "Doolin is the leader of the gang of desperadoes who have been terrorizing the eastern part of Oklahoma for the past two or three years." Dale suggested that with evidence hard to come by anyway, maybe a deal "was the best way to go."

The problem, though, was that the gang could not stop its terrorizing. In January 1894, Doolin, Tulsa Jack, and Dynamite Dick robbed the Farmers' and Citizens' Bank in Pawnee. Doolin, not willing to waste time, had gone up to the clerk, C. L. Berry, put his pistol to the man's head, and said, "Open the vault or I'll blow your brains out."

As frightened as he was, Berry convinced the bandit that the

---

* To rub his nose in it, when Madsen got back to Guthrie, he found someone had delivered a message from Bill Doolin promising to repay him for the breakfast after his next withdrawal from a bank.

vault was on a timer and would not open until 4:00, an hour away. Instead, the robbers scooped up what cash they could and exited. When the three thieves rode away, Berry sat behind Doolin atop his horse, which discouraged any shooting during the escape.

In March, in the middle of the night, Doolin and Bill Dalton entered a hotel room in Woodward and with guns drawn woke the occupant. George Rourke was the train station agent, and after he was dressed, the outlaws escorted him down to the depot, where he took over $6,000 from the safe. Rourke was found in the morning bound and gagged but otherwise unharmed.

Still, the fact that no one had been killed during the crimes the gang committed left the door open to some kind of deal. Then came the events at Longview, Texas, in May . . . and all deals were off the table. Marshal Nix made it crystal clear he wanted the Doolin-Dalton Gang wiped off the map.

As Glenn Shirley put it, "Heck and Bill Tilghman were to spearhead the campaign until the last member of the Doolin gang 'was in prison or under the sod.' Chris Madsen soon joined them. Through their efforts in the desperate months to follow, they became known as the 'Three Guardsmen of Oklahoma.'"

CHAPTER 33

A DOOMED DALTON

Sometime in the spring of 1894, Bill Dalton and Bill Doolin decided to go their separate ways. There may have been several reasons, but probably the overriding one was they would be harder to find if not together. Doolin could secretly continue to visit his wife and child, and the same went for Dalton and his wife, Jane, and their two children.

And their fame made it increasingly harder to hide. Headlines continued to adorn the tops of newspapers, and it did not seem to matter much if they were true. MET THEIR DOOM blared the April 20 edition of *The Coffeyville Journal*, with the article describing a furious gun battle in which three marshals, a woman, and a little girl were killed along with Dalton, Doolin, and Bitter Creek Newcomb. Five days later, *The Cherokee Advocate* had the headline THEY DIED WITH THEIR BOOTS ON, reporting that a posse led by Heck Thomas had confronted the outlaws. The result: "The gang was exterminated!"

All the while, Bill Dalton was making his way to Longview. It was founded in 1869, and the following year, Ossamus Hitch Methvin Sr., a Georgia native who had come to East Texas about 1848 and bought 1,200 acres, sold 100 of those acres to the Southern Pacific

Railroad. The price was just a dollar and a promise—which was kept—that the railroad would build its line in the direction of land he owned. Methvin prospered and constructed a three-story home on Rock Hill (eventually known as Methvin Hill). Once completed, he looked out from a third-floor window and pronounced, "What a long view!" The growing community now had a name, and in June 1871, it was incorporated as the first town in Gregg County.

It was still thriving enough by May 1894 that Bill Dalton decided to make a withdrawal from the First National Bank of Longview. On the twenty-third, two men later described as "rough looking" entered. One was wearing a long slicker coat that concealed a Winchester rifle. He handed a note to the bank president, Joe Clemmons: "This will introduce you to Charles Speckelmeyer who wants some money and is going to have it. Signed B and F." It was later assumed that "B and F" stood for "Bill [Dalton] and Friends."

Two more rifle-toting men were in an alley next to the bank, ready to prevent any interference. But they turned out not to be very good at their assignment. Somehow, word of a robbery in progress had gotten to the Longview marshal, Matthew Muckleroy, who grabbed his guns and immediately deputized several armed citizens. As they approached the bank, the two would-be thieves began firing wildly, and the local peace officers fired back, with dozens of shots exchanged.

The bullets took their toll. A local man, George Buckingham, was killed outright. Marshal Muckleroy was struck in the abdomen, but his life was spared when the bullet was deflected by silver dollars in his pocket. A local saloonkeeper, J. W. McQueen, was hit and would later die. Charles Learned was walking across the courthouse square and took a round to the leg, and that would result in the leg being amputated. Another Longview citizen, Theodore Summers, was shot in the hand. One of the bandits firing back, George Bennett, was hit more than once and died. Subsequently, he would be identified as Jim Wallace, who had recently married a local girl. For the former Jenny Renfro, it was a quick transition from bride to widow.*

Inside the bank, its president, Clemmons, tried to be a hero by grabbing Bill Dalton's pistol. He got off easy when the hammer came down on his hand, and he suffered only a flesh wound. Dalton and Speckelmeyer collected what cash they could, about $2,500, plus $450 in unsigned banknotes, and ran out a side door and made a run for their horses. Dalton had the presence of mind to have bank employees run with them, and their fellow citizens were reluctant to shoot. He and Speckelmeyer were joined by the third thief, and all three galloped away. It was later learned that in addition to Dalton, the escaped bandits were brothers Jim and Judd Nite. A posse was pulled together, but they rode off too late to pick up the gang's trail.

Bill Dalton headed back up to Oklahoma Territory—specifically, to near Ardmore in the Arbuckle Mountains, where he had a hide-out. The Nite brothers were not found . . . at least, not right away. Three years later, a posse, acting on a more recent warrant, found them in Menard County. After Judd, whose full name was Christopher Columbus Nite, was discovered, he was killed. Jim was shot three times but survived. He was captured, tried, and convicted for the Longview bank robbery for which he was sentenced to a seven-year term.

Two years into his sentence, apparently determining that another five years was too long to wait, Jim Nite, who was in a Tyler jail awaiting transfer under a change of venue for another trial, escaped. But he was captured again, and on August 5, 1899, he received a twenty-year sentence. This time, he stayed put for fourteen years, then was either pardoned or paroled by Texas governor Oscar B.

---

* After the shooting stopped, a crowd gathered around Wallace. They cut off the dead man's beard and shredded his clothes. After a rope was placed around his neck, Wallace was dragged across the Longview public square and hanged from a telegraph pole.

Colquitt. In 1920, Jim Nite got into an argument with a man in Tulsa, who shot him dead.

Bill and Jane Dalton, with Gracie and Jack, hid out in a borrowed cabin near Elk in Indian Territory. A couple of quiet weeks passed, then on the morning of June 7, 1894, a man and two women entered a shop in Ardmore. What attracted the clerk's attention was that in addition to the usual items purchased was an unusually large amount of ammunition of various calibers. Also purchased was a suit of clothes for a man, but it was much larger than the size of the man accompanying the women.

To the clerk's credit, after the trio left, he did not simply shrug and turn his attention to the next customer. Instead, he was suspicious. As he examined the banknotes, he realized that they were new bills from the First National Bank of Longview, over in Texas, and several were not signed. The clerk took the notes to the Ardmore marshal's office; the marshal immediately telegraphed his counterpart in Longview. It was soon found that the serial numbers of the notes matched some of the stolen ones.

Separately, local lawmen were notified that a suspicious package had arrived by train from Texas at the Ardmore freight depot. When they opened it, they found three one-gallon containers of whiskey. Introduction of whiskey into the Indian Territory was still a serious offense, and deputies kept watch on the freight depot to see who claimed the package.

Most of the day passed with the man and two women spending freely during a shopping spree. Late that afternoon, the man appeared at the freight depot and claimed the package containing the whiskey. At this point, U.S. marshal Selden Lindsey arrested the man, who he recognized as Houston Wallace, brother of Jim Wallace, the dead bandit at the Longview bank robbery. Lindsey also took the two women into custody. They identified themselves as Mrs. Pruitt and Mrs. Smith.

One of the women had three hundred dollars hidden in her bosom, and the other had four hundred dollars hidden in her stocking. The money was identified as having been taken from the First National Bank. Houston Wallace was locked up on the whiskey charge, and the women were to be held in custody until noon the next day. Lindsey immediately formed a posse and set off for the Wallace ranch in the Arbuckle Mountains near Elk.

The marshal and his men had extra motivation to solve the case, because by then, rewards totaling $35,000 had been offered by various organizations for the capture of Bill Dalton, dead or alive. This was quite a handsome sum at a time when a Stetson hat cost $4.50 and a good saddle cost $10. To be on the safe side, Marshal Lindsey divided his men into two posses who would keep their eye out for suspicious riders on their way to rendezvous at the ranch.

There was a glitch right as the trip to Elk began. The competing marshal, hoping to delay Lindsey's arrival at the Wallace ranch, got hold of the confiscated whiskey and gifted it to Lindsey's posse, hoping to get them drunk enough so they would pose no threat to his posse earning all that reward money. One man in Lindsey's posse passed out and fell dead drunk on the way to the hideout. By the time the posse arrived at the Wallace ranch on the morning of June 8, 1894, only Lindsey and one member of the posse, Caleb "Loss" Hart, were in good enough shape to perform as peace officers.

The reunited posse surrounded the Wallace ranch house. Lindsey and Hart were stationed behind the house, in a ravine. All was seemingly peaceful around the house as the sun began to break across the Arbuckle Mountains. A man was observed playing in the front yard with several children. One of them, a young girl, peeled off to the pasture to fetch the milk cow. As the girl and the cow passed the ravine behind the house, she spotted Lindsey and Hart but had the presence of mind to ignore them and continue quietly on to the house. Once she had the cow tied up, she called out to the man in the front yard playing with the children.

Bill Dalton hurried to the house and in a few seconds jumped out the back window with a pistol in his hand. He ran a few hundred feet toward the timber and the ravine when Marshal Lindsey called for him to surrender. Dalton turned and fired his pistol at the lawmen crouched in the ravine. Lindsey had heard that the Daltons were good shots and wondered if Bill Dalton would miss a second time.

He would not risk it. The reward, after all, was dead or alive. Lindsey hoisted his Winchester to his shoulder and fired. At almost the same instant, Hart fired his Winchester at the fleeing man. The first shot struck Dalton in the chest, spinning him around so the second shot hit him in the back. He fell facedown on the grass.

Hart and Lindsey cautiously approached the wounded man. Slowly, Dalton rolled over on his back, smiled, and breathed his last breath. It was at that moment when Hart and Lindsey confirmed the dead man was Dalton. *The Fort Worth Gazette* would report the next day, "A .44 Winchester hole at the pants band on the right side of the spinal column, near the hip, shows where the little messenger of justice had rid the country of the worst outlaw who ever stole a horse or shot a man in the Southwest."

A minute later, a woman was found in the house who identified herself as Jane Dalton. Assisted by the sympathetic lawmen, she went out and confirmed that the dead man was her husband of eleven years, Bill.*

Jane had the body shipped back to California for burial on the property her parents owned in Livingston.† However, when the

---

* Two days after her husband's death, Jane Dalton was arrested on a charge of receiving stolen money. The Ardmore marshal ordered her released "as he did not propose to allow any such outrage perpetrated while he bore a commission," the *Daily Ardmoreite* reported.
† An account of this published in *The Weekly Oklahoma State Capitol* was curiously headlined, "Mr. Dalton Continues Dead."

ranch was sold, Bill's body was moved to nearby Turlock Memorial Park, where it remains.

The Dalton Gang was no more. But Bill Doolin was still very much alive and continuing his outlaw ways. And he was not the only one.

CHAPTER 34

END OF THEIR DAYS

Very likely, when he learned about Bill Dalton's death, Bill Doolin saw his own future. Perhaps seeing the bigger picture, he may have considered himself the last of the last outlaws. Even so, he intended to put off his demise for as long as possible.

However, several members of his gang were unable to do so. The Wild West was in the history books, but that did not prevent them from dying in gun battles.

With the tales of Dynamite Dick Clifton and Arkansas Tom Jones having already been told, the next gang member to meet his maker after Bill Dalton was William "Tulsa Jack" Blake. On the night of April 3, 1895, Blake and fellow gang member George "Red Buck" Waightman were leading their own mini-gang when they stopped a southbound Rock Island train. The messenger inside the express car, J. W. Jones, defied an order to open the door. His resistance softened considerably when the bandits fired twenty rounds into the car, with two of the bullets striking him in the wrist and leg. Jones opened the door, and the robbers came aboard.

Leaving the other members of the gang to try to get the safe open, Tulsa Jack and Red Buck, waving their six-shooters, roamed the other cars, relieving passengers of their wallets, watches, and other valuables. Then, with as much as they could carry off, the outlaws reunited outside the train, climbed on their horses, and disappeared into the night. But they did not ride far enough.

The next afternoon, a seven-man posse headed by U.S. deputy marshal William Banks caught sight of the impromptu Blake-Waightman Gang, who had been resting in a sand basin along the Cimarron River near Dover, Oklahoma. After quietly closing in, Banks called for the thieves to surrender. Tulsa Jack's response was to begin firing. Immediately, the air was full of flying bullets.

This went on for over a half hour, with the two sides making liberal use of their pistols and rifles. When the bandits' ammunition ran low, Tulsa Jack tried to make a run for it. He did not get far—a fusillade of shots ended his life. While this was happening, the rest of the gang took off in a different direction and were able to escape.

Two more Doolin-Dalton Gang members died during a similar event a month later. Their outlaw life caught up to them thanks to the woman who would become known in legend as the "Rose of Cimarron."

As mentioned before, Bitter Creek Newcomb enjoyed visiting the Dunn ranch near Ingalls because he was infatuated with Rose Dunn, who at the time of the Ingalls shoot-out was fifteen years old. Though she was of a poor farming family and it was unusual for the time, Rose received a formal education at a convent in Wichita. Her older brothers taught her too—how to ride, rope, and shoot as well as they did. Apparently, no one taught her to steer clear of outlaws. She fell for Newcomb, and the rest of the Doolin-Dalton Gang looked at her as a kind of kid sister.

Complicating matters was that her brothers would later become bounty hunters. The gang of two went under the imaginative name of the Dunn Brothers.

After the bloody Battle of Ingalls, the wounded Newcomb and

Charley Pierce were hidden and nursed back to health by Rose. Possibly as many as three other gang members hid out at the ranch until some of the lawmen lost interest while others hurried off to follow up on reports from all over the territory of gang member sightings. Finally, Bitter Creek and Charley were well enough to move on.

Over time, Rose may have been visited by her outlaw lover, but it is known that on May 2, 1895, Newcomb and Pierce returned to the ranch outside Ingalls. As soon as they climbed off their horses, they were ambushed by the now-inhospitable Dunn Brothers, who were quite aware that by this time the reward for getting Bitter Creek had accumulated to $5,000. It was believed that both bandits had been killed.

However, as the brothers hauled the bodies to Guthrie in a wagon, Newcomb tried to sit up, and he pleaded for water. His thirst went unquenched as one of the brothers shot him dead for sure.

To anyone who would listen, Rose Dunn insisted—as did her brothers, who feared reprisals—that she had nothing to do with the deaths of Bitter Creek Newcomb and Charley Pierce. Soon after, the Dunn Brothers team was halved. They were suspected of cattle rustling, and when a sheriff named Frank Canton went to investigate, Bill Dunn confronted him.* The latter whipped out his pistol and fired twice. He missed, but Canton did not, killing Dunn.

Three years after her lover's killing, Rose married a local politician, Charles Noble, and in 1900, they moved away from Oklahoma. After Noble's death in 1930, she reconnected with Richard Fleming,

---

* Frank Canton was born in Virginia as Josiah Horner. After the family moved to Texas, he became a cowboy and then a bank robber, and spent time in jail for it. Aiming to go straight, he changed his name to Frank Canton, and in 1882, he was elected sheriff of Johnson County, Wyoming, participating in the Johnson County War. He was investigating the Dunn brothers because in 1894 he had relocated to Oklahoma and hired on as an undersheriff of Pawnee County.

who had been a teenage suitor, and they married. The so-called Rose of Cimarron died in 1954 at age seventy-six in Salkum, Washington.*

NEXT UP—OR DOWN, six feet under—would be George "Red Buck" Waightman, who had been luckier and faster than Tulsa Jack Blake a few months earlier. After his escape from the posse, he stopped at the home of a Baptist minister, who objected to the outlaw's demand for a hot meal and a fresh horse. Waightman shot him dead. He probably did not get the meal, but he did steal the horse.

By September, he had teamed up with a man named Charlie Smith, and the two tried to rustle cattle belonging to Gus Holland. When the rancher tried to stop them, he was killed. They then shot another rancher who refused to buy the stolen beeves. He survived, but the bandits were able to get away.

Red Buck hoped to reunite with Bill Doolin, but the latter was angry about the murder of the Baptist minister, so Waightman went out and recruited his own gang. The members consisted of Joe Beckman, Hills Loftis, and Elmer "Kid" Lewis, who indeed was only eighteen years old. This new gang must not have been too ambitious because they eschewed a train or a bank to instead rob a store in Arapaho, Oklahoma.

Vowing to catch them was U.S. deputy marshal Joe Ventioner, who led a posse after Waightman's bunch of two-bit bandits. They fled west where on the other side of the border Texas Rangers took up the chase. In a skirmish, Beckman was killed and Red Buck wounded, but he, Loftis, and Lewis escaped.†

---

* The legend of this highly fictionalized young lady was burnished over the years in pop culture, helped by a 1952 western feature titled *Rose of Cimarron* and the title song of a Poco album released in 1976.

† The following year, the now-nineteen-year-old Kid Lewis was caught after killing the employee of a bank he was robbing in Wichita Falls, Texas. While he waited in jail for a formal arraignment, townsfolk dragged him out onto the street and lynched him.

Waightman returned to Oklahoma to recuperate. His new out-law companion was a Texas man, George Miller. They were hiding out near Arapaho in a dugout owned by a W. W. Glover. Unwisely, Glover decided to go to town to give up the fugitives and collect the reward, and on his way, Red Buck flagged him down and killed him. As soon as Ventioner heard of the murder, he collected two other deputy marshals, William Holcomb and Bill Quillen, and they set off on the bandits' trail.

That trail led them into Custer County, where the lawmen were told that Waightman and Miller were hiding out on a farm. It was owned by Dolph Picklesimer, who, perhaps to compensate for such an unenvi-able name, was known to cozy up to outlaws. Thus, his farm was where a deadly shoot-out occurred on the morning of March 4, 1896.

Ventioner and his fellow deputy marshals arrived with arrest war-rants. They were met with gunfire. Finally getting his man, Ventioner shot and killed Red Buck Waightman. But George Miller, in turn, shot Ventioner, striking him in the abdomen. William Holcomb fired at Miller, with a startling result—the bullet struck the bandit's cartridge belt, and several rounds lodged in it exploded, blowing off Miller's right hand. This was the gruesome end to the gunfight.

Holcomb and Bill Quillen tended to Ventioner, who would sur-vive the grievous wound and return to his lawman role. The deputies also put handcuffs on Picklesimer for harboring fugitives. George "Red Buck" Waightman, after the ritual photographing of his dead body, was buried in the Arapaho Cemetery.

What of the severely maimed George Miller? After serving some prison time in Texas, his right wrist was fitted with a steel hook. He too wound up with an unenviable name: "Hookie" Miller. He resumed his outlaw ways but apparently saw the light, because he applied for the job of a deputy U.S. marshal and was appointed. (This might say more about the depleted marshals' ranks than it does about Miller.) He did his duty for many years, though, so well that he was still a lawman in July 1923 when he was killed while serving an arrest warrant.

Speaking of unenviable names: Richard "Little Dick" West did not escape the Doolin-Dalton Gang fate of violent death. After Bill Dalton left, West continued to ride with Bill Doolin, but he free-lanced too. The latter included forming a gang with the brothers Frank and Al Jennings. They were not very good bandits, bungling attempts to rob trains and banks in various parts of Oklahoma. Pre-dictably, given such a poor track record, the gang broke up, and West went his own way.

Before offering Little Dick's bullet-riddled farewell, one must de-tour to discuss the life of Alphonso Jennings, an unusual legendary life in that the legend was mostly fact. Born in November 1863, he became a lawyer and did well enough that in 1892, he was appointed the prosecuting attorney of Canadian County, Oklahoma. Jennings had two other brothers who were also lawyers, Ed and John, and three years later, he joined them in their own private practice.

And then the troubles began. In October 1895, there was a dis-pute in the Cabinet Saloon in Woodward, Oklahoma, with another attorney named Temple Lea Houston, and gunfire was exchanged, wounding John and killing Ed. Houston was charged with murder but acquitted, which was not surprising, as the flamboyant attorney was well known and popular in those parts.

He had been the only one of Sam Houston's eight children to be born (in 1860) in the governor's residence in Austin, Texas. Raised by an older sister after his parents' death, Houston left home at thirteen to join a cattle drive and later found himself working on a Mississippi River steamboat. Even as an attorney, the tall Tem-ple Houston wore buckskin clothing and a sombrero, imitating his father, and his auburn-colored hair fell to his shoulders. He was no-torious for his dramatic courtroom presentations, which included frequent quotes from classic literature as well as the Bible.

Another feature of Houston's attire was he always kept at his waist "Old Betsy," a Colt revolver. Perhaps the Jennings brothers were un-aware that he was often referred to as the "best shot in the West."

They found out the hard way, and the violent event and Houston's subsequent release was like a burr under Al Jennings's saddle.*

He left Woodward, and after some wandering, in the summer of 1897, he and Frank formed the Jennings Gang, which included Little Dick West. Attempts to rob banks and trains often went awry. Fortunately, no one was killed, though during an unsuccessful effort to rob a Santa Fe train just south of Edmond, Oklahoma, a passenger had part of one ear shot off. An indication of the gang's paltry production as thieves was that when they stopped a train near Chickasha, Oklahoma, that October, they were unable to open the safe, but they did rob passengers of a bottle of whiskey and a bunch of bananas.

The following month, Al Jennings was wounded while being captured in McIntosh County. There was no more of the outlaw life for him—in fact, things took quite a turn, or several turns. Jennings was sentenced to life in prison but was freed after three years. In 1904, he was pardoned by President Theodore Roosevelt, and that same year, O. Henry had a short story about Jennings published, titled "Holding Up a Train." *Beating Back* was the title of a novel Jennings wrote based on his life. And Jennings became a silent-era movie star.

In his first film, he played himself in a screen version of his novel. Other films followed, and his career even lasted into the sound era, with his last motion picture being *Song of the Gringo* in 1936. Jennings cowrote the screenplay and played a judge, and the film marked the big-screen debut of the popular singing star Tex Ritter.† Meanwhile, in 1914, Jennings ran for governor of Oklahoma, but his political career turned out to be as unsuccessful as his outlaw one.

---

* The fall of 1963 saw the debut of the TV series *Temple Houston*, which ran for twenty-six episodes. The series was produced by Jack Webb of *Dragnet* fame and was coproduced by Jeffrey Hunter, who played the title role; then he moved on to play Captain Christopher Pike in the original pilot episode of *Star Trek*.
† The blandly titled movie *Al Jennings of Oklahoma* was released in 1951, with Dan Duryea playing the title character.

After leaving the law and crime and politics behind, Jennings was a traveling evangelist, warning crowds about the mistakes he made. This itinerant life must have suited him fine, because he did not die until December 1961, at age ninety-eight, his life having spanned the presidencies of Abraham Lincoln to John F. Kennedy.

After the arrest of Al Jennings and the breakup of the gang, Little Dick West was on his own again. In 1898, his outlaw days as well as his life ended. He had been targeted by the Three Guardsmen, and two of them finally caught up with him near Guthrie. As Heck Thomas and Bill Tilghman approached and called for him to surrender, West whipped out his pistol and began firing. But he was not fast enough to do any damage before a bullet fired by posse member Deputy Bill Fossett finished him. Little Dick was buried in the city's Summit View Cemetery . . . where Bill Doolin already rested.

But before telling the tale of Doolin's death, there is one more gang member to dispose of: Little Bill Raidler. He had escaped the ambush in April 1895 that had resulted in the death of Tulsa Jack Blake, but he was not on the loose long. In September, he was found by a three-man posse headed by Bill Tilghman. Raidler reached for his rifle and was shot in the wrist, and then when he tried to flee, Tilghman shot him twice more. Raidler was down but not dead. He was convicted and sentenced to ten years in prison.

He was still only thirty-three years old when released in 1903, but Little Bill Raidler had never fully recovered from his wounds, and he died a year later.

CHAPTER 35

THE LAST DESPERADO

Bill Doolin's recovery from his foot wound was slow and painful. One doctor told him that he had developed rheumatism in the foot. To help the healing along and to avoid the various posses crisscrossing Oklahoma, Doolin and Edith and their son, Jay, who was born in January 1894, sought out the medicinal waters in Eureka Springs, Arkansas.

And that was where, in January 1896, Bill Tilghman found him.

After the apprehension of Little Bill Raidler, Tilghman had learned that a man fitting Doolin's description, favoring a bad leg, and calling himself Tom Wilson had been spotted with his wife and baby buying supplies at a store in Kansas. Late that December, he tracked Edith and her son to Burden. They were living in a tent and apparently were so impoverished that at Christmas, several local women had collected and donated to Edith some cash and a basket of food.

Expecting Doolin to join his family, Tilghman kept watch on the trains. No luck. Curiously, Edith and Jay traveled to nearby Winfield, and the deputy sheriff followed them. After she left the post office there, Tilghman learned she had picked up a letter from a Mr.

Wilson sent from Eureka Springs. Edith and Jay boarded a train to Perry, back in Oklahoma. The lawman went on to Guthrie to report to Marshal Evett Nix and declare that he was going to Arkansas to arrest the outlaw. And, to better his chances of surprise, Tilghman was going alone.

"Doolin will shoot you on sight," Nix warned.

The deputy left, visited a local tailor, and returned dressed as a preacher, including a Prince Albert coat and a derby. After receiving grudging approval from Nix for the mission, Tilghman boarded a train that afternoon. The search for the outlaw was stunningly short.

The lawman arrived in Eureka Springs at 1:30 in the morning. As he walked from the railroad station to a hotel, the first person he encountered was Bill Doolin, who did not recognize the "preacher" and continued on to the Davy Hotel, where he was staying.

Later that morning, Tilghman hired a carpenter to construct a box that would conceal a shotgun. While the work was being done, the deputy sheriff decided to experience the mineral waters for himself, and he stepped into a nearby bathhouse. Among the people in the gentleman's waiting room was Doolin, sitting in a far corner, reading a newspaper. He glanced at the preacher, who hastily repaired to an available bath room.

Tilghman determined there was no use waiting for the shotgun box. With his six-shooter in hand, the deputy emerged and strode across the waiting room. When he got to Doolin, he ordered the bandit to surrender. "What do you mean?" Doolin responded, standing. "I have done nothing."

Still, his right hand went for his gun, and Tilghman grabbed his wrist. Then, pointing his pistol at Doolin's face, he again ordered him to surrender. Meanwhile, the gentlemen's waiting room emptied out fast.

"Bill, don't make me kill you," Tilghman implored.

Zoe Tilghman supplied the purple prose of what happened next: "Their eyes met. In the marshal's was power, purpose, an invincible spirit; in the outlaw the fury and desperation of the trapped wild beast. Two strong men; but one was stronger. Doolin's gaze faltered. His straining body relaxed, his arms moved upward. Bill kept his gun steady."

With help from the bathhouse owner, Tilghman completely disarmed Doolin. It was as he was shackling him that Doolin, peering closely, said, "You're Tilghman."

Later that day, Marshal Nix received a telegram from Eureka Springs: "I have him. Will be home tomorrow. Tilghman."

On the train to Guthrie, Doolin was no longer in shackles. He had given his word not to cause any trouble, and the lawman believed him. Still, during the trip, Tilghman was perched in the seat behind the outlaw with his gun ready.

News of the outlaw's capture spread faster than the train could travel. When it arrived at 12:25 on January 16, 1896, people were packed rows deep at the Santa Fe Railroad depot and had gathered at the jail. "There was a great pushing, scrambling, and crowding for a glimpse of the 'King of Outlaws,'" Tilghman later reported. However, "instead of a booted, spurred, and bearded desperado [they saw] a tall, slender man, with sandy mustache and pleasant blue eyes, with a smile on his face, dressed in a well-worn suit of clothes and walking with a cane."

One woman inched close to Doolin, looked up at him, and said, "Why, Mr. Doolin, I believe I could capture you myself."

His smile widening, the outlaw replied, "Yes, ma'am, I believe you could."

Waiting at the station with a cab was Marshal Nix and Heck Thomas. After Tilghman and Doolin got in, they rode off to the federal jail . . . but not before Nix had the cab make a tour of the city so that more people could see the captured outlaw and the proud lawmen. And when that was done, the marshals and Doolin had a luxurious lunch at the Royal Hotel.

Finally, at 3:30 p.m., as Bailey Hanes puts it, "the steel door of the federal jail clanged shut behind Doolin, and for the first and only time in his life he was behind bars. The most notorious of all western outlaws was at last a federal guest."

For over six months, Doolin cooled his heels in the Guthrie jail as something of a celebrity. Among his fellow prisoners was Dynamite Dick Clifton. Together, they hatched a plot to escape and let about a dozen other inmates in on it. The plot worked—on July 5, a careless guard unlocked the wrong cell. "Doolin sprang through the door and snatched his revolver," Glenn Shirley writes. "His docility was gone. His eyes shone, the hair on his head bristled, and his teeth set in a death's head grin. He shoved his gun against [the jailer's] breast and ordered him to open the combination lock to Dynamite Dick's cell or die."

Soon, thirteen prisoners were on the run. They ran fast and fled, each going his own way.* For Doolin, that meant reuniting with his wife and son in Lawson.

THIS TIME, IT was Heck Thomas who found him after he'd had only a few weeks of freedom.

On the evening of the jailbreak, Thomas was dropping off letters at a post office in Guthrie when he heard about it. He immediately hurried home to grab his Winchester. He told Matie to hide his other guns, because Doolin and possibly a few of the other escapees knew where he lived and might come by to steal them. He would later be angry when he learned his wife had put his rifles and pistols in some brush behind the house, where they were exposed to rain. His daughter, Beth Thomas Meeks, notes sardonically, "Since they were the tools of his trade, I guess those guns were about the most important thing in the world to him."

---

* Other than Doolin and Clifton, only two of the escapees were ever recaptured. One of them, George Lane, was tracked down and apprehended by Chris Madsen and Heck Thomas in Greenwood, Missouri.

During the next few weeks, accompanied initially by his son Albert, Thomas focused on tracking down Doolin. Let other deputy marshals try to find Clifton and the like, Heck wanted the head guy. Along the way, he added to his posse and asked questions wherever he stopped for supplies. A tipster told him that Edith Doolin had returned to live at her father's house near Lawson. To Thomas, that meant Bill Doolin was also in the area.

Once in Lawson, according to a letter written to Bill Tilghman and dated September 3, 1896, Thomas received some "fresh news" that led him and his posse to stake out the Ellsworths' house. For several hours, the veteran deputy marshal gazed through what he called "field glasses," hoping for a sign of Doolin.

Inside the house, Bill and Edith Doolin had dinner with her parents. He vowed that he was quitting the outlaw business and he and his family were going to relocate to West Texas or possibly as far as New Mexico. He had a wagon of their possessions ready to go. Finally, about 8:00 p.m., Heck Thomas saw a tall man step out of a stable on the property and begin walking in bright moonlight down the lane.

It was definitely Bill Doolin, and he held out in front of him a Winchester. "He was walking slow," Thomas wrote Tilghman, "looking first on one side and then on the other."

When Doolin had come close enough, Thomas called out to him to surrender. Instantly, Doolin raised the rifle and fired. That bullet missed, as did the second one, while Thomas was having trouble firing his shotgun. Another member of the posse fired, and the bullet struck the Winchester. Doolin dropped it and pulled out his pistol, firing once. "At about that time," Thomas reported, "I got the shotgun to work and the fight was over."

Edith Doolin had heard the shots, and she ran out of her parents' house and down the road, shouting, "Oh, my God! They've killed Bill!" Heck Thomas caught and restrained her before she could see her husband's body.

The slain outlaw was loaded into a borrowed spring wagon and brought to Guthrie. In the wagon behind it was a distraught Edith Doolin.* In Guthrie, there was the obligatory taking of photographs of the body. Beth Thomas Meeks reported, "The town went wild in celebration, relieved at the death of the noted desperado."

During the embalming process, twenty-one buckshot holes were counted in Bill Doolin's body. The embalmer was also the owner of a furniture store, and he had to repeatedly shoo away the curious crowds who climbed all over his goods to try to observe the procedure. He later lamented, "I could have made plenty of money if I had charged 25 cents admission to view the body of Bill Doolin."

Speaking of money: In a bizarre bit of fundraising, Edith, with some help from her brothers, wrote a poem about her husband and printed it with one of the photographs of his perforated body on postcards that were sold for twenty-five cents each. The proceeds went toward burial expenses. Perhaps embarrassed by the ploy, Oklahoma authorities stepped in and picked up the tab for burial of Bill Doolin in the Boot Hill section of the city's Summit View Cemetery.† A rusty buggy axle was driven into the ground to mark the grave. *The Stillwater Gazette* opined, "His left leg will get a rest."

Heck Thomas was well compensated for finding and finishing off the remaining leader of the Doolin-Dalton Gang. The Wells Fargo Company gave him $500, and the same amount was soon paid by

---

* Sometime during the next few months, Edith Doolin filed a wrongful death lawsuit against the U.S. Marshals Service. It was dismissed in February 1897.

† Buried next to Bill Doolin in 1977 was Elmer McCurdy, an outlaw who was killed in a shoot-out with police after robbing a Katy train in October 1911. Where was the outlaw's body for sixty-six years? In mummified form, it was first put on display at an Oklahoma funeral home and then became a fixture in traveling carnivals for decades. After changing ownership several times, sometime in the 1960s the late robber's remains wound up at the Pike amusement park in Long Beach, California. Eventually, they were discovered by a film crew of the TV show *The Six Million Dollar Man* and were positively identified in December 1976. Five months later, Elmer McCurdy was finally laid to rest, probably for good, becoming Doolin's neighbor in Summit View.

the state of Missouri, and the railroads came up with an additional $300. Of this $1,300 total, Heck kept $400 and doled out the rest to the members of his posse and to Tilghman, who had not received any reward for tracking Doolin down the first time because it required "arrest and conviction."

The end of the Dalton Gang and its spin-off the Doolin-Dalton Gang was further and arguably final confirmation of the end of the Wild West. With few and less notorious exceptions, bands of bandits would not roam the back roads of Oklahoma, Kansas, Texas, and beyond. It would be left mostly to the writers of books and the directors of movies to keep the Wild West alive. And, certainly, the death of Bill Doolin in 1896 meant the end of the direct line of outlaws that had begun with the James and Younger brothers back in the 1860s.

There was, yes, an outlaw gang often referred to as "the Wild Bunch," led by Butch Cassidy and the Sundance Kid. This subsidiary of the Hole-in-the-Wall Gang in northern Wyoming was rather short-lived, and in 1901 the two leaders left the United States for Argentina. The kind of rampant crime attributed to the outlaw gangs of the American West would not be seen again until the Prohibition years and then the Depression of the 1920s and '30s, and much of it was urban violence among rival criminal gangs.

By then, none of the last outlaws were left in the American West.

EPILOGUE

Once the Dalton Gang and the bloodbath of Coffeyville were no more, it was left to the family members and citizens of that city to pick up the pieces. Coffeyville for the most part prospered during the twentieth century, and today, it entertains aficionados of the shootout during the Dalton Defenders Days, two days of storytelling and reenactments held during the weekend nearest the anniversary of the October 1892 event.

Of the outlaw Daltons, Grat and Bob never married and did not leave any children behind. Bill's widow, Jane, and two children returned to California. Jane married a man named Adams and had two more children and was known as Jane Bliven Adams. She died in 1941 at age seventy-eight.

Edith Doolin also remarried, to Samuel Meek, but her son, Jay, with Bill Doolin remained her only child. She was just fifty-seven when she died in 1928 in Ponca City, Oklahoma. Jay Doolin Meek lived there too, working for an oil company until he retired at age sixty-five, and died there in 1980 at age eighty-six.

It can be said that Bill Doolin's true descendants are how many times he has been portrayed in books and on the big and small screen. Of the latter, one example is the film *Return of the Bad Men,* released in 1948. Robert Armstrong—mostly known for his role in *King Kong* fifteen years earlier—plays Doolin as the leader of a gang more powerful than the Wild Bunch. This almost purely fictional account added the Sundance Kid, Billy the Kid, and two of the Younger brothers to the known members of Doolin's gang. Marshal Vance Cordell, played by Randolph Scott, is a composite of the lawmen like Bill Tilghman and Heck Thomas who pursued Doolin. The sturdy Scott was back the following year in *The Doolins of Oklahoma,* playing Bill Doolin himself, who by the final reel learns the errors of his outlaw ways. The World War II hero Audie Murphy portrayed Doolin in the 1952 feature *The Cimarron Kid.* The burly Leo Gordon played Doolin being shot to death in the 1950s television series *Stories of the Century.*

Even with all the heartache she was burdened with, Adeline Younger Dalton lived a long and, at least in her later years, peaceful life. She died in January 1925 at age eighty-nine at her home in Kingfisher. According to a local obituary, "Her surviving children were Ben of Kingfisher, Littleton and Emmett in California, Mrs. E. D. Whipple of Siloam Springs, Ark., Simon of Okweemah, OK, and Miss Leona of Kingfisher."

Of the prominent people in Coffeyville who were present the day of the shoot-out, no one had a more dramatic—and, alas, short— second act in life than the newspaper editor David Stewart Elliott. In May 1898, to do their bit in the Spanish-American War, Company G of the Twentieth Kansas was recruited at Independence, Kansas, and Elliott, the Civil War veteran, was its captain. But it was the following year that the Twentieth Kansas distinguished itself, in the Philippines. While in the line of duty at Caloocan, just north of Manila, on February 28, 1899, Captain Elliott was shot by a Filipino sharpshooter and died a few hours later.

His remains were brought home, and on April 14, 1899, they were laid to rest at Coffeyville with military honors. Elliott was fifty-six years old. A Montgomery County history noted, "As a writer he was terse, graceful and effective," and, "At his death he was a member of sixteen lodges."

During the 1890s and beyond, the "Three Guardsmen of Oklahoma" burnished their somewhat regal reputation by apprehending or killing over three hundred outlaws.

Chris Madsen was born during the administration of Millard Fillmore and he died at age ninety-two as Franklin Roosevelt was soon to be sworn in for his fourth term, in January 1944. In 1898, Madsen had taken a break from lawing to serve as a quartermaster sergeant in the Rough Riders unit commanded by Colonel Theodore Roosevelt.* When the Spanish-American War ended, he returned to being a deputy U.S. marshal in Oklahoma. Madsen was in his sixties when he became the Oklahoma City chief of police, and from 1918 to 1922, he was a special investigator for the governor of what by then was the state of Oklahoma. During this stint, he tried to reenlist in the U.S. Army to serve during World War I but was rejected because of his age. Madsen retired to Guthrie, where he passed away.

In 1899, Bill Tilghman established the Oakland Stock Farm, which bred thoroughbred horses. One of his two initial stud horses was Chant, winner of the Kentucky Derby five years earlier. Immediately prosperous as well as popular, Tilghman easily won election as sheriff of Lincoln County in 1900 and was reelected two years later. His wife, Flora, was only thirty-nine when she died that same year. In 1903, the forty-nine-year-old Tilghman married Zoe Agnes Stratton, who was twenty-six years younger. The couple would have three sons, Tench, Richard, and Woodrow.†

---

* Also along on the mission to storm San Juan Hill in Cuba that year was Albert Thomas, Heck's son.
† Dick Tilghman was only twenty-two when he died, in 1929, shot while trying to hold up a card game. His brother Woodie was a career criminal who spent most of his life behind bars.

Tilghman remained active in Democratic Party politics. In the Democratic National Convention held in St. Louis in July 1904, Alton Parker was nominated for president. Tilghman was a member of a group of delegates who journeyed to Parker's home in New York to inform him of his nomination. While there, he looked up an old friend from Dodge City, Bat Masterson, who had begun reporting for *The New York Morning Telegraph*. Masterson introduced Tilghman to President Theodore Roosevelt, who would go on to defeat Parker in the 1904 election.

Tilghman being a Democrat probably accounted for his failure to receive the appointment from Roosevelt that he coveted above all others—U.S. marshal of Oklahoma. Back home, a few years later, Tilghman easily won election as an Oklahoma state senator. He did not stay in that chamber long because he missed lawing. In 1911, he became the Oklahoma City chief of police, preceding Chris Madsen in the position. Tilghman served two years and was credited with a sharp reduction in crime.

It was not necessarily artistic ambitions that propelled Tilghman into the motion picture business. As one-reel and two-reel and longer films were being released featuring western frontier scenarios, he was dismayed that some of them offered glamorous depictions of outlaws while lawmen were sometimes seen as buffoons. To produce what he thought were more accurate depictions, Tilghman, with Madsen and their former boss Evett Nix, formed the Eagle Film Company.

The result of this collaboration was the popular *The Passing of the Oklahoma Outlaws,* which was released in 1915. Tilghman, as director, and his cinematographer, Benny Kent, filmed on location at many of the former outlaw hideouts in Lincoln and Payne Counties and at the 101 Ranch, which had become a favorite movie backdrop.* Tilghman played himself, as did Madsen and Arkansas Tom Jones, before his return engagement as a real outlaw. *The Passing of*

---

* As you will see later, Tilghman had already made his debut as a movie director.

the Oklahoma Outlaws was well received when the film was released to theaters. For several years afterward, Tilghman toured the country with the movie, telling stories to supplement what was portrayed on-screen. When his tour stopped in Los Angeles, he visited with another old Dodge City friend, Wyatt Earp.

Unfortunately, Tilghman did not remain in the safer world of cinema. In 1924, the year he turned seventy, he agreed to become city marshal of Cromwell, Oklahoma, a booming oil town experiencing some violent growing pains. He had previously clashed there with a U.S. prohibition agent, Wiley Lynn. On October 31, hearing that Lynn was drunkenly discharging his gun, Tilghman attempted to take the agent into custody. With the help of a bystander, he disarmed Lynn, but Lynn pulled out a second pistol and shot Tilghman several times. Tilghman died the following day.*

Governor Martin Trapp directed that Tilghman's body lie in state in the rotunda of the Oklahoma capitol building and be attended by an honor guard. He was buried in Chandler, where a park would be named for him. His widow, Zoe, would live another forty years, dying at eighty-three in 1964.

By 1902, Heck Thomas was the police chief of Lawton, Oklahoma.† This allowed him to spend more time at home rather than on the trail, and the job provided a steady income. Though now in his fifties, Heck was not much better off financially than when he'd first stuck on a badge. As Glenn Shirley points out, "Many of the old officers had spent their lives in Federal service. Few had saved anything. Some found jobs with the state or municipalities." Plus, Heck did not have the same stamina for spending day after day in the saddle,

---

* In an outcome that outraged Tilghman's family and friends, Lynn was tried and acquitted after pleading self-defense. In July 1932, in Madill, an intoxicated Lynn was shot and killed in a gunfight. Zoe Tilghman commented, "No jury can acquit him now."

† Until he built his own house, Thomas and his family rented a house in Lawton. His landlord was Al Jennings.

thanks to the combination of mileage and the lingering aches and pains of having been wounded six times over the years.

Six years later, Heck was a movie star. Well, briefly. One of the more notable productions inspired by the Wild West was *The Bank Robbery*, made and released in 1908. This was Bill Tilghman's first foray as a movie director and at the time was something of a lark. The leader of the bandit gang was played by Al Jennings, and Thomas played the lawman who assembled a posse to chase him and his accomplices. (Playing a minor role was the Comanche warrior Quanah Parker.) Some of the movie was shot in the Wichita Mountains Wildlife Refuge. During the filming at the "crime scene," a bystander thought the bank was really being robbed, and he jumped out a window to run for help.

Heck's responsibilities as police chief included heading Lawton's volunteer fire department. While responding to a call one night in 1909, he suffered a heart attack. His recovery was slow enough to convince him to retire as a lawman. After this, his income depended on being a process server. But he did not stay completely retired. When Chris Madsen became acting U.S. marshal at Guthrie, he appointed Heck as one of his five deputies.

The reception after the swearing-in ceremony on the night of January 1, 1912, was the final reunion of the Three Guardsmen. Bill Tilghman traveled from Oklahoma City to join them. Not surprisingly, much of the evening was spent swapping stories of outlaws like the Dalton brothers, Bill Doolin, Sam Bass, Jim and Pink Lee, and the many others they had handcuffed or killed over the years. The other newly sworn-in deputies listened in awe of such adventures and of the men who had helped tame what had been left of the American frontier.

Heck's deteriorating health did not allow him to perform any deputy duties. In early August, he wrote Madsen about his "malady"— which was diagnosed as Bright's disease: "I know I have not the strength to resist it, so no matter what happens don't you and Bill come down here, and no flowers." On August 14, 1912, Heck died, surrounded by a few friends and Matie and their daughters.

Beth Thomas Meeks later reported, "A public subscription was taken up to pay my father's funeral expenses, and we buried him in Highland Cemetery . . . a poor reward, I felt even then, for one of Oklahoma's most courageous frontier lawmen who had devoted his entire life to law and order."

The headline of the article about his passing in *The Lawton Constitution* was: THE NAME OF HECK THOMAS, ONCE A TERROR TO OUTLAWS.

And, finally, the only outlaw to survive the shoot-out in Coffeyville on October 5, 1892: Emmett Dalton.

After his release from prison and a pardon from Governor Edward Hoch of Kansas in 1907, Emmett saw that he could trade on his notorious name to make a living in show business. His new wife, Julia—whom we now know was *not* his childhood sweetheart, as he maintained—traveled with him as he performed with the Pawnee Bill Wild West troupe. Then he envisioned an even brighter future in the new town that would be called Hollywood. Emmett sold real estate in Los Angeles while studying the emerging industry and grasped that a fundamental virtue—indeed, the very reason for its existence—was making stuff up, and people would buy it if it was entertaining enough.

In 1912, Emmett cowrote the script and portrayed himself in the three-reeler *The Last Stand of the Dalton Boys.* He remained in and around the rapidly growing industry. Six years later, both the book and movie *Beyond the Law* came out. As previously noted, the book was a mixture of contrition and lingering defiance. As he proclaims in the very first chapter, "Our fight was not with the law, but the law as it was enforced. In those wild days what we knew of law and order was merely graft and corruption masquerading under the cloak of the law. The land-stealing railroads, the grasping express companies, the 'mushroom' banks were guilty of more misdeeds than all the crowds of bandits who terrorized the west."

In the screen version of *Beyond the Law,* Emmett plays himself. As Bill Tilghman had done with his version of events, Emmett hit the road with the film. Wisely, he did not try to glorify bandits who stole people's money but instead advocated for prison reform and provided bromides like, "The biggest fool on Earth is the one who thinks he can beat the law. It never paid and it never will, and that was the one big lesson of the Coffeyville raid."

Emmett was back into real estate in the 1920s and briefly back in the headlines when he was baptized by Sister Aimee Semple McPherson, one of the more famous evangelists in the country. His health declined after his visit to Coffeyville and the touring required to promote his book *When the Daltons Rode* in 1931.* His days on the road were over, and he and Julia lived quietly in Los Angeles until his death in 1937 at age sixty-six. His grave can be found in Kingfisher. His widow, Julia, married yet again, to a man named John Johnson. She died in 1943 and is buried next to her last husband in Dewey, Oklahoma.

What was written about Julia in *The Coffeyville Leader* in the May 27, 1943, edition resonates beyond her: "With her death the winds of time have blown out the last spark of glamor in the Dalton family."

---

* In 1940, Emmett's second memoir was turned into a feature film directed by George Marshall and starring Brian Donlevy, Broderick Crawford, Kay Francis, Andy Devine, and that man again, Randolph Scott.

ACKNOWLEDGMENTS

I remain convinced that without the dedicated staffers at various research centers, I would not have a career. So once more, this time with *The Last Outlaws,* my thanks go to those librarians and curators in Kansas, Missouri, Oklahoma, and elsewhere who helped me along the arduous research road and whose unflagging courtesy made the journey an enjoyable one. I am always both delighted and humbled by the expertise and enthusiasm of such research professionals.

In particular, I want to mention Lisa Keys, Lauren Gray, Dylan Sweyko-Kuhlman, and Michael Church at the Kansas State Historical Society; Jackie Reece and Melissa Weiss at the Western History Collections at the University of Oklahoma; editors and archivists at *True West* magazine; the volunteers at the Coffeyville Historical Society and the Dalton Defenders Museum; Matthew Menke at the Tulare County Historical Society; and Samantha Dean and archivists of *The Coffeyville Journal* at the Coffeyville Public Library.

Closer to home, I am also grateful for the efforts of staffers at the John Jermain Memorial Library, especially Susan Mullin, for their long-standing assistance and kindness.

My research was aided by the work of authors who inspired as well as informed me, including members of the Wild West History Association and the Western Writers of America. In particular, I would like to cite the Missouri native and U.S. Air Force veteran Nancy B. Samuelson. I benefited greatly from her indefatigable research and detailed books on the Dalton family (she herself is distantly related) and frontier lawmen.

This book would not have originated let alone been completed without the encouragement and steadfast support of my editor, Marc Resnick. Others at St. Martin's Press who have also made *The Last Outlaws* a happy and productive adventure include Sally Richardson, Andy Martin, Rebecca Lang, Danielle Prielipp, Tracey Guest, Lily Cronig, Kelly Too, and Mac Nicholas. Another "founder" of this book is Nat Sobel, a friend as well as agent, and I appreciate everything done for me by him and his staff, especially Adia Wright.

My dear friends continue to wait for me to not work so much so we can get together more often. Their support, especially while *The Last Outlaws* was being written, was a big reason why every day still mattered. And finally, my love to Leslie, Katy and James, Vivienne, and Brendan.

SELECTED BIBLIOGRAPHY

Allin, David. *The Dalton Boys: The Real Story of the Dalton Gang.* Middletown, DE: Independently published, 2017.

Barndollar, Lue Diver. *What Really Happened on October 5, 1892.* Denton, TX: Roots and Branches, 1992.

Brant, Marley. *The Illustrated History of the James-Younger Gang.* Montgomery, AL: Elliot and Clark Publishers, 1997.

———. *The Outlaw Youngers: A Confederate Brotherhood: A Biography.* Lanham, MD: Madison Books, 1992.

Coffeyville, KS at 100: 1869–1969: History and Centennial Celebration. Coffeyville, KS: Coffeyville Journal Press, 1969.

Croy, Homer. *Cole Younger: Last of the Great Outlaws.* Lincoln: University of Nebraska Press, 1999.

Dalton, Emmett. *Beyond the Law.* New York: Pelican, 2009.

———. *When the Daltons Rode.* Garden City, NY: Sun Dial Press, 1937.

Elliott, David Stewart. *Last Raid of the Daltons: Battle with the Bandits at Coffeyville, KS, October 5, 1892.* Coffeyville, KS: Coffeyville Journal Press, 1954.

Eye Witness [pseud.]. *The Dalton Brothers and Their Astounding Career of Crime.* New York: Frederick Fell, Inc., 1954.

Gardner, Mark Lee. *Shot All to Hell: Jesse James, the Northfield Raid, and the Wild West's Greatest Escape.* New York: William Morrow, 2014.

Green, Carl R., and William R. Sanford. *The Dalton Gang.* Springfield, NJ: Enslow Publishers, 1995.

Hanes, Bailey C. *Bill Doolin: Outlaw O.T.* Norman: University of Oklahoma Press, 1968.

History Unleashed. *The Dalton Gang: Myths, Legends, and Stories About the Wild West's Most Wanted.* Kindle.

Howes, Charles C. *This Place Called Kansas.* Norman: University of Oklahoma Press, 1984.

Kinney, John J. *Captain Jack and the Dalton Gang: The Life and Times of a Railroad Detective.* Lawrence: University Press of Kansas, 2005.

Latta, Frank F. *Dalton Gang Days.* Santa Cruz, CA: Bear State Books, 1976.

Meeks, Beth Thomas, with Bonnie Speer. *Heck Thomas, My Papa.* Norman, OK: Levite of Apache, 1988.

Nash, Jay Robert. *Encyclopedia of Western Lawmen & Outlaws.* New York: Da Capo Press, 1994.

Ohnick, Nancy. *The Dalton Gang and Their Family Ties.* n.p.: Ohnick Enterprises, 2005.

Preece, Harold. *The Dalton Gang: End of an Outlaw Era.* New York: Hastings House, 1963.

Pryor, Alton. *The Dalton Gang.* London, UK: Stagecoach Publishing, 2014.

Ray, Clarence E. *The Oklahoma Bandits: The Daltons and Their Desperate Gang.* North Haven, CT: Forgotten Books, 2022.

Samuelson, Nancy B. *The Dalton Gang Family: A Genealogical Study of the Dalton Outlaws and Their Family Connections.* Meade, KS: Back Room Printing, 1989.

——. *The Dalton Gang Story: Lawmen to Outlaws.* Eastford, CT: Shooting Star Press, 1992.

——. *Shoot from the Lip: The Lives, Legends, and Lies of the Three Guardsmen of Oklahoma and U.S. Marshal Nix.* Eastford, CT: Shooting Star Press, 1998.

Schuck, L. E. *The Last of the Dalton Gang.* Pittsburgh, PA: Dorrance Publishing, 2021.

Shirley, Glenn. *Guardian of the Law: The Life and Times of William Matthew Tilghman 1854–1924.* Fort Worth, TX: Eakin Press, 1988.

——. *Heck Thomas, Frontier Marshal.* Norman: University of Oklahoma Press, 1981.

——. *West of Hell's Fringe: Crime, Criminals, and the Federal Police Officer in Oklahoma Territory, 1889–1907.* Norman: University of Oklahoma Press, 1978.

Smith, Robert Barr. *Daltons!: The Raid on Coffeyville, KS*. Norman: University of Oklahoma Press, 1996.

———. *The Last Hurrah of the James-Younger Gang*. Norman: University of Oklahoma Press, 2001.

———. *Tough Towns: True Tales from the Gritty Streets of the Old West*. Guilford, CT: Two Dot, 2007.

Steele, Phillip W. *In Search of the Daltons*. Springdale, AR: Frontier Press, 1985.

Sterling, Hank. *Famous Western Outlaw Sheriff Battles*. n.p.: Literary Licensing, 2011.

Tilghman, Zoe A. *Marshal of the Last Frontier: Life and Services of William Matthew (Bill) Tilghman*. Glendale, CA: Arthur H. Clark, 1964.

Younger, Coleman. *The Story of Cole Younger, by Himself*. St. Paul: Minnesota Historical Society Press, 2000.

INDEX